A
SINGING
SOMETHING

A SINGING SOMETHING

Womanist Reflections on Anna Julia Cooper

KAREN BAKER-FLETCHER

CROSSROAD • NEW YORK

1994

The Crossroad Publishing Company
370 Lexington Avenue, New York, NY 10017

Library of Congress Cataloging-in-Publication Data

Baker-Fletcher, Karen.
    A singing something : womanist reflections on Anna Julia Cooper /
Karen Baker-Fletcher.
        p.   cm.
    Includes index.
    ISBN 0-8245-1399-1
    1. Cooper, Anna J. (Anna Julia), 1858–1964—Religion.   2. Black
theology–History.   3. Feminist theology—History.   4. Afro-American
women—Religion.   I. Title.
BT82.7.835   1994
230'.092—dc20   94-22622
                                                                      CIP

*Dedicated to the memory of my great-grandparents,
T. J. Harris and Desiree McBeth Harris,
teaching ancestors who gave inspiration
to generations;*

to my spouse and companion, Garth Baker-Fletcher;

*and to our children, Kristen and Kenneth,
who give hope for the future.*

Contents

Acknowledgments

I AM INDEBTED to many institutions and persons for assistance I have received in completing this project. I am grateful to the Fund for Theological Education, the Harvard Minority Prize Fellowship, and Christian Theological Seminary (CTS) for their financial and spiritual support of the dissertation phase of this project. Rufus Burrow and Ursula Pfafflin at CTS asked important questions during my early revisions of the manuscript. I am also thankful to Esme Bahn, research assistant at the Moorland-Spingarn Research Center at Howard University, and to Roland Baumann of the Oberlin College Archives for their bibliographical and historical knowledge as well as their assistance in accessing archival materials.

When, as a Ph.D. student, I began researching Anna Cooper's life and thought as a resource for contemporary womanist theology and ethics, my advisor, Richard Niebuhr, asked incisive and helpful historical and philosophical questions about Cooper in relation to other nineteenth-century thinkers. I appreciate his genuine interest in examining the similarities, as well as differences, between Black and White thinkers, male and female. I am thankful to Preston Williams for his advice regarding the initial stages of the project and for suggesting that I consider writing on Cooper. For several years he has been a wonderful source of advice on references, sources, and consultants. I am grateful to Margaret Miles for immensely helpful suggestions on consistency and style and to Clarissa Atkinson for her suggestions on historiography.

Conversations with Sharon Welch have given me hope in the possibilities of genuine feminist/womanist dialogue. Katie Cannon, a womanist mentor, has been a longstanding source of inspiration and support for my interest in Black women's literature and theology. Cheryl Sanders encouraged my research of Cooper and provided shelter, dinner, and encouragement during my visit to the Moorland-Spingarn Research Center in Washington, D.C.

I have enjoyed Barbara Johnson's advice on literary theory and analysis. Conversations with friend and colleague Marcia Riggs of Columbia Theological Seminary regarding the religious social ethics of the Black women's club movement in all its diversity across class lines have been invaluable. Cheryl Townsend Gilkes, likewise, has provided helpful insights regarding womanism and class analysis. Delores Williams served as a reader. Her insightful, challenging voice has encouraged me to examine Cooper in all her complexity. Emilie Townes, a womanist sister-friend, has contributed much moral wisdom on the value of the *humanness* — with all the strengths and weaknesses involved — of prophetic leaders as models for Christian theology and ethics.

This project could not have been completed without the assistance of several people at the School of Theology at Claremont: Gloria Johnson, who served as my editorial assistant, Karen Torjesen, who served as a reader, and Marjorie Suchocki, who encouraged me in numerous ways in the publishing and rewriting of this manuscript.

I appreciate George Lawler's love for language and his recommendations for initial revisions. The book could not have been completed without the assistance of Bob Heller. Thanks to Debra Haynes, friend and colleague, for lively conversations during my early research. Thanks also to Chandra Taylor-Smith, Bennie Smith, Jerry and Gayle Davis Culp, Dawn Scott, and John Henry Scott, dear friends, who gave sisterly and brotherly support. Family members Kay Jett Baker, Taylor Baker, Jr., and Superia P. Fletcher gave support at various stages along the way. Garth Baker-Fletcher, my spouse, colleague, and friend, has been a tireless companion. Finally, our children, Kristen and Kenneth, have been a source of great joy and delight.

Preface

I HAVE BEEN INTERESTED in women's writings since childhood when my mother's mother would recite original poems and read from my great-grandmother's autobiographical writings. My maternal great-grandparents were educators in Meridian, Mississippi, and T. J. Harris Junior College was named after my great-grandfather. Aunts, uncles, mother, grandmother, and great-grandmother would give voice to the family history with a sense of joy and dignity regarding Black Americans' capacity not only for survival but for rising to the occasion to thrive in the midst of loss, danger, and injustice.

My paternal grandmother and grandfather, Lizzie and Taylor Baker, Sr., migrated from Arkansas to Indianapolis during the Depression. They journeyed from the deeply segregationist, exploitive labor market of the South to relative economic independence in the somewhat less segregated but equally discriminatory North through mother wit and "makin' do." I first witnessed the kind of perseverance that historical Black women like Maria Stewart, Ida B. Wells-Barnett, and Anna J. Cooper are famous for in my paternal grandmother. My education began in the midst of an extended, mixed-class family system of persevering, quick-witted, rigorous-thinking people. My intellect was enlivened by family members whose diverse educational backgrounds (whether college-, graduate-, or life-educated) were equally rich and demonstrated that the life of the mind was an ongoing, everyday event that was not limited or confined to formal educational institutions. Rather, it involved a willingness to engage in lifelong collective and independent thinking and learning about the world one lived in. Book learning was valued, but not apart from the living knowledge and application of knowledge that transcends the written text. More and more, I find that my quick response to my paternal grandfather when he asked me what I was going to learn at Harvard ("Nothing I haven't already learned at

11

home") is true in many respects. Yes, I have gathered rich details of information and certain theoretical skills. But all this would be meaningless without the living foundation of knowledge that I learned at home, which gives life and meaning to what I have found in books and archives.

I am indebted to my family for the rich heritage they have passed on to me. I am especially grateful to my grandparents on both sides and my maternal great-grandmother. I have never tired of their stories about life in the late nineteenth and early twentieth centuries, of "makin' do" during the Depression, or their living analyses of American history and society. I first heard preachments on the concrete location of heaven and hell ("Right here on this earth!") not in a textbook on Black theology but from my paternal grandfather (who is a barber, not a preacher) just about every time the topics of Church, the Bible, or religion came up. I learned about the significance of collective work and the effects of Machiavellian "divide and conquer" strategies against Black people in the name of White Western progress from this same grandfather. I first learned about the Spirit and the healing power of Jesus not from texts, but from my women elders. I learned about segregation from family members and about the Civil Rights movement from an aunt who was a recording secretary for the Southern Christian Leadership Conference (SCLC). Through this same aunt, Desiree Jett, I briefly met Ella Baker, acting director of the SCLC in the early days of the Civil Rights movement, who later gave credibility to student organizations in the Civil Rights movement and helped them pull together to organize the Student Nonviolent Coordinating Committee (SNCC). Through her I also met Wyatt T. Walker, director of the SCLC in Atlanta, and the South African photographer Peter Magubane. After that, I learned more about these people through textbooks. My aunt, however, made them real for me and others even as she recommended more texts.

I first learned of the value of women's everyday creativity not from Alice Walker, whose writings I value, but from the teaching, working, and artistic hands of mother, grandmothers, and aunts. My cousins and I (I have no siblings) found our intellectual curiosity nurtured by debates at family gatherings and conversations around kitchen tables. My interest in the lives and thought of historical African Americans begins with my family, magnificent storytellers and debaters all.

From my mother and father, Kay J. and Taylor L. Baker, Jr., I learned about the rich heritage of historically Black colleges. My mother taught me about the profound contributions of Black leaders and educators in Atlanta, where she grew up and graduated from Spelman College and Atlanta University. From my father I learned of Benjamin Mays, president of Morehouse and a great mentor to my father's generation. From both parents I learned of Frantz Fanon, Leroi Jones, James Baldwin, Maya Angelou, and later Judge Leon Higginbotham, whose books were scattered around our house. I learned of the accomplishments of African Americans in American history. Teachings in "Negro" and, later, Black History were part of my home training year round. My parents bought literature by Black authors about Black Americans that was not available in the classroom. Aunts and uncles provided yet more literature for birthdays and Christmases, with Aunt Mila Baker introducing me to the poetry of Nikki Giovanni. Aunt Mila and Aunt Desiree shared accounts of their experiences in graduate school and their roles as professors. As a girl, I found that the contributions made by women and persons of color were most often excluded in textbooks. I found it peculiar and illogical that such rich accounts of persons of heroism, survival, genius, faith, and creativity had been bypassed. I came to attribute the absence of their thought and accomplishments to selective ignorance in the dominant American culture.

The "Voices" of Black Women

I first became interested in the theological issue of women's voices as an M.Div. student at Harvard Divinity School. I found that Black women's "voices" were largely absent from theological conversation in the classroom and in the publications of the scholarly world. Discussions in feminist theology often centered around the problem of the absence and silencing of women's voices. The traditional theological canon of literature overlooked and excluded women's religious and theological thought.

I specifically found myself asking, how does one begin to access women's religious thought? I found the argument that there was too scarce a body of extant material by women inadequate. I was concerned that very few scholars had bothered to look for the materials. I had a sense of belonging to a tradition that had not been named.

Until the last twenty years, entire traditions of thought have been overlooked because they belonged to women and people of color. I find Michel Foucault's metaphor of an "archaeology" of knowledge to describe the subjugation of certain intellectual histories helpful.[1] Both Euro-American and African American feminists are engaged in a process of recovery, retrieval, quite literally the excavation of women's thought.

Historically women have recorded their religious and theological ideas in a variety of forms. The construction of the theological treatise has been primarily the domain of the male theologian. Until recently, women traditionally have been excluded from formal theological education. Thus they have often recorded their ideas in forms other than formal theological treatises: autobiographies, essays, poetry, artwork such as quilts, and music.

Only with the women's movement of the late twentieth century have women had the freedom to consider formulating their ideas in the traditional forms of academic scholarship. At the same time, women are bringing with them new insights into the importance and value of art, poetry, and narrative for representing the God-human relationship. I find Black women's literature — historical, fictional, and poetic — a valuable resource for constructing theologies for the late twentieth-century world.

Research on historical texts by literary scholars has contributed greatly to recent African American women's religious scholarship. In recent years, African American literary and historical scholars such as Marilyn Richardson, Mary Helen Washington, William L. Andrews, and Darlene Clark Hine have been responsible for the republication of a number of nineteenth-century Black women evangelists and social reformers.

Perhaps the singlemost massive recovery and republication of historical writings by African American women is the series of texts by African American women writers published by the Schomburg Library in cooperation with the Oxford University Press, with Louis Gates as general editor. In 1988, Anna Julia

Cooper's *A Voice from the South,* originally published in 1892 by Aldine Printing House in Xenia, Ohio, was reissued as part of this series.

This book explores the life and thought of Anna Julia Haywood Cooper (1858–1964), with special emphasis to her symbolization of human being, particularly womanhood, in relation to God, Christ, and the world in Western culture. Cooper advocated equal rights for women of every color and cultural heritage, but she was particularly concerned with civil, educational, and economic rights for Black women. Cooper was a prominent educator and writer from the late nineteenth to the mid-twentieth century. She was a "race woman," proud of the darker-raced people, brought to America primarily as slaves, that we now call African Americans. In affirmation of her race, she referred to her people with a sense of pride and dignity as "Black women" and "Black men." At times she used the terms "colored" or "Negro."

Several theological themes are foundational to Cooper's concept of human development, and these same theological themes, along with a social-analytical critique of the world, motivated her as an educator. These themes are a valuable resource for contemporary womanist and feminist theologians engaged in the task of generating new symbolizations of human being in relation to God. Particularly significant is the attention Cooper gives to "voice," a term that occurs in the title and is discussed in the text of her best-known publication, *A Voice from the South*. The title is striking and serves as the primary text of discussion for this book.

The theme of voice is central to my discussion. I examine Cooper's argument for women's movement from silence and subjugation to a model of bold vocalization and independence to consider how her concept of woman's voice provides a resource for a contemporary theological concept of women's embodiment and prophetic message of freedom and equality. Today, as womanists both build on and move beyond Cooper's thought, we will find it necessary to consider a diversity of women's voices among Black women.

Cooper's consciousness of the importance of women's voices is striking. She decried the injustice that muffles tones of the Black community in a White world and suppresses the cries of Black women against injustice in an oppressive social system. As an author she was conscious of the difficulties of creating a narrative voice that would be given a serious audience in a world that discriminated against persons based on their gender and the color of their skin. She criticized American society, Northern and Southern, for inadequately listening to the voices of Black Americans, male and female. Because women's voices were the most "muted" voices in American and world cultures, she emphasized that it was time for women's voices of every color to be heard. Most important, the voices of Black women of the South remained the most muted of all and deserved an audience because of their particular sensitivity to the problems of racial and gender inequality.

As I have researched Anna Cooper's writings, I have found that she introduced an interesting metaphor of God in relation to voice in her doctoral defense, describing God as a "Singing Something" that rises up within humanity in every nation to cry out against injustice. On the one hand she had a traditional understanding of humankind being created in the image of God. Human being was a "divine spark," an "urge-cell" from the very being and substance of God. But her metaphor of a *"Singing Something"* suggests an epistemic shift. Human being is not simply created in the image of God. Human being is created in the voice of God. This suggests the presence of a prophetic element within humanity that must be exercised with wisdom and discernment. Her metaphors for describing the embodied and ontological nature of God and humanity are well worth building on in the contemporary world, a world in which we are seeking new or overlooked metaphors for God and human being.

Critical of words and practices that violated the sacredness of human being, God's message as described in scripture and taught by the historical Jesus, in Cooper's view, denounced the domination of the weak by the strong. She and her contemporaries, like Black religious leaders today, interpreted God's message as one that valued the sacredness and inviolability of human nature. Humankind was created in ontological freedom and equality, both of which ought to be realized in society. This meant that human beings were required to respect the sacredness of one another's lives across racial, cultural, economic, national, religious, and gender boundaries. In addition, militarism represented brute force at its worst by devastating entire populations of people.

Structure of the Book

Chapter 1 explores Anna Cooper's life, placing her in her social-historical context as a leader in the post-Reconstruction era with its emphasis on racial uplift and the organization of the Black women's club movement. Here I seek to present something of the invincible spirit of the woman. She appears at a superficial glance to have been an eternal optimist, and yet her consistent caution that it would take millennia for God's movement of reform, initiated by Jesus of Nazareth, to realize itself in human culture suggests a strong measure of realism and commitment to perseverance in her thinking. Working with perseverance for political freedom and equality was essential whether these ideals were fully realized for women and men of color in her own time or not.

In chapter 2, I consider what such a strategy of persevering faith in a God of justice might contribute to our own age of increasing pessimism and nihilistic tendencies. We are in danger of losing the faith of prophetic leaders of a previous generation, who in some respects had far less hope for actual change in the matter of human rights than we do today. Anna Cooper, Ida B. Wells-Barnett, Mary Church Terrell, Charlotte Forten Grimké, Fannie Barrier Williams, Frances Ellen Watkins Harper, Frederick Douglass, W. E. B. Du Bois, Booker T. Washington, Francis and Archibald Grimké, and Kelly T. Miller were very close to the realities of both slavery and apartheid-like segregation. The freedom they had longed for and hoped for was partially realized with the end of the Civil War and the abolition of slavery. And yet, with Jim Crow segregation in the South, modelled on segregation in the North, they witnessed the threatening rise of new forms of slavery in America: sharecropping with its system of forced indebtedness and the relegation of the masses of Black women to work as exploited and underpaid domestic servants who were provided little time off to raise their own families.

The pessimistic spirit that threatens our own age is undoubtedly a result of the promise of political and economic freedom and equality being held back one time too many as far as concrete programs are concerned. The Civil Rights movement was not the final step toward full freedom and equality for all peoples in America.

Indeed, since the 1980s some of the gains of the civil rights and
Black power movements have been rescinded or are being considered for rescindment in much the same way that the gains of the
Reconstruction era were rescinded after the 1870s. It is precisely
because our own age is similar to that of Cooper's in such respects
that we benefit from examining the type of religious perspective
that empowered and enabled her to persevere in the face of the
backward, backlashing movement that has tended to follow political and economic gains for Black people in America. Like Black,
liberation, feminist, and womanist theologians today, Black Americans of Cooper's generation sought a wholistic vision of freedom
and equality in society that would value the cultural pluralism of
the United States.

A close analysis of Cooper's work reveals that theological
themes are foundational to her concept of human development.
These theological themes, along with a social-analytical critique of
human culture, are foundational for her essays on social progress
and for her choice of a life of service as an educator. Moreover,
Cooper's symbolizations of Christ, God, Church, and womanhood are of value for generating new symbolizations, particularly
for womanist and feminist theologians engaged in a critique and
reconstruction of Christian thought and practice. In Chapters 2
and 3, therefore, I examine her religious thought.

Chapter 2 examines Cooper's symbolizations of Christ, Church,
culture, and womanhood. Like other Black women involved in
the nineteenth-century women's movement and racial uplift, she
appealed to a symbolization of Christ and a concept of God
that affirmed the humanity of Black women and men. Her interpretation of the meaning of Christ and Church were important
components of her reconstruction of a symbolization of Black
womanhood that affirmed a status of equality, leadership, and dignity in relation to the rest of humanity. Her symbolizations of
Christ and Church were also important in her appeal for a reformation of ideas of what constitutes human being in the larger
society. Her arguments for belief in social progress and development indicate that she was familiar with nineteenth-century liberal
Christian theories of history, biblical hermeneutics, and social evolution popular among the Social Gospel leaders in the 1880s and
1890s.[2]

Like her contemporaries, Anna Cooper was influenced by ideals of true womanhood popular in the nineteenth century and sought to transform them. The dominant image of woman was of a gentle, kind, loving, mother who was moral instructor of the family in the domestic sphere — and physically frail, ill-suited for hard labor.[3] This White middle- or upper-class image was not inclusive of Black women or of working-class White women. Black women, in particular, were negatively stereotyped as promiscuous, slothful, of male or brute animal strength, and lacking in moral virtue.[4] Cooper successfully employed the moral elements of the image of true womanhood as descriptive of Black women to gain an audience supportive of providing educational opportunities for Black women. She was not immune to the rhetoric regarding delicacy but transformed it to emphasize moral sensitivity. Some womanist theologians and ethicists, like Emilie Townes and Delores Williams, have carefully questioned whether women like Cooper, Ida B. Wells-Barnett, and Mary Church Terrell failed to fully represent the wisdom of the masses of working Black women in their own words. To some extent, as Mary Helen Washington has observed, the answer is yes. The masses of Black women would have found it difficult, impossible even, to appreciate the emphasis on physical frailty and emotional delicacy in dominant ideals of true womanhood. Such characteristics would have been inauthentic to the experience of work and survival in the midst of socio-economic suffering most Black women were engaged in. Some of the mannerisms Anna Cooper ascribes to the morally virtuous Black woman — "subtle whisperings" — contradict her examples of women leaders who confidently and boldly spoke for reform. Survival required emotional and physical fortitude that fit neither categories of true womanhood nor stereotypes of Black women as Amazons. And yet, as Evelyn Brooks Higginbotham has suggested in *Righteous Discontent,* many working Black women aspired to the *moral* ideals of true womanhood.[5] White women, Black women of all classes agreed, had no exclusive claim to righteousness. While the rhetoric of the ideal of true womanhood was intended for White middle- and upper-class women in the dominant culture, who were regarded as having exclusive possession of virtues of moral purity, chastity, innate religiosity, and compassion, Black American women adapted the ideal to their own situations to claim their place among the most morally virtuous of women.

Chapter 3 continues the themes in chapter 2 as they pertain to Cooper's thought on philosophy and religious belief. Belief in this intellectual's thought is faith and action that works for reform. Using faith synonymously with belief, she posited "faith that works" against the skeptical philosophy of David Hume and the agnostic philosophical positivism of Auguste Comte, as popularly understood. Religion for this reformer was an embodied, intuitive form of reason — a living coal that unsealed the lips of the dumb and provided the reason for human existence. Her belief in the power of religion informed her faith in human potential and women's contribution to culture.

Chapters 4–5 examine Anna Cooper's concept of "womanhood" and her analysis of Black and White feminist relations. Critical of racism among White women's clubs, she contended that the world needed to hear "woman's" voice across racial lines, a point women of color and some liberation White feminists are still arguing today. Cooper tended to refer to women as "woman" and to Black women as "the Black Woman." She also referred to "woman's voice." Her sense of the contributions women could make for social reform was grand, larger than life, so she painted women with large, sweeping strokes as "woman." Today, such language appears to represent women as a monolithic group and fails to capture the pluralism Cooper sought to embrace.

Chapter 5 considers Cooper's representation of the "voice" of the "Black Woman" in light of her social-historical context. I consider why she may have found it necessary to paint Black women with seemingly monolithic strokes. Further, I examine Cooper's metaphors of "muteness" to refer to the subjugation of women and "voice" to represent speech as an expression of freedom from domination. Her overarching goal was the universal freedom and development of the human race — male and female.[6] The struggle for freedom was a complex struggle of men *and* women, Blacks and Whites, Christians and people of diverse religions, whose voices needed to be heard.[7]

It is ineffective to reappropriate the thought of historical figures uncritically. While Anna Cooper's thought, practice, and faith have much to contribute to continuing generations, my task is not to place her on a pedestal. A woman who believed reformers of any age caught only a glimpse of God's will and movement for reform, she would not have desired unthinking praise for herself. Quests for freedom and equality vary from generation to generation as new questions emerge in response to shifting social norms. And yet, something of the past is preserved in our present society for good and for ill. Freedom and equality along gender and racial lines remain inadequate. Some of our present concerns resonate with those of Black women reformers of the turn of the twentieth century, but some do not. Throughout the text I critically consider the meaning of Cooper's thought for her own social-historical context and those aspects that are problematic for our own time. In chapter 6 I focus on a critique of Cooper's understanding of Christ, culture, and womanhood as a resource for contemporary theologians and ethicists.

I engage in a womanist reflection on the constructive significance of Cooper's work for Black womanist theologians in chapter 7. I also seek to construct an ethics of virtue or *power.* The original Latin meaning of *virtus* is "power." Because "virtue" has been employed to connote an ideal of passivity among women in popular American culture, I prefer the term to suggest women's active power. In this chapter, I move well beyond a discussion of the power of voice to consider four other powers: the power of "making do," the power of "tar" as derived from Toni Morrison's understanding of Black women's power to "hold things together," the power of "memory" derived from Morrison's narrative on "re-memory" in *Beloved,* and finally the power of "regeneration." "Regeneration" is an overarching power that is distinctive in that it enables the passing on of wisdom and power to future generations; the power of regeneration is necessarily embodied in the first four powers.

Hermeneutics

One can read Cooper's *A Voice from the South* as a *theological* text. There are many forms in which theology has been recorded. The most widely known and accepted form among traditional academic circles is the formal theological treatise. Very

few women in Christian history have been trained to write formal
theological treatises; nor have they possessed status for recognition in a male-dominated world if they mastered such training.
But women have recorded theology — their reflections and ideas
about the nature of God and the world — by adapting the forms
that were available to them and accepted as gender-appropriate
by the dominant society.

Richard R. Niebuhr uses the term "theographia" to refer to
the variety and multiplicity of writings and graphics that inform
our theological understanding in Christian history and culture. Included in the notion of theographia are letters, sermons, myth,
narrative, religious autobiographies, hagiography, hymns, liturgies, markings and graphics, as well as the traditional formal
theological treatise.[8] I see the work of writers such as Jarena Lee,
Amanda Berry Smith, Maria Stewart, and Anna Julia Cooper —
like the writings of Augustine, Anselm, Julian of Norwich, Teresa
of Avila, and Margery Kempe — as forms of theography. The
varied genres of writing and their content point to the multiplicity of theological symbolizations and religious experiences in the
Christian tradition.[9] Also, the varied, changing social-historical
contexts in which African American women write indicate the
processual nature of African American women's symbolization of
self in relation to symbolizations of God, Christ, and the world.

The systematic theologian often prefers to construct two categories: first-order theology and second-order theology. First-order
theology would include scripture, hymns, sermons, and religious
autobiography. Second-order theology is seen as self-conscious,
reflective, and as drawing on first-order theology — sermons,
scripture, popular literature — to create formal theological treatises. This concept of theology obscures the interdependence of
the varieties of theological writings. I find this division of theology
into two categories to be too rigid and tightly drawn. It obscures
the fluidity and reciprocity between various media.

For this reason I find Niebuhr's concept of "theographia" to
be a particularly valuable and appealing alternative. Formal theological treatises and religious narrative are types of theographia,
which exist in a complex environment of multiple symbol systems. Narrative, sermons, autobiography, markings, and so on
form the soil from which formal theological treatises are writ-

ten, but formal theological treatises also form a soil from which emerge new narratives, sermons, autobiographies, and so on.[10] The relationship is a reciprocal one.

My employment of Niebuhr's symbol theory is influenced by feminist and womanist critiques of theology and culture as discussed by theologians like Mary Daly, Sharon Welch, Carol Christ, Jacquelyn Grant, and Delores Williams — all of whom are engaged in various approaches to criticizing Christian symbols for the purpose of effecting social change. Moreover, womanist and to some extent feminist liberationist theories suggest a wholistic vision of theology that is inclusive of a variety of materials as part of what one might consider the canon of theology.

Thus theologians like Mary Daly, Carol Christ, Sharon Welch, Katie Cannon, and Delores Williams turn to literature as a theological resource. Margaret Miles engages in a theological analysis of literature, art, and devotional manuals as well as traditional theological treatises. These are all methods of rethinking how we can gain greater access to and understand the religious thought and practice of historical and contemporary people.

Feminist and womanist theologians demand inclusiveness in the understanding of what theology is and who constructs it. They share with Richard Niebuhr an understanding of the participation of theological symbols in an ever-changing process of personal and social-historical experience, an awareness of the impossibility of true objectivity, and the necessity of ongoing critiques of symbols for the purpose of an endless interpretation and reformation of our understanding of God, Christ, and culture.

A Note on Language: Race, Ancestry, and Nationality

When quoting Cooper, I employ the terms that she used to refer to African Americans: "Black," "colored," "Negro." When referring to contemporary culture, I use a variety of terms that I currently see reflected in current literature. The term "African American" affirms culture and national ancestry of Black women and men in America. It is not inclusive of Third World nations or of people of African descent outside North America and has some limitations when one begins to consider global concerns. The term "Black" continues the task of the Black power movement to affirm the beauty and power of African Americans. The term "Black" affirms the African ancestry, the culture, and the beauty of the skin color of persons of African descent across the globe. The human race is best envisioned as a rainbow or garden of varied colors and cultures, with Blackness as one that must be valued and recognized. The term "White" refers to persons of European descent in America and across the globe. The expressions "women of color" or "people of color" are reflective of social-political solidarity with Third World nations and a valuation of all those descended from darker-skinned peoples. Some people think that one must choose among the many terms used to refer to persons of African descent in America. However, I am delighted by the rich variety of descriptive terminology available to describe myself and others of African descent and of color.

It is important to resist efforts to neatly categorize persons. Rigid categorization reeks of a lack of freedom to define self and community. There is no one term that adequately describes a person, a people, or a nation. A multiplicity of terms is descriptive of individuals and communities. I have chosen several terms currently prevalent in the literature of the academic arena and folk culture to affirm freedom of choice in self-naming and cultural identity among peoples of African descent in America.

NOTES

1. I have been influenced to some extent by Michel Foucault's criticism of Western intellectual history and culture. I am intrigued by his metaphor of "an archaeology of knowledge" and his concept of "subjugated" knowledges to describe knowledge that has been historically and disdainfully regarded by intellectuals as primitive or incomplete. I agree with Sharon Welch that women's thought has been effectively subjugated historically and requires an archaeological retrieval. See Michel Foucault, *The Archaeology of Knowledge, and the Discourse on Language* (New York: Pantheon Books, 1972), and Sharon Welch, *Communities of Resistance and Solidarity* (Maryknoll, N.Y.: Orbis Books, 1985), 9–14, 16–20. Also important is Jacques Derrida's deconstruction theory as taught by Barbara Johnson. Deconstruction theory's analysis of difference, self, other, and marginalization is helpful in critiquing the exclusion of texts,

social and literary. See Jacques Derrida, *Dissemination,* trans. Barbara Johnson (Chicago: University of Chicago Press, 1981).

2. See Ronald C. White, Jr., *Liberty and Justice for All: Racial Reform and the Social Gospel (1877–1925),* Rauschenbusch Lectures, new series 2 (New York: Harper & Row, 1990), xvii–xxiv. Cooper was friends with Alexander Crummell, who criticized Josiah Strong's racist, conservative Social Gospel teachings, and with Francis Grimké, who began developing Social Gospel motifs in his sermons in the 1890s. Moreover, Cooper wrote at least one letter to the editor of the *Outlook* regarding the writings of Lyman Abbott, Social Gospel leader and editor of *The Outlook,* requesting an expansion of the social ideals published in the *Outlook* to include teachings on racial equality. Perhaps most important, the content of Cooper's writings is reflective of Social Gospel ideals and nineteenth-century liberal interpretations of evolutionary theory: the concept of society as an organism, evolutionary optimism, correlations between happiness and progress, and familial metaphors to describe God and society. Also, Cooper's repudiation of theories of "the survival of the fittest" and the domination of the weak by the strong resonate with Walter Rauschenbusch's later address on the race question in 1913. See White, *Liberty and Justice for All,* 209–10.

3. See Barbara Welter, *Dimity Convictions* (Boston: Beacon Press, 1976), 21–41, for a discussion of the cult of "True Womanhood" in nineteenth-century America. "True Womanhood" was a phrase used by writers in women's magazines and religious literature in reference to women's piety, purity, domesticity, and submissiveness.

4. See Barbara Hilkert Andolsen, *"Daughters of Jefferson, Daughters of Bootblacks": Racism and American Feminism* (Macon, Ga.: Mercer University Press, 1986), 45ff, for a discussion of nineteenth-century understandings of "True Womanhood" and its impact on Black womanhood.

5. See Evelyn Brooks Higginbotham, *Righteous Discontent* (Cambridge: Harvard University Press, 1993).

6. See Anna Julia Cooper, *A Voice from the South,* ed. Mary Helen Washington, Schomburg Library of Nineteenth-Century Black Women Writers (1892; New York: Oxford University Press, 1988), 121.

7. Ibid.

8. See Richard R. Niebuhr, "The Tent of Heaven: Theographia I," printed in the *Alumnae Bulletin, Bangor Theological Seminary* 52, no. 2 (Fall–Winter 1977–78): 9–22.

9. Ibid.

10. Ibid.

1

Living into Freedom

OW DOES ONE go about the task of constructing a theology of hope in a time when optimism is questioned? How does one call for a revival of faith and belief in an empowering God of freedom and equality in a time when promises of freedom and equality have been too often thwarted? How does one find strength to press forward for social change, when, as Martin Luther King, Jr., prophesied, the gains of the Civil Rights movement have not brought America nearly far enough?[1] The night before his assassination, King proclaimed he had been to the mountaintop, that he might not get there with us, but he had seen the promised land. When King died, Black America found itself in a wilderness of despair, with the promised land a far-off dream. With King's death, a movement that had pulsed regularly in African American history — from the revolts of Nat Turner and Denmark Vesey in the eighteenth century, to the underground railroad leadership of Harriet Tubman and Frederick Douglass in the nineteenth century, to the racial uplift and the Black women's club movements with leaders like W. E. B. Du Bois and Anna Julia Cooper in the late nineteenth and early twentieth centuries, to the Civil Rights and Black power movements represented by Martin Luther King, Jr., and Stokely Carmichael in the middle of this century — gave way to disillusionment.

It is vital for the life of the movement of reform that historically has empowered the hearts of Black Americans and those who have stood in solidarity with them to be revived in full force. It is vital to remember that wilderness experience is part of the journey to freedom envisioned by historical Black Americans. If they somehow found hope for freedom and equality in the midst of slavery and Jim Crow, surely hope is possible today. There is a charge often preached from African American pulpits to "remember *who*

27

you are and *whose* you are." There is a charge often given in African American secular culture to "remember where you came from." Only by remembering who one is and to whom one belongs can there be a revival of hope. Only by knowing God's activity in the lives of the ancestors and God's continued activity in the lives of contemporary women and men of color is it possible to fully recover hope in a God of social change.

It is tragic that with all the gains of the Civil Rights and Black power movements, African Americans must continue to fight to write and teach themselves into history through the public institutions and media of this land. White history and culture is the norm in integrated schools and in the media. It is tragic that the gains of desegregation have been violent to the souls of Black folk. Desegregation has been construed simplistically to connote the mere presence of African American bodies in previously segregated institutions. America has been desegregated in its public institutions, but little integration or desegregation of power has taken place. Moreover, African Americans of the last two generations have lost the rich education in Black history, literature, and culture that their parents and grandparents received from Black teachers in Black schools.

This does not mean that we need to go back to segregation, but it does mean that African Americans must demand and take every opportunity to teach and write themselves into American history and culture in order to reclaim their souls. It means that White Americans must listen and re-vision American history. This is a political act of a spiritual nature. It is deeply tied to the Afrocentric practice of naming (*nommo*). By recovering and passing on Black history and culture from generation to generation African Americans participate in the power of naming, passing on the soul-life heritage of Black folk.

Recovering and passing on a heritage of Black history and culture from generation to generation is important because there is a virus of nihilism at work in Black America that afflicts both spiritual and socio-economic well-being. For too many this nihilism has taken the place of faith in a God of freedom and equality. In 1990, 50 percent of deaths among Black men were the result of gunshot wounds in Black-on-Black, gang-related shootings. Suicide is increasing among young Black men. Nihilism is

evident among young women and men who commit a slow suicide through drug use. It is evident in young women and girls
who grasp at early childbearing as one of few rather than many
means of fulfillment available to them. These are problems that
afflict *all* Americans, but particularly threaten the lives of African
Americans. As Cornel West has noted, the Black folk saying that
"When White folk have a cold, Black folk get pneumonia" is all
too true.[2] Such crisis threatens the very spiritual and physical life
of a community.

Nihilism is not new to African Americans. J. California Cooper
and Toni Morrison in their historically based novels *Family* and
Beloved describe well the attempts of slave women to kill themselves and their children to escape slavery. But the nihilism that
afflicts Black Americans today is insidious, because it is coupled
with disillusionment regarding true freedom and opportunity in
the midst of "freedom" and "opportunity." Black leaders and
scholars like Marian Wright Edelman, Cornel West, and bell
hooks observe that the cohesion of the Black community is in
threat of being lost and needs to be recovered. They discuss feelings of defeatism among young Black men and women. We need
only look at the numbers of Black men who are dying in the
streets or who are in prisons to understand the meaning of the
term "defeatism." Defeatist attitudes in the Black community are
the product of limited economic opportunity, culturally biased
education, and political inequality.[3]

Young Black women and men are more likely to drop out of
school than their White peers. They are less likely to receive support from school officials regarding racial conflict and tension and
more likely to be suspended or expelled than White students.[4] The
bungling methods by which desegregation has been administered
in public schools has been a major disappointment for African
Americans. Black students are still segregated by means of track-
ing programs, which are reinforced by low expectations from the
White majority population of teachers. Black teachers continue to
struggle to teach African American history and culture (beyond
Black History Month) as integral to their curricula in overt and
subversive ways. Until a revision of American history and culture
takes place, the dominant cultural norm will continue to disrupt
the history and symbols that give meaning and life to African

American people. Until such revision happens, Black churches, which have been historically the bedrock of African American faith and culture, must intensify their efforts to pass on history and culture.

By recovering their history and culture African American people today can remember God's revelation and activity in the lives of Black foremothers and forefathers. By remembering who they are (African and American) and whose they are (God's), a recovery from the spiritual deaths of apathy, defeatism, and despair can take place. It is possible, then, to remember that there is a power in the universe that is greater than classism, greater than racism, greater than sexism, greater than xenophobia in all its manifestations.

In order for people to begin to believe again that there is a power in the universe greater than evil and suffering, churches must instill more knowledge of the ways in which our ancestors believed God empowered them to work for social reform. Such knowledge provides a basis for new hope and faith across class lines. Black middle-class Americans need to relearn a faith in God that requires active love for the entire community and respect for the intellect of the masses. There is a tendency to ascribe "intellect" exclusively to people with academic degrees. But Patricia Hill Collins has aptly redefined the meaning of "intellect" to include the reason of both the highly educated and everyday people — women like Anna Cooper, a scholar/activist, and Sojourner Truth, an unlettered preacher/activist, each of whom reinterpreted the meaning of human rights. The teachings and insights of a diversity of people make for a fuller vision of a just society.[5] Finally the God of historical and contemporary Black Americans who "makes a way out of no way" is a source of strength for peoples across class, racial, and gender lines. What seems impossible for us is possible for God, as we work with God in the task of social change.

For a revival of hope to take place, Black churches must accept Black women as equal partners with Black men in ministry. Black churches all too often resist accepting women in pastoral ministry, although Black women make up 75 percent of most Black congregations. Certainly, the fact that Black men are the minority in most Black congregations indicates that outreach to Black males is necessary.[6] But the need for outreach to Black men does not necessitate excluding Black women from outreach programs or pastoral ministry. It is important to institute some gender-specific programs, but this should not dictate who stands in the pulpit on Sunday morning. God calls entire people, male and female, to ministry. God's salvation is for the entire community. Black women *and* men together have gifts that are vital for what Jacquelyn Grant calls a "wholistic liberation" of the Black Church and community.[7]

These are not new ideas. They are old ideas that are being considered in a new and ever-changing context. A century ago and more, Black American women and men made similar challenges to America's politically and economically powerful elite and to their own communities in their calls for social reform. In Black churches, historically the religious and the political go hand in hand. Black Christians have understood the oppressive power of religion as well as its liberating power. From David Walker to Henry Highland Garnett to Sojourner Truth and Jarena Lee to Anna Julia Cooper and Ida B. Wells-Barnett to Martin Luther King, Jr., African Americans have questioned what constitutes true Christianity. False Christianity is politically oppressive; it supports slavery, discrimination, lynching, racism, sexism, classism, and imperialism. True Christianity seeks social, economic, and political justice *as well as* personal spiritual perfection. Historical Black women and men have passed on a legacy of prophecy in action to contemporary Black Americans.

The ancestral legacy of prophecy in action is a rich and valuable resource. Yet there are certain social justice issues that previous generations did not address that must not be overlooked today. The prophetic, socially transforming legacy of our ancestors is not something to appropriate uncritically. To move toward a wholistic realization of freedom and equality requires attention to the full dignity, humanity, and human rights of all. The problems of sexual violence, spousal abuse, and child abuse need to be addressed explicitly and consistently in both Church and community. The practice of denying homophobia as a justice problem needs discussion. Contemporary Black churches and community organizations must wrestle with prejudice regarding gays and lesbians in the Black community.

Black Americans can no longer afford to see no evil, hear no evil, speak no evil when it comes to internal problems of oppression. The excuse for denying such problems usually amounts to someone arguing that "we don't need to air our dirty laundry." But it is the same laundry that every other community has to deal with, so the Black community does not single itself out by openly addressing such problems. This is not to belittle the fact that the media disproportionately sensationalizes social problems in the Black community. But rather than live in fear of the negative racial stereotypes the mass media engages in, it would be more productive to continuously challenge such distortions while actively correcting the problems that do exist.

Rather than remain silent, it would be far more fruitful to begin appreciating the Black community's talents for preventing and addressing such problems. Why not challenge the media to publicize such positive activities? According to sociologist Andrew Billingsley, statistics reveal fewer incidents of child abuse among Black families than White families in America.[8] He attributes this to the strength of the extended family system. Why not find ways of more fully reviving and strengthening this system in Church and community? Why not share the practices and values that are a part of this system with the larger society? Moreover, rather than deny the existence of sexual and domestic violence among Black families, why not consider the values and practices among Black Americans that have been effective in preventing such violence? In other words, it is time to move away from a shame-based reaction of denial when confronted with such issues to an esteem-based proactive response to our God-given gifts for transforming such evils where they really do exist. Such gifts need to be acknowledged, strengthened, built upon, and shared with the larger society.

Anna Cooper: From Servitude to Service

With the vital need for a recovery of Black historical theology in mind, I now turn to the life and thought of a historical African American Christian woman who struggled with the triple jeopardy of racism, classism, and sexism. Like so many women of color today, she lived on the boundaries of oppression and freedom, of spiritual annihilation and spiritual survival. How does one bring her voice to life so that it can be heard today as people across the globe continue to struggle for freedom, justice, and equality? And what might such a woman's Gospel message of freedom mean for Christians and non-Christians in this post-modern world?

Dr. Anna Julia Cooper lived on the boundary between two centuries — the nineteenth and the twentieth. Born in slavery, she reached out for freedom and was shaped spiritually and intellectually by the optimistic worldview of the Reconstruction period in America. We today do not live in such an optimistic age. We today live in a world where nihilism and despair increase daily. We today live in a world where the promise of freedom, equality, and justice has been undermined in the eyes of so many. It is not easy, given the shifts in social-historical contexts, to apply a message from such an optimistic age as Cooper's to our pessimistic nuclear age. And yet Anna Julia Cooper's thought has so much in common with womanist, liberationist, and contemporary feminist thought that these newer schools echo many of her beliefs and the beliefs of her contemporaries. From the standpoint of womanist theology it is important to listen in on what Cooper had to say in order to better understand our heritage as Americans, as women, as men, as people of color. All of us in this nation belong to one or more of these three groups and can identify with some of Cooper's concerns.

Dr. Anna Julia Haywood Cooper was one of the most highly educated Black women of her time, a major player among turn-of-the-century literary figures. Her most famous collection of writings, *A Voice from the South,* was published in 1892, prior to the work of W. E. B. Du Bois, a contemporary with whom she is often compared. Along with James Weldon Johnson and others, Cooper encouraged Du Bois in the research and writing of his massive volume *Black Reconstruction in America.*[9] A respected woman in Black intellectual circles, she gained recognition internationally for her work as a scholar and educator.

By the 1890s, with the organization of the National Association of Colored Women (NACW), Black women had developed a national platform from which to speak.[10] Anna Julia Cooper addressed the problem of the *muting* of Black women's voices in *A Voice from the South*.[11] She addressed the ethics of the race problem, higher education for women, and the role of the Church in developing educational programs for Black women and men. Challenging White supremacist ideology among feminists like Anna Howard Shaw, she argued that women's voices of *all* races are part of God's movement of social reform. Such arguments are similar to Ida B. Wells-Barnett's challenges to Frances Willard discussed in her autobiography, *Crusade for Justice*.[12]

In *Womanist Hope/Womanist Justice* Emilie Townes warns that tendencies in African American cultural analysis to characterize the turn of the century as the age of Booker T. Washington and W. E. B. Du Bois limit the conceptual framework of historical interpretation to theories of exceptional male genius.[13] Excluded are the works of African American women like Frances Ellen Watkins Harper's *Iola LeRoy* and *Shadows Uplifted* (1892) and Ida B. Wells-Barnett's *Southern Horror* (1892), *A Red Record* (1895), and *Mob Rule in New Orleans* (1900). Such foundational works for African American social ethics, along with Cooper's *A Voice from the South*, predate Washington's *Up from Slavery* (1901) and Du Bois's *Souls of Black Folk* (1903).

The Selected Works of Ida B. Wells-Barnett,[14] for example, reveals Wells-Barnett's genius as a journalist who gathered statistics on lynching and Black socio-economic conditions at the turn of the century. Her discussions on race, miscegenation, lynching, mob brutality, boycotting, the power of the press, education, Black leaders, and the women's movement and temperance movement form compelling arguments in American social ethics. She demonstrates that African Americans have long employed the media and boycotting to resist racism.

The 1890s were an important period in the development of Black intellect. A founding member of the National Association of Colored Women's Clubs, Cooper was part of a national network of Black intellectual leaders who emphasized racial uplift for the masses. Like her contemporaries, Mary Church Terrell, Fannie Barrier Williams, Josephine St. Pierre Ruffin, and Ida B. Wells-Barnett, she spoke out against racial and gender discrimination. Such women dedicated their lives to improving conditions of newly freed but economically deprived and illiterate slaves. They started schools, self-help organizations, literary societies, and clubs to improve the lives of former slaves and their children. Cooper's contribution was first and foremost through service to others as an educator and administrator.

Anna Cooper was born Annie Julia Haywood in Raleigh, North Carolina, on August 10, 1858. Her mother, Hannah Stanley Haywood, was a slave, and her father was her mother's master. It was not uncommon for slavemasters to force slave women to engage in sexual relations with them. Slave women were considered chattel and were not only raped but were often forced to serve as concubines to their masters. Such a system of forced concubinage amounted to the slavemasters engaging in continual sexual abuse of the women they chose to victimize in this way. To be conceived in a situation of forced concubinage was not unusual, so there were laws to ensure that the children of slavemasters were granted no legal privileges to property, including ownership of one's body. In accordance with the laws governing slavery, Cooper, known in childhood as Annie Julia Haywood, followed the slave condition of her mother. Angered by her biological father's abuse of her mother, Cooper acknowledged his paternity with disdain in her brief, albeit telling, autobiographical writings. "Presumably my father was her master," she wrote. "If so I owe him not a sou."[15]

Describing her mother as too "modest" to ever discuss her daughter's paternity, Cooper resisted popular notions among White Americans that slave women could not possibly be sexually moral. Her description turned the stereotypes of promiscuity so often levied against Black women upside down. Her mother lived in a world where Black women were blamed for the rapes their masters perpetrated against them. By refusing to acknowledge indebtedness to her slavemaster father, Cooper implied that *he, not* her oppressed mother, was the moral transgressor whose name was unfit to be mentioned or recognized.

Cooper's experience of slavery was brief compared to that of her mother and older brothers, Andrew and Rufus. She matured in a system of freedom where she could receive an education without secrecy. She was only four or five years old, when in 1863, Abraham Lincoln's Emancipation Proclamation freed slaves from bondage. It was not until 1868, however, that she began to experience one of the concrete social benefits of that freedom — a formal education. Until then who knows what kinds of dreams she may have had for her life? Who knows what possibilities may have seemed realistic to her?

We will never know what direction Cooper may have chosen to take if the Episcopal Church had not established St. Augustine's Normal and Collegiate Institute in Raleigh, North Carolina, in 1868 for the "Education of Teachers for the Freedmen."[16] Cooper credits that school as the place where she learned not only reading, writing, and mathematics, but classical languages and religious discipline. She writes of her years there as if the school offered an entirely new world for her, a world where she could dream infinite possibilities for herself and humankind.

The knowledge of her slave birth and early childhood must have had a profound effect on Cooper's developing sense of freedom and equality, because when she describes her early childhood she writes with constraint. She writes with respect of the longing for freedom in the slave community, with anger about her paternity, and with compassion for her mother. In her later years, she recalled stories told her about "anxious slave's superstition to wake the baby up & ask directly which side is goin' to win de war?"[17] Hope for freedom seems to characterize her memory of her earliest years.

Of her St. Augustine years, Cooper does not write about *hope* for freedom as much as she writes about *living fully into freedom*. Freedom and equality for all became her life endeavor, with education as a particular means for making socio-economic freedom and equality realities for more Black people in America. Like so many former slaves during the Reconstruction period, Annie and Hannah Haywood believed that education was a gateway to fuller freedom and equality. While Hannah continued to work as a domestic, she encouraged her daughter to take advantage of every opportunity St. Augustine's had to offer.[18] Annie would be spared the physical, psychic, and economic abuses involved in working in White people's homes. Through her educational achievements, young Annie escaped some of the constraints that the masses of Black women in the South faced. Many Black women faced a "new slavery" as underpaid, overworked, emotionally and physically abused domestic servants, sharecroppers, or laundry women in a South resistant to change. A teaching career was a way to escape poverty and a way to help others.

While an education carried certain advantages with it socially and economically, such advantages were limited. Formally educated Black Americans in the South found themselves increasingly segregated and denied equal access to public institutions as the Reconstruction period gave way to the Jim Crow period. In the North, Black Americans experienced only a relatively freer lifestyle. But Anna Cooper, committed to serving Black women and men in the South throughout her life, possessed an irrepressible spirit. Her commitment to the vocation of teaching and to scholarship has been noted by several Black women historians and literary critics in recent years.[19]

Cooper viewed teaching as "the noblest of callings." Teachers, like missionaries and theologians, responded to a call to minister to those who have a need. Teaching was a calling whose worth was greater than any material wealth. She suggested that the nobility of the call to teach transcended race: "I believe that if I were white I should still want to teach those whose need presents a stronger appeal than money.... It is human to be stimulated by appreciation where it is genuine."[20]

What is most striking about Cooper is the passion and motivation that gave great energy to her commitment to education, scholarship, and the intellectual life. She was motivated by belief in the power of religion and in a Christian faith that saw the teachings of Christ as calling for social reform.[21] She is part of a wide range of Black women in African American history who were inspired by a missionary impulse and strong moral and theological values. Jarena Lee (1783–185?), an itinerant preacher in the African American Episcopal Church, and Maria Stewart (1803–79), America's first Black woman political orator, were earlier African American women speakers with whom Cooper shared a similar missionary impulse.

Marilyn Richardson aptly observes that such women, with varying perspectives, have held in common "a strong sense of the Christian imperative as a call to change conditions in the here and now.... By various roads," Richardson explains, "these women came to see their faith as an impetus to lives of social activism."[22] Grounded in a concept of God as an agent of both personal and social change, they held a strong commitment to racial pride and dignity, freedom and equality, and the liberation of positive human potential.

Cooper, like her contemporaries and earlier figures like Maria Stewart, often synthesized democratic principles with a social interpretation of scripture. Such women, along with Black men like David Walker and Frederick Douglass, tested whether the central principles, beliefs, and history of American experience would ever truly be respected for Black Americans. They challenged America to move beyond "empty rhetoric" to proactive moral agency, claiming Christian and democratic principles for Black and White people alike.

Altruism, for Cooper, was an important principle for capturing the spirit of both democracy and Christianity. Her "philosophy of life," as she called it, included an ideal of social altruism, Social Gospel principles, and a concept of the Church as a civilizing influence. For the Church to serve as a civilizing institution meant that it must engage in social reform. Altruism was not simply a private affair between individuals; it was a social one involving institutions. "The greatest happiness comes from altruistic service & is in reach of all of whatever race & condition," she explained.[23]

Altruism is certainly a noble value. But it is very difficult for many contemporary Christians who are women and/or African American to appreciate "service" as central to Christian faith. Today there is much talk about solidarity or unity in diversity, engaging in conversation, being on the side of the God of the oppressed. "Service," like "solidarity" and "unity," is a metaphor for describing Christian relationship, true. But it is a metaphor that feminist, womanist, Black, and liberation theologians debate because of its associations with slavery. Jacquelyn Grant, for example, underscores the problem of euphemizing language of servanthood. Building on the work of womanist biblical scholar Clarice Martin, she criticizes the tendency to interpret the Greek *doulos* as "servant," when it really means "slave."[24] Historically, women have been viewed as servants to men and children. During the slave period, "servant" was a euphemism for "slave." African Americans were exhorted by their slavemasters "to be obedient" as the New Testament exhorted "servants" to do. Cooper was much closer to the experience of slavery than we are today.

Cooper did not employ the term "service" to describe altruism without conflict. Rather, conscious that the idea of service had been abused and could be abused again, she employed it with some difficulty. She wrestled with the question of what it meant to engage in *service,* just as feminist, womanist, and liberation theologians do today. She explained that she did not mean to imply a "pious idea of *being used*" in her use of the term "service." Rather, she had in mind a voluntary commitment to act benevolently toward others. Making a distinction between *servitude* and *service,* she equated servitude with slavery. Servitude was a form of exploitation, a "hateful" practice employed by dominating cultures. But service was *voluntary* and altruistic. Later, during her years as a teacher at the M Street and Dunbar High Schools in Washington, D.C., Cooper wrote and produced a pageant entitled "From Servitude to Service," honoring great Negro leaders in American history. The title is reflective of her own life. Born in servitude, she saw freedom as an opportunity to willingly dedicate her life to Christian service. Service for Cooper meant unselfish commitment as an educator to principles of freedom and equality. She had a sense of being called out to serve the children of newly freed slaves.

Although Cooper does not emphasize the expression "lifting as we climb," which was a motto of many of the Black women's clubs at the end of the last century, she certainly did participate in the movements that employed the motto. The expression "lifting as we climb" meant that it was not enough to gain material and educational success for oneself. It called people out of their self-centeredness to an ethic of service. The motto also, however, carries certain elitist connotations, especially to contemporary ears. It is important to ask, "Who is doing the lifting?" Not all of the women who employed the motto were middle-class, but there was indeed a sense that those who were educated and had attained some measure of success were doing the lifting. Today we are critical of such a perspective. It would be easy to see such a motto as untenable, but it is important to be cautious in our criticism. We must ask what we are going to replace it with. Better, what have we replaced it with?

We live in a world where people are more isolated than in the past, where we do not know our neighbors and feel little responsibility to be our brother or sister's keeper. The African ethic of community solidarity, care, and uplift that undergirds traditional African American social values finds itself in competition with a Western philosophy of individual rights in the midst of competing interests. While a high valuation of the rights of individuals is certainly important, it is not helpful when it is construed hierarchically and when it fails to consider the rights of individuals from a relational, community perspective that emphasizes the interdependence of all life.

In examining values of the past, like the "lifting as we climb" ethic, it is important to retain something of the power of such ethics as we discard the oppressive aspects. Today middle-class communities, in particular, risk moving toward a "lift yourself up by your own bootstraps" ethic, which in the nineteenth century competed with the "lifting as we climb" ethic. An alternative is an ethic of *lifting one another up*. As a popular hymn in Black churches goes, so often Black people in this country have been "climbing up the rough side of the mountain." In lieu of opting for a "lifting as we climb" ethic or "lift yourself up by your own bootstraps" ethic, it is time for Americans across racial, ethnic, gender, and class lines to lift one another up the mountains of oppression, evil, and suffering to move powerfully toward the goals of spiritual and social freedom. To lift one another up across classes, sharing knowledge and wisdom from our various contexts, is to act in solidarity with one another. We begin creating freedom and equality by acting in solidarity with each other across race, class, and gender lines. Solidarity is a new way to conceive and practice altruistic service, a new way of understanding what it means to help one another survive and transform evils of oppression.

Call for Equality in Higher Education and Christian Service

Vehemently opposed to separate programs for women in higher education, Cooper emphasized the importance of providing equal educations to women and men. This issue was central to Cooper's thought and one that she spoke about with ire, sarcasm, and wit. She spoke from her general social observations, from statistics, and from her own experience. Although St. Augustine's was a world where Cooper could live more fully into freedom, it was also binding in certain ways. While it played an important role in her understanding of teaching as an altruistic service, it was also a sexist school. It was the school where Annie Haywood became proficient in languages and developed a love for the classics but it was also the school where she had to fight to take Greek, a class organized for male students. St. Augustine's failed to adequately redress the problem of sexism.

A fast learner who "had devoured what was put before" her, and, "like Oliver Twist, was looking to ask for more," Cooper explained that she felt a "thumping within" of the type felt by any "ambitious girl" desirous of more knowledge and learning. In contrast, she portrayed her male ministerial classmates as sleepy and less ambitious than herself.[25] Cooper's ideas on women's education began at St. Augustine's, where she sought an education equal to that provided for male ministerial candidates. The school provided free tuition and reduced or omitted board for needy pupils but was less generous toward its female students than toward its male ministerial candidates.[26] She criticized St. Augustine's for placing her, "a self-supporting girl," in the position of having to struggle to pay her board by teaching in the summer and after school.

Angered that she had "to fight her way against positive discouragements to the higher education," she criticized the school's practices toward women. She objected to the practice of limiting classes like theology, Greek, and the classics to men. When first advised that a Greek class was being formed for "candidates for the ministry," Annie Haywood responded to the principal, Dr. Smedes, that "the only mission opening before a girl in his school was to marry one of those candidates."[27] She was admitted to the Greek class only after challenging sexist conventions. While continuing her studies at St. Augustine's, Annie did marry one of its candidates for ministry, George Cooper, from Nassau in the British West Indies, a Greek teacher. They were married on June 21, 1877, and continued to study and teach at St. Augustine's.[28] George died in 1879. Cooper, free to develop a long teaching career, never remarried. In the District of Columbia, where she spent most of her adult life, women teachers who chose to get married were required to resign. She devoted her life to her vocation.

In March 1880, in the year after George's death, Cooper argued against the sexist practices she had experienced at St. Augustine's in her address "The Higher Education of Women."[29] Moreover, she contended that the Christian woman is as "potent a missionary agency among our people as the theologian."[30] For Cooper, the contributions of women who were wives, missionaries, mothers, and teachers carried significant weight. Therefore, she argued, young girls must "feel that we expect something more of them than that they merely look pretty and appear well in society."[31] She despised the notion that girls ought to be trained only as much as necessary to make a good wife.

Although she never challenged sexism in the Church regarding women's preaching, Anna Cooper sought equality in the Church and its understanding of ministry. Rather than challenge gender exclusiveness in the pastorate, she placed teaching on an equal par with preaching. The Episcopal Church until 1977 did not sanction the ordination of women. If she was interested in ordination, it is not evident in Cooper's writings. She approached the problem of women's equality in ministry from a different vantage point. Preaching and teaching, she argued, were equally vital stimulants for the regeneration of the race.[32] One was not inferior to the other. She felt her own calling was to improve the race through teaching, a vocation many women were taking up during this period. Now, on the eve of the twenty-first century, far more thorough eradication of sexism from the Church is long overdue. True, teaching is vital to the growth of Church and society as much as preaching. But it is also important to question division of labor along gender lines. In the nineteenth century, women were just entering the work force as teachers. For women to choose the vocation of teaching was considered progressive, because it had been dominated by men. Today, we must continue to value women's choice to teach, particularly at the university level, which is still predominantly male. But we must also challenge the notion that preaching and pastoring are the exclusive domain of men.

In order to move more fully into the vocation of teaching, in 1881 Cooper wrote to Oberlin College in Oberlin, Ohio, requesting admission and free tuition. She was admitted into the sophomore class and graduated with two other Black women in the class of 1884: Mary Church Terrell, who later became president of the National Association of Colored Women, and Ida A. Gibbs (later Ida Gibbs Hunt), who from 1895 to 1904 taught English at the M Street High School in Washington, D.C. She also received an M.A. degree from Oberlin in 1887.

The college experience at Oberlin, with its liberal Christian dedication to the service and education of the underprivileged, further fueled Cooper's already intense desire to dedicate herself to her vocation. Oberlin also fostered her burning intellectual curiosity and scholarly interests. When questioned about Oberlin College's religious training, Cooper responded that Oberlin helped broaden her understanding of Christianity beyond the myopic faith of a "bigoted" churchwoman entrenched in denominational doctrines.[33] Just as Cooper found a caste system of race and gender intolerable, she also found supremacist views of religion intolerable. But she remained an Episcopalian and preferred an Anglo-Catholic liturgy rather than indigenous Black cultural-religious practices.

After graduating from Oberlin, Cooper turned down an invitation to serve as "teacher in charge of girls" at St. Augustine's, a proposition she found sexist. Instead she accepted a position at Wilberforce College in Xenia, Ohio, in charge of the "department of modern languages [and] science."[34] In September of 1885 she returned to St. Augustine's at a lower salary to teach mathematics, Latin, and Greek, apparently because her mother, Hannah, was reaching seventy and Cooper wanted her to retire from domestic work.[35] While at St. Augustine's she was as productive as ever and founded a Sabbath school with other faculty. But she was not content to remain at St. Augustine's. A critic of the Church's perspective on the education of women, she quickly became well-known for her views on the educational status of women in her lectures and essays. She exhorted the Church to take more active responsibility for women's education. At Oberlin, Cooper had been able to take classes in fields conventionally reserved for men, such as philosophy. Having experienced an unconventional model of education, Cooper became the Church's harshest critic when it came to higher education for women.

Sexism and the Church

While she criticized sexism at St. Augustine's and American educational institutions generally, Cooper appreciated the education she received at St. Augustine's. Moreover, she appreciated the Episcopal worship and doctrine she encountered there. Part of her love for the Episcopal Church was aesthetic: for example, the beauty and dignity of the prose in the Prayer Book and the high standard of decorous worship. As a mature woman past retirement age who had traveled abroad and worshiped in foreign lands, she was able to look back on her church experience and give it new meaning. The Episcopal Church, with its Anglo-Catholic roots, gave her a profound sense of connection to the Church across the centuries and around the world. She referred to herself as a sojourner — a pilgrim in the world — who found the Church wherever she traveled.

Although Cooper respected the Episcopal Church, she was not uncritical. She criticized the Church for its racism and its sexism, at the same time indicating the importance of the Episcopal Church's role in proselytizing the American Negro. By the mid-1880s, she was an outspoken Black woman intellectual in demand as a speaker for her analysis of the need for the development of Black womanhood in the South. In 1886 she championed the plight of Southern Black womanhood before a convocation of "colored clergy of the Protestant Episcopal Church at Washington, D.C."[36] She argued that the Church needed to take an expanded and more active role in the education and development of Black women.[37]

In her address entitled "Womanhood a Vital Element in the Regeneration and Progress of a Race," Cooper argued that the Episcopal Church needed to take seriously the concerns of Black women and men. The Church needed to respect the "manhood" of the "Black man's personality" and defer to his conception of the needs of his people. Moreover, it needed to develop Negro womanhood "as an essential fundamental for the elevation of the race, and utilizing this agency in extending the work of the Church."[38] The development of Negro womanhood had been neglected too long by both Black and White churchmen, she charged. Therefore, the Church needed to aid in the education of the "head, heart, and hand" of the Black woman. Cooper saw women as workers for the renewal of humanity. She saw women as a starting point of a race's regeneration: "Now the fundamental agency under God in the regeneration, the re-training of the race, as well as the ground work and starting point of its progress upward, must be the *black woman*."[39]

After all, the young intellectual argued, men and women receive their earliest educations as children at their mothers' feet. This was a popular understanding of womanhood in the nineteenth century. Because women were society's earliest educators and passed along moral virtues to children, Cooper's argument went, they required education for the development of their intellect and moral sympathy. The Black woman was the fundamental agency under God in the development of the race.[40]

Like womanist theologians today, Cooper sought freedom and equality for Black women and men. She challenged colored and White clergy alike to establish educational programs for Black women. She challenged White clergy to look at the entire Negro race as equal to the White race. She turned around the presumption that Black people were barbaric, reminding her audience that the Germanic tribes that encountered the Roman Church, and later the English, were seen as quite barbaric during earlier historical periods: "...surely the task of proselytizing the American Negro is infinitely less formidable than that which confronted the Church in the Barbarians of Europe."[41]

The Episcopal Church effectively turned away Black ministers who professed that they were Episcopalians, Cooper charged. There would be more Black clergy in the Episcopal Church if it divested itself of its racial bias. She criticized a White Southern clergyman who claimed that "the Church is not adapted to the rude untutored minds of the Freedmen, and that they may be left to go to the Methodists and Baptists whither their racial proclivities undeniably tend."[42] Angered by such a bigoted statement, she argued that there were Black Americans who would find Episcopal thought and practice appealing if encouraged to participate.

The problem in Cooper's thought here is that unlike Black male and womanist theologians today, who argue for the value of Black folk culture and African syncretism in religious worship, she engaged in an elitist perspective of the Church in which practices such as clapping, shouting, and call and response were unappreciated. At the same time, she correctly challenged the Episcopal Church to view Black Americans as equal, concluding that not until the Episcopal Church realized that "only sympathy and love can draw" would they be able to "come in touch with our life and have a fellow feeling for our woes." Until then, she argued, White bishops would continue to be "perplexed" by the small percentage of Black Episcopalians.[43]

Today one must go beyond Cooper's acceptance of a Eurocentric model of worship to include religious practices from Black folk culture. An ethic of standing in solidarity with diverse members of Church and community requires that contemporary theologians and ethicists take seriously the contributions of Black folk culture to religious faith and practice. This is a theme that Du Bois addressed more progressively in *The Souls of Black Folk,* published some seventeen years after she published *A Voice,* although he too writes of folk life with a distant air. It was not a theme Cooper addressed except in passing. Her proper theme, as she described it, was the development of the Black woman.

It was the Church's failure to take seriously such development that most concerned Cooper. Where in the Episcopal Church might such a woman find an ally? Someone with power and standing in the community? Dr. Alexander Crummell had delivered his views on the Black Woman in his address "The Black Woman of the South: Her Neglects and Her Needs," before the Freedman's Aid Society of the Methodist Church in Ocean Grove, New Jersey, August 15, 1883; his address was later published as a pamphlet. It is unclear when she first met him, but Cooper and Crummell soon shared their mutual concerns.

Crummell, born a free Black in New York City, March 2, 1819, received a degree in divinity from Queen's College in Cambridge in 1853 and worked as a missionary for twenty years. He returned to a post–Civil War and post-slavery America in 1873.[44] Angered by the racial oppression he saw and experienced, he wrote and delivered speeches of protest in which he described the degradation and abuse of the Black woman and called for aid and assistance in her development.[45] By the time Cooper arrived in Washington, D.C., he was well established nationally and internationally as a renowned orator. As pastor of the District's only colored Protestant Episcopal Church, he was a key member of the audience she addressed.

This Black woman from the South, Anna J. Cooper, criticized the Church for making "no motion towards carrying out Dr. Crummell's suggestion" to dedicate itself to the development and education of Black women.[46] In her address before the colored clergy of the Protestant Episcopal Church of Washington, D.C., in 1886, she related her appreciation of Crummell's proposals for developing Black womanhood. She referred metaphorically to his prophetic role in the Episcopal Church by calling him Moses, Prophet, and King, chastising her audience for failing to take seriously his call to develop Black women in the South.

After acknowledging Crummell's earlier work on the subject, Cooper proceeded to present her own views. With acerbic wit she queried her audience about whether they would listen to her — a Black woman who had come up from the South — if they had ignored Crummell, whose prophetic voice was already well known to them and established in the Black community:

> "Woman's influence on social progress" — who in Christendom doubts or questions it?...Nor, on the other hand, could it have been intended that I should apply the position when taken and proven, to the needs and responsibilities of the women of our race in the South. For is it not written, "Cursed is he that cometh after the King?" and has not the King already preceded me in "The Black Woman of the South"? They have had both Moses and the Prophets in Dr. Crummell and if they hear not him, neither would they be persuaded though one came up from the South.[47]

Through a play on words, Cooper recalled the biblical story of the rich man and Lazarus, the poor man who begged for crumbs outside the rich man's doors (Luke 16:19–31). Like the rich man who went to hell when he died and yearned to come up from the dead to warn his relatives about the imminence of death and the threat of hell, Cooper "came up from the South" to plead deliverance from socio-economic inequality for Black women. Just as Abraham told the rich man that "though one came up from the dead" none would hear him, Cooper questioned her audience's ability to hear what she had to say.

Six years later, in her preface to *A Voice from the South,* Cooper stated that only Black women could speak adequately on behalf of Black women and their needs. In her address before the

Episcopal clergy, she spoke authoritatively of Black women's conditions in the South. She questioned the Episcopal clergymen's commitment to Black women. Appealing to popular sentiments of protectiveness by men toward women, she sought to gain her audience's interest in responsible social action toward Black Southern women.

Apparently Cooper's speech made a favorable impression, because in 1887 she left Raleigh for Washington, D.C., to accept a position at the city's only Black high school, the M Street School (also known as Washington Colored High School). She taught science and mathematics to male and female students. The M Street School was one of the most prestigious Black high schools in the United States. In 1916 the school relocated and became known as the Dunbar High School. Black students from across the country sought enrollment there.

The young scholar stayed at the home of Dr. and Mrs. Alexander Crummell during her first year in the District of Columbia. In Crummell she found a friend and ally for the needs and concerns of Black women. She also found a church home through Crummell and became a member of St. Luke's Church. The product of Crummell's great fundraising campaign, St. Luke's architecture was modeled after an Anglican country church. Founded by Crummell in 1873, it was the first "separate colored Episcopal Church of the District of Columbia."[48]

Apparently, these two champions of Black women mutually respected one another, because when Crummell founded the American Negro Academy in 1897, an organization of the most prominent Black scholars in America, the group invited Anna Cooper to attend. The Academy's membership included W. E. B. Du Bois, Rev. Francis Grimké, and Archibald Grimké. There is some dispute as to whether Cooper was a member. Although biographer Louise Hutchinson writes that she was the only female member of the Academy, no formal documentation of her membership has been found. Cooper herself wrote in her review of the Academy's first meeting that the organization limited their membership to "men of African descent."[49]

While members of the Academy respected Cooper's scholarship, their appreciation was constrained by a conservative attitude regarding women's roles in intellectual discourse. Washington correctly observes that Frederick Douglass, Du Bois, Francis Grimké, and Crummell did not acknowledge Cooper's work in print as she did theirs. The relationships between Cooper and Black intellectuals of the period were far from equal or truly mutual.

When asked by Monroe A. Major to provide names of Black women for his historical volume on prominent Black women, Frederick Douglass responded: "I have thus far seen no book of importance written by a negro woman and I know of no one among us who can appropriately be called famous." This was a peculiar statement given that it was made in 1892, the year Cooper published *A Voice from the South*.[50] There were any number of other women Douglass could have named as well, since this was a vital period for Black women writers and lecturers: Frances Ellen Watkins Harper, Ida B. Wells-Barnett, Mary Church Terrell.

W. E. B. Du Bois, who praised Cooper's biographical sketch of her friend Charlotte Forten Grimké, a leading Black woman writer, educator, and activist, failed to follow through on Cooper's request that he publish the manuscript. Moreover, he failed to credit Cooper for her very famous statement that "Only the Black Woman can say, 'When and where I enter, in the quiet, undisputed dignity of my womanhood...then and there the entire race enters with me" in his essay "On the Damnation of Women," in his book *Darkwater*.[51] Often reputed to be a feminist for his sensitivity to the social and intellectual subjugation of Black women in *Darkwater* and other writings, Du Bois participated in such subjugation by overlooking an opportunity for a genuinely collegial relationship with Cooper. In the midst of an intellectual world dominated by men, Anna Cooper never received the full respect or credit she deserved for her work.

Cooper's Friendship with the Grimké Family

From the first year of their acquaintance in 1887, Cooper and the Grimkés were aware that their friendship would deepen.[52] The friendship became a lifelong one, and after Charlotte's death, Anna Cooper and Francis Grimké corresponded by letter. The Grimkés formed the core of Cooper's social-intellectual life and were her closest friends. Charlotte Forten Grimké (1837–1914), though older than Anna by about twenty-one years, became her dearest friend. She was a granddaughter of the famous free Black abolitionist, James Forten of Philadelphia. Born a member of Philadelphia's free Black elite, she had strong scholarly interests and served as a teacher for several years. She had studied French, German, Latin, and English literature.[53] Deeply religious, she believed God had called her to use her talents to inspire and improve her race.[54] A published author of poetry and essays, she was also well known for her work teaching contraband slaves in South Carolina from 1862 to 1864. She moved to Washington, D.C. in 1872.[55]

Charlotte's husband, Francis Grimké, was twelve years younger than Charlotte. Born in Charleston, South Carolina, in 1850, of a White slavemaster, Henry Grimké, and a slave woman, he and his brother, Archibald, were nationally prominent. Archibald, a graduate of Harvard Law School, was a member of a prominent law firm in Boston and had served as consul to Saint-Domingue (modern-day Haiti). The brothers were the nephews of Sarah Grimké and Angelina Grimké Weld.[56] Angelina Grimké Weld recognized Francis as her legitimate nephew and helped finance his education. Francis and Charlotte met in Washington, marrying in 1878, when Grimké graduated from Princeton Theological Seminary and became pastor of the Fifteenth Street Presbyterian Church where he served until his death.[57]

Cooper and the Grimkés met at one another's homes on weekends for cultural and intellectual stimulation for a period of thirty years or more. They invited others with similar interests into their "circle of kindred spirits," as Cooper described it. Weekends with the Grimkés were "something to look forward to." The two homes were blended "in planned, systematic and enlightening but pleasurable and progressive intercourse of a cultural and highly stimulating kind."[58] Friday night meetings were held at the Grimkés and Sunday evenings were spent at Cooper's home. Guests included Dr. Edward Blyden, missionary to Liberia; Mrs. Anne Douglass, the second wife of Frederick Douglass; the Black composer Samuel Coleridge-Taylor; and the Harvard-trained Black philosopher, Alain Locke.

Sunday evenings were a time for gathering to hear music. Cooper would play classical music at the piano in her home. They sang songs like "He Shall Feed His Flock," "I Know My Redeemer Liveth," and "Consider the Lilies." They would end in hymns, with Francis joining in. The Friday meetings were spent studying art.[59] Discussions lasted a full hour, after which Mrs. Grimké served tea and the group engaged in general conversation.[60]

Sometimes discussions became heated. Grimké and Cooper did not always agree. He disapproved of Cooper's poem "Simon of Cyrene," arguing that she made Simon a volunteer when the scripture read that "him they compelled to bear His Cross." Claiming poetic license, Cooper portrayed Simon of Cyrene as "One elect thruout the Ages to play his part in that Drama when Asia betrayed and Europe crucified — Africa, predestined to come forward humbly and gladly to give Service, the peculiar contribution of Ethiopia's blameless Race." With this interpretation in mind, she donated a stained-glass window depicting St. Simon of Cyrene to St. Augustine's College in memory of her deceased husband. She eschewed a portrayal of Simon as "a slave, dumb driven, as an accidental beast of burden happening at the moment to be caught in the denouement of the greatest Drama of the Universe."[61]

Grimké, arguing for a literal translation, called Cooper's thinking "pure rationalism." She, liberal in her outlook and influenced by the broad ecumenical spirit of Oberlin College, viewed Grimké as a "fundamentalist."[62] Given the fact that the experience of slavery was a few decades away, it is not surprising that the question of whether Simon served as slave or volunteer generated such heated debate. If Simon were a slave, what would his service to Christ mean symbolically for Black Americans? Would it entail questioning one's faith and Christian service? While Cooper's distinction between servitude and service is helpful, it is eisegetical here and imposes a preferred meaning onto the text. It does not apply well to this particular text, as Grimké argued. The disagreement on Simon's story was part of the strength and bond of their friendship. Cooper explained:

> A lasting friendship is not conditioned on identity of views nor dependent on the self-immolation of either personality. Dr. Grimké bore with my "rationalism" quite graciously, I trust, as I with his fundamentalism... neither ever tried to win over the other.[63]

Although she remained a member of St. Luke's Episcopal Church, Cooper regularly visited the Fifteenth Street Presbyterian Church to hear Grimké's special sermons. She included some of the sermons in her *Life and Writings of the Grimké Family.*[64] She also discussed his sermons in her Tuesday night classes at Frelinghuysen University. Grimké's special sermons emphasized the moral and intellectual development of the Negro. He began developing Social Gospel motifs in the sermons in the 1890s. Social Gospel scholar Ronald White has observed that White and Black Social Gospel leaders alike appealed to both Christian and civic "Scriptures." This is evident in both Grimké's and Cooper's work. Each made appeals to America's consciousness regarding democratic and Christian principles. For example, in a letter to Woodrow Wilson, Grimké appealed to the Constitution and the Declaration of Independence as well as to Wilson's "Christian character." He condemned segregation as undemocratic and un-Christian.[65]

Similarly, in her 1925 doctoral defense Cooper appealed to social progress in a democratic sense as part of the very nature of God that is also inherent in human being. In her earlier work, democratic principles are similarly synthesized, conflated even, with Christian ones. Both Grimké and Cooper interpreted the religion of Jesus as standing for "the fatherhood of God and the brotherhood of man," which was a popular, often quoted expression in the Social Gospel movement.[66] Grimké and Cooper shared a common bond in their social interpretations of the Gospel.

The M Street School and Dunbar High School

The Social Gospel interpretation of Christ's teachings that Cooper propounded was optimistic, even idealistic. But in reality, she faced many obstacles in her efforts to apply the democratic ideals she saw in the Gospel to the society she lived and worked in. White Social Gospel leaders were far more ready to deal with class issues among European immigrants than among Black women and men. Moreover, such ideals did not adequately challenge the sexism and racism of America's public educational institutions. In 1901–6, Cooper was principal of the M Street School. With her new college preparatory curriculum, the school was accredited for the first time by Harvard and successfully placed several students at schools like Harvard, Yale, Radcliffe, Dartmouth, Amherst, Oberlin, and Brown.[67]

In 1904–5, the predominantly White Washington, D.C., school board took measures to oust Cooper from her principalship. They thought that Washington's colored high school should emphasize industrial and vocational subjects, which Cooper refused to do.[68] She saw a diversity among Black students. Such subjects were most appropriate for some Black students but not for all. She focussed on a college preparatory curriculum. In response the school board attacked her moral character, turning to gossip that Cooper and her teaching colleague John Love, also her foster son and twelve or thirteen years her junior, were having an affair. Cooper, widowed, was a single woman, and single women were not looked on kindly by the school board.[69] Despite the lack of damaging testimony, the board voted to dismiss Cooper on the charges that she refused to use a textbook authorized by the board, was too sympathetic to unqualified students, did not maintain discipline, and did not maintain a "proper spirit of unity and loyalty." They decided not to rehire her.[70] She taught languages at Lincoln Institute in Jefferson City, Missouri, until 1910, when the M Street School rehired her.

Undoubtedly some of the outrage surrounding Cooper's principalship was sparked by the glowing reviews she received in a book by the Abbé Felix Klein, which brought international attention to her work as a principal. In 1903, Klein, a professor from the Catholic Institute of Paris, was engaged in writing *Au pays de "la vie intense"* (In the Land of the Strenuous Life), a study of Canadian and U.S. religious and educational institutions. In his journeys, Klein visited the M Street School, where Anna Cooper was principal. He was impressed by her grace and dignified bearing. He was further impressed by her exegesis of Vergil's *Aeneid* in her Latin class. He esteemed the quality of the school's college preparatory curriculum and the structure of its administration.

The two scholars parted good friends, with Klein expressing hope that he would see Cooper some time in Paris. Later, Klein's passages on Cooper in his book created an outrage in Washington. Many Whites were offended that Klein esteemed the colored high school as the best high school in Washington. Such an estimation of a colored high school — especially directed by a single

Black woman — was unheard of. Klein and Cooper wrote one another on a fairly regular basis, particularly around Christmas and Easter. Klein sent Cooper pictures of the Black Madonna of Chartres in one letter, noting that his countrymen had long seen Black women as beautiful.[71]

Accepted as a doctoral student at Columbia University in New York City, based on course work in Paris, Cooper did go to Paris for four summer sessions of study in Romance languages. Doctoral studies were no easy task for Cooper, since in 1915 she had adopted and begun raising the grandchildren of her brother Andrew, who was hospitalized with a serious illness. The children ranged in age from twelve years to six months: Regia, John, Andrew, Marion, and Annie Cooper Haywood, an infant and Cooper's namesake. Well into her middle years, she was determined to fulfill two callings she viewed as "most noble": motherhood and teaching. With multiple responsibilities, she found it most difficult to fulfill her residency requirement. Contemporary Americans are becoming accustomed to working mothers as a result of economic necessity and the feminist movement. But it was a very strong break with convention for a single professional woman to work as mother, student, and teacher in 1915. Women today find such triple callings challenging, often daunting. Cooper took on multiple roles in a social-historical context even less supportive than our own. She was undaunted.

In 1923 Cooper came down with the flu, an illness she believed was providential, because she had an opportunity to ask for a year's sick leave from the Paul Laurence Dunbar High School. She decided to recover from the flu *and* complete her Ph.D. residency in Paris.[72] After overcoming initial disagreement from the secretary to the dean at Columbia, in 1924 she began study at the Sorbonne, which accepted her credits from Columbia. She wrote to the Abbé Felix Klein for spiritual support. Sending God's blessings and protection for her "courageous plans," he helped her make travel arrangements and find lodging in Paris.[73]

After completing fifty semester hours at the Sorbonne, Cooper received a letter warning her that she would be dropped from her position at the Dunbar High School if she did not return within sixty days. Savoring every last moment of each day, she returned five minutes before 9:00 A.M. on the sixtieth day. She completed work on her dissertation at the Library of Congress in Washington, D.C. Klein helped her find a "collaboratrice" to copy archival material and send it to her at the Library of Congress.[74]

In her dissertation, "Slavery and the French Revolutionists," Cooper examined France's attitudes toward human rights during the French Revolution in contrast to its attitudes toward slavery in Saint-Domingue (Haiti). The abolition of slavery, she argued, became a major issue during the French Revolution. Moreover, revolutionary France could have avoided the loss of Haiti as a province if it had been consistent in its principles on human rights. Slavery could have been easily abolished through legislation if the people it dishonored most, the French colonists, had felt they could no longer violate their moral laws. That France abolished slavery not by appeal to moral law and legislation but in response to violent revolution was tragic.[75]

Although France was inconsistent in its principles of liberty, equality, and fraternity during the Revolution, Cooper argued, these principles triumphed less than half a century later. She credited "les Amis des Noirs" (the Friends of the Blacks) with leaving an indelible mark on France's memory by awakening the African people to an awareness of their individual human personality and right to liberty. The principles of liberty, equality, and fraternity finally triumphed, because these were *immortal* principles inherent in human nature.[76] The Friends of the Blacks did not introduce Africans to democratic principles but helped awaken them to a priori principles they already possessed. The philosophic mind, she argued, recognizes that there is no such thing as supremacy among human nations and cultures.

Against the wishes of her supervisor, who denied her request for a leave, Cooper left for Paris in March 1925 to defend her dissertation.[77] Her defense on March 23, 1925, was a success. Employing familial metaphors from Social Gospel theology in her defense, she referred to God as "the father of us all." Her emphasis on the brotherhood of man and the fatherhood of God and her metaphor of democratic progress as an "urge-cell" of the Creator reflect the merging of sociology and theology in Social Gospel thought. Social Gospel theologians borrowed Paul's metaphor of the interdependence of one body as a biblical basis for appealing to this idea of Christian society as well as to the emerging social sciences symbolization of society as organic or solidaristic.

The Frelinghuysen Years

Five years later, in 1930, Cooper was of retirement age and required to leave her position at Dunbar High School. But far from ready to retire, she was elected in 1929 to serve as the second president of Frelinghuysen University. She accepted the offer and was installed as president after retiring from Dunbar High School in 1930. By 1930, educated Black women in Washington, D.C., had begun to take on more untraditional roles in Black community life.[78] Cooper was representative of a shift in women's roles during this period.

Frelinghuysen, founded in 1906, was established to provide educational, social, and moral uplift programs for the children of former slaves. Originally a network of schools in buildings and homes throughout Washington, D.C., especially the poorer sections, by 1926–27 it offered a complete high school education, business high school, junior college, and college-level courses in liberal arts, sociology, applied science, fine arts, applied Christianity, theology, law, and pharmacy. But the school was in financial trouble. Forced to relocate several times, Frelinghuysen finally relocated to Dr. Cooper's home at 201 T Street, N.W., in the Fall of 1931. When there was some dispute about making 201 T Street the permanent home of Frelinghuysen, Cooper along with a small group of trustees established an annex to Frelinghuysen named after her mother, the Hannah Stanley Opportunity School, which would remain under her management and control. This group was concerned about potential mismanagement of funds by the school's business officers. Eventually Cooper bequeathed her property to Frelinghuysen and then apparently removed Frelinghuysen from her will when the school went defunct in mid-century.[79] An elegant structure, Anna Cooper's home still stands, its former grandeur evident.

Unable to raise funds for Frelinghuysen to meet new accreditation rules as a university,[80] Cooper changed the school's name to "Frelinghuysen Group of Schools." Holding fast to her philosophy of altruistic service, she encouraged teachers to volunteer or to work for very little. She practiced this ideal herself by accepting only $50, which she supplemented with her pension from Dunbar High School. In a letter to Francis Grimké in 1937, she lamented that it seemed "increasingly difficult to get anything like sober consideration of big basic principles and even the least concerted action for the common good." She deplored that working in "self-forgetful devotion for the general welfare" was considered by too many to be foolish and impractical.[81] She resigned from the presidency in 1939 but worked as registrar until 1949, when, at age ninety, she retired. The school closed in 1964.

In 1958, in an interview for her one-hundredth birthday, Cooper explained, "It isn't what we say about ourselves, it's what our lives stand for."[82] She died in 1964 at the age of 105. Her life stood for unfailing, persevering commitment to Christian service and hope in a God of freedom and equality. Service was public and required participation in God's activity of reform. It required Social Gospel theology and ethics. It required the application of biblical principles to a wholistic analysis of racism, sexism, and classism.

Discontented with things as they were, Cooper sought with unwavering hope to change them. She was not naive, but tempered her optimism with a dose of realism. She knew she would meet resistance; when challenged, she did not sink to despair but pressed on to demand that America become consistent in its moral principles of freedom and equality. Inequality between Whites and people of color, women and men, contradicted the principles on which the nation was founded. Basing her social-political ideas on biblical principles, she envisioned Christ as the exemplar of human cooperation with God's movement of reform. The Church was called to teach a Gospel of reform, with women of all races taking up leadership positions to work equally with men. Such is the legacy she leaves contemporary Americans.

NOTES

1. See Martin Luther King, Jr., *Where Do We Go from Here: Chaos or Community?* (Boston: Beacon Press, 1968), 155–66. King argued for the elimination of poverty among both Blacks and Whites, noting that it was time to move beyond "civil rights" legislation to an establishment of effective social-economic mandates.

2. See Cornel West's discussion of nihilism in *Prophetic Fragments* (Grand Rapids: Eerdmans, 1987).

3. See Marian Wright Edelman, "The Black Family in America," in *The Black Women's Health Book,* ed. Evelyn C. White (Seattle: Seal Press, 1990), 128–48; Bell Hooks and Cornel West, "Black Women and Men: Partnership in the 1990s," in Bell Hooks, *Yearning* (Boston: South End Press, 1990), 203–14; and Cornel West, *Prophetic Fragments* (Grand Rapids: Eerdmans, 1987).

4. Statistics from a study by the Rev. Anne Byfield, "Workshop on Black Women and Men," Conference on the Family, Martin University, Indianapolis, April 27, 1991.

5. See Patricia Hill Collins, *Black Feminist Thought* (New York: Routledge, 1990), chapter 1.

6. The research of C. Eric Lincoln and and Lawrence H. Mamiya indicates that there are so few Black men available for the ministry that by the year 2000 there will be a shortage in urban Black churches (*The Black Church in the African-American Experience* [Durham, N.C.: Duke University Press, 1990], 400–401).

7. See Jacquelyn Grant, *White Women's Christ and Black Women's Jesus* (Atlanta: Scholars Press, 1988).

8. See Andrew Billingsley, *Climbing Jacob's Ladder: The Enduring Legacy of African-American Families* (New York: Simon & Schuster, 1992).

9. See David Levering Lewis, introduction to W. E. B. Du Bois, *Black Reconstruction in America: 1860–1880* (New York: Atheneum, 1992), viii–ix. Mary Helen Washington in her introduction to Cooper's *A Voice from the South,* Schomburg Library of Nineteenth-Century Black Women Writers (1892; New York: Oxford University Press, 1988), criticizes Du Bois's failure to properly credit Cooper's influence on his work.

10. Marcia Riggs's dissertation, "Toward a Mediating Ethic of Black Liberation" (Ann Arbor: University of Michigan, 1991) provides a helpful ethical analysis of the Black women's club movement.

11. See Cooper, "Our Raison d'Être," *A Voice from the South.*

12. See Alfreda Duster, ed., *Crusade for Justice* (Chicago: University of Chicago Press, 1970).

13. Emilie Townes, *Womanist Justice, Womanist Hope* (Atlanta: Scholars Press, 1993), 175.

14. Jualynne Dodson, ed., *The Collected Works of Ida B. Wells-Barnett* (New York: Oxford University Press, 1991).

15. Undated autobiographical document by Anna Cooper, Anna Julia Cooper Papers, courtesy of the Moorland-Spingarn Research Center, Howard

University, reproduced in Louise Daniel Hutchinson, *Anna J. Cooper: A Voice from the South* (Washington, D.C.: Smithsonian Institution Press, 1981), 4.

16. "Cooper's Account of Her Entry to St. Augustine's Normal School," Anna Julia Cooper Papers, courtesy of the Moorland-Spingarn Research Center. Reproduced in Hutchinson, *Anna J. Cooper*, 20.

17. See Hutchinson, *Anna J. Cooper*, 3–5, 15–16.

18. Ibid., 23. Hutchinson notes that in a questionnaire to "Negro College Graduates" by Dr. Charles S. Johnson of Fisk University in 1930, Anna Cooper wrote: "My mother's self-sacrificing toil to give me advantages she had never enjoyed is worthy [of] the highest praise and undying gratitude." Hutchinson notes that we know from Cooper's own testimony that Hannah would not have been able to adequately instruct her daughter herself. Most likely Cooper does not mean the self-sacrificing toil of academic instruction, but the self-sacrificing toil of her mother's labor to support herself and her daughter. Rather than demand that her daughter work full-time to bring in more income, she made her daughter's education top priority.

19. See Hutchinson, *Anna J. Cooper*, chapter 1; Leona C. Gabel, *From Slavery to the Sorbonne and Beyond: The Life and Writings of Anna J. Cooper* (Northampton, Mass.: Department of History of Smith College, 1982), 83–92; and Mary Helen Washington, introduction to *A Voice from the South*, xxvii–xxxi.

20. Cooper, "Negro College Graduates' Questionnaire," Anna Julia Cooper Papers, courtesy of the Moorland-Spingarn Research Center. See also Hutchinson, *Anna J. Cooper*, 38.

21. Gabel, *From Slavery to the Sorbonne*, 83–92. Gabel describes Cooper as "essentially" a "religious" person in "a broad, liberal sense."

22. Marilyn Richardson, *Black Women and Religion* (Boston: G. K. Hall, 1980), xvi.

23. "Negro College Graduates' Questionnaire," question 65, Anna Julia Cooper Papers, courtesy of the Moorland-Spingarn Research Center.

24. Jacquelyn Grant, "The Sin of Servanthood," in Emilie Townes, ed., *A Troubling in My Soul* (Maryknoll, N.Y.: Orbis Books, 1993), 211; Clarice Martin, "Womanist Interpretations of the New Testament," *Journal of Feminist Studies in Religion* 6, no. 2 (Fall 1990): 44–45.

25. Cooper, "The Higher Education of Women," in *A Voice from the South*, 76.

26. See Gabel, *From Slavery to the Sorbonne and Beyond*, 13–15.

27. Cooper, "The Higher Education of Women," 77.

28. See Hutchinson, *Anna J. Cooper*, 29.

29. Anne Allen Shockley, *Afro-American Women Writers: 1746–1933* (New York: G. K. Hall, 1988), 204ff.

30. Cooper, "The Higher Education of Women," in *A Voice from the South*, 79.

31. Ibid., 78.

32. See Cheryl Townsend Gilkes, "Some Mother's Son and Some Father's Daughter," in *Shaping New Vision: Gender and Values in American Culture*, ed. Clarissa Atkinson, Constance Buchanan and Margaret Miles (Ann Arbor:

UMI Research Press, 1987), 80. Gilkes notes that the early recruitment of women as teachers in the Afro-Christian tradition helped established their status and inclusion as "educators," which was also a status claimed by male preachers.

33. "Negro Students Questionnaire," question 37, Anna Julia Cooper Papers, courtesy of the Moorland-Spingarn Research Center.

34. See Hutchinson, *Anna J. Cooper*, 40. Hutchinson notes that Cooper left her position at St. Augustine's College at a monthly salary of $30 and that Smedes offered to double her income only after she announced her plans to attend Oberlin. Hutchinson suggests that the challenge of the position and the salary at Wilberforce were more satisfactory to Cooper's needs and interests.

35. Hutchinson notes a letter from Anna Cooper to her mother, mailed on October 7, 1884, which suggests that Cooper's mother was concerned and disappointed when her daughter went to Wilberforce instead of returning home. Also, Cooper's brother, Rufus, had died leaving a widow and six children, most of whom were school age (ibid., 43).

36. Cooper, "Womanhood a Vital Element in the Regeneration and Progress of a Race," in *A Voice from the South*, 9.

37. Ibid. See chapter 2 for further discussion on Cooper's thought regarding the role of the Church in the development of Black womanhood.

38. Ibid.

39. Ibid., 28.

40. Ibid.

41. Ibid., 33–34.

42. Ibid., 35–36.

43. Ibid., 41.

44. Richard Barksdale and Kenneth Kinnamon, *Black Writers of America* (New York: Macmillan Company, 1972), 101–2. See also W. E. B. Du Bois, *The Souls of Black Folk* (New York: Signet Classic, New American Library, 1969), 237. Du Bois devotes a chapter to Alexander Crummell, whom he personally met. Du Bois notes the "temptation of Despair" Crummell faced when he was turned down because, as Crummell was told, "the General Theological Seminary of the Episcopal Church cannot admit a Negro."

45. Barksdale and Kinnamon, *Black Writers of America*, 102–3.

46. Cooper, "Womanhood a Vital Element in the Regeneration and Progress of a Race," 43.

47. Ibid., 24.

48. See Clotilda A. Barnett, "St. Luke's Episcopal Church, 1873–1879," in *One Hundred Years: St. Luke's Episcopal Church*, a yearbook published on St. Luke's one hundredth anniversary in 1973.

49. See Gable, *From Slavery to the Sorbonne*, 34, Hutchinson, *Anna J. Cooper*, 107–10. See also Alfred Moss, *The American Negro Academy* (Baton Rouge: Louisiana State University Press, 1981).

50. See Washington, introduction to *A Voice from the South*, xxxix–xli.

51. Ibid.

52. Cooper, *Personal Recollections of the Grimké Family*, 8: "In spite of absorbing cares and worries of house hunting and home prospecting...,

even in that first year we met we knew the meeting to be of no chance acquaintanceship."

53. See Brenda Stevenson, introduction to *The Journals of Charlotte Forten Grimké*, ed. Brenda Stevenson (New York: Oxford University Press, 1988), 24.

54. Ibid.

55. Ibid., 50.

56. Carter G. Woodson, ed., *The Works of Francis James Grimké*, vol. 1 (Washington, D.C.: Associated Publishers, 1942), vii.

57. Ibid. Francis Grimké was attending Howard Law School in 1874 and probably met Charlotte at that time. He later transferred to Princeton Theological Seminary.

58. Cooper, *Life of the Grimkés*, 8–9.

59. Ibid., 11.

60. Ibid., 11–12.

61. Ibid., 15.

62. Ibid., 15, 21.

63. Ibid., 21.

64. Ibid., 22.

65. Ronald C. White, Jr., *Liberty and Justice for All: Racial Reform and the Social Gospel (1877–1925)*, Rauschenbusch Lectures, new series 2 (New York: Harper & Row, 1990), 110, 112. White notes that Henry Justin Ferry in "Francis James Grimké: Portrait of a Black Puritan" (Ph.D diss., Yale University, 1970) has noted the development of Social Gospel themes in Grimké's work, although Grimké never abandoned his understanding of the primary locus of ministry as the parish. The U.S. Constitution is an example of "civic scripture."

66. Ibid., 108.

67. See Hutchinson, *Anna Julia Cooper*, 61–81.

68. See ibid., 61, 67–81. See also Washington, introduction to Cooper, *A Voice from the South*, xxxiv.

69. Washington, introduction to Cooper, *A Voice from the South*, xxxv–xxxviii.

70. Ibid., xxxiii–xxxviii. Washington lists these as the four grounds on which Cooper was dismissed. See also Sharon Harley, "Anna J. Cooper: A Voice for Black Women," in *The Afro-American Woman*, ed. Rosalyn Terborg-Penn and Sharon Harley (Port Washington, N.Y.: Kennikat Press, 1978), 92. Harley notes that although Cooper's failure to be rehired by the school board may be attributable to objections at having a female principal, "a more likely explanation is that she was being punished for her opposition to White superiority by refusing to use inferior curriculum and textbooks." I concur with Harley's analysis, but suspect Cooper's gender exacerbated negative sentiment regarding her spirit of independence.

71. Letter From Abbé Felix Klein to Anna Julia Cooper, Anna Julia Cooper Papers, courtesy of the Moorland-Spingarn Research Center.

72. Cooper, *The Third Step*, privately printed, n.d., Anna Julia Cooper Papers, courtesy of the Moorland-Spingarn Research Center, Howard University, Washington, D.C.

73. Ibid., 3 and 7. The French reads "Que Dieu vous protége et benisse vos courageux desseins." See also Gabel, *From Slavery to the Sorbonne*, 46–48.

74. Gabel, *From Slavery to the Sorbonne*, 65.

75. Cooper, *L'attitude de la France a l'égard de l'esclavage pendant la Révolution* (Paris: Imprimèrie de la Cour d'Appel, 1925), 12.

76. Ibid., 160. Cooper quotes A. Cochin, *L'abolition de l'esclavage* (Paris, 1861). See Frances Richardson Keller, trans., *Slavery and the French Revolutionists, by Anna Julia Cooper* (New York: Edwin Mellen Press, 1988), 221, for notes.

77. Cooper, *The Third Step*, 11.

78. See Sharon Harley, "Beyond the Classroom: The Organizational Lives of Black Female Educators in the District of Columbia, 1890–1930," *Journal of Negro Education* 51, no. 3 (1982). See also Darlene Clark Hine's definitive series *Black Women in United States History*, which includes this same essay by Harley, along with hundreds of essays by Harley, Evelyn Brooks [Higginbotham], Rosalyn Terborg Penn, Darlene Clark Hine, and numerous other Black women historians.

79. Hutchinson, *Anna J. Cooper*, 147–52, 165–67. The decision to relocate the school to Cooper's home was reached by the majority of the trustees. Some, like John Lankford, opposed.

80. Melinda Chateauvert, "The Third Step: Anna Julia Cooper and Black Education in the District of Columbia, 1910–1960," in *SAGE: A Scholarly Journal on Black Women, Student Supplement 1988*, 7–13. Chateauvert notes that Frelinghuysen was unique, being the only university in Washington, D.C., besides Howard University that admitted Black students.

81. Cooper, "Letter from Anna J. Cooper to Francis J. Grimké," February 28, 1937, in *The Works of Francis J. Grimké*, vol. 4, *Letters*, ed. Carter G. Woodson (Washington, D.C.: Associated Publishers, 1942), 566–67.

82. Hutchinson, *Anna J. Cooper*, 175. See also "Negro Educator Sees Life's Meaning at 100," *Washington Post*, August 10, 1958, courtesy of the Oberlin College Archives.

2

God, Christ, Church, and Society

DURING THE LAST DECADE, African Americans have experienced the painful sting of White backlash in governmental legislation regarding civil rights for people of color. It is now more difficult, for example, to file a racial discrimination suit against an employer than it has been for some twenty-odd years. Moreover, affirmative action has become a target of attack, the most vicious criticism being that it is a form of "reverse racism." Worst of all, racially motivated hate crimes are on the rise, affecting not only Black Americans but Latinos, Asians, and Jews as well. Just as Black women and men today struggle with White backlash against the socio-economic gains of the Civil Rights and Black power movements, so Black women and men in the late nineteenth and early twentieth centuries struggled with backlash against the gains of the Reconstruction period. Emerging White supremacist groups like the Skinheads and Neo-Nazis, as well as the seemingly ever-present Ku Klux Klan, call to mind the rise of the Ku Klux Klan during the late nineteenth century, who were also broad in their hatred of non-Protestant people of color.

On the one hand, the world of contemporary African Americans seems remote from that of nineteenth-century African American women and men. In the twentieth century, W. E. B. Du Bois's "talented tenth," educated, middle-class African Americans, grew to 33 percent, in large part because of the effects of desegregation and to some extent because of affirmative action programs, which were created as an effort at redistributive and compensatory justice. But on the other hand, it seems that very little progress has been made at all since such a percentage growth is not large and

63

is in threat of shrinking if America continues to perceive Black people's demand for an equal share in the economic, political, educational, and social life of the nation as a threat. The masses of Black Americans have not benefitted from the programs set in place in the 1960s and 1970s, leaving many African Americans pessimistic about the possibilities for real change in American society.

Americans, Black or White, cannot go back to the kind of optimism in the evolution of society that Anna Julia Cooper embodied one hundred years ago, because too many promises have been made and broken in the interim. All too often it appears that society is *regressing* rather than *progressing*. But neither need those most directly affected by xenophobic attitudes give way to an extreme pessimism, which leads to despair resulting in fatalism and nihilistic actions. It is still necessary to press forward to demand progress in American society. And, although America cannot recover the kind of optimism Cooper embodied at this particular moment in history, faith in a transforming God who empowers commitment to social progress and reform provides strength and hope in the continued work for freedom and equality. The Church, as Anna Cooper argued, has a direct responsibility to call for progress and social reform if we understand salvation as social and not exclusively personal. Therefore, it would be fruitful to examine her understanding of Christ and culture in relation to the Church to consider the liberating emphasis of her Christology, which prefigures contemporary liberationist thought.

God and Reform

For Cooper, the most sacred and noble lesson of the Gospels was love for one another regardless of color. This, in her view, was the most important message of Christ's teaching. Only in receiving all of God's people equally, she suggested in her choice of scripture, can one receive Christ. She implied that those who claim to be Christians and limit their understanding of equality to people of their own race are not true Christians at all.

In her essay "Has America a Race Problem? If So, How Can It Best Be Solved?" Cooper wrote of race as being like a family.[1]

Like other women in the Black women's club movement, she was concerned about White attempts to exterminate Black men and women. Following the lead of Ida B. Wells-Barnett, she and her contemporaries sought an end to the practice of lynching. Extermination of the race, particularly in the South, was a real threat. There is no need, she argued, to exterminate others:

> Men will here [in America] learn that a race, as a family, may be true to itself without seeking to exterminate all others. That for the note of the feeblest there is room, nay a positive need, in the harmonies of God. That the principles of true democracy are founded in universal reciprocity, and that "A man's a man" was written when God first stamped His own image and superscription on His child and breathed into his nostrils the breath of life.[2]

In the harmonies of God, race is not at all problematic, because all of humankind bears God's image and is God's child. These are familiar principles to contemporary readers. But Cooper wrote during a time when Black writers were challenging the White supremacist views of those who identified with the Ku Klux Klan, the "night riders," for the first time. She wrote during a period when many White Americans openly questioned the humanity of Black Americans. To claim that Black people were created in the image of God undoubtedly sounded as radical to the ears of many White Americans then as the Black liberationist claim that God is Black sounds to many White people today.

Criticizing White supremacist claims, Cooper contended that the supremacy of one race could not ultimately prevail in America, a continent "held in equilibrium by such conflicted forces and by so many and such strong fibred races."[3] She questioned the viability of racial supremacy on American soil, arguing that with its multiracial makeup America would inevitably be required to recognize God's image as being stamped on all races. In 1925, in her doctoral defense, "Equality of Races and the Democratic Movement," Cooper argued against theories that democracy, progress, and equality manifested themselves only in Western civilization. For Cooper, these principles were not the property of a superior race. Rather they were innate principles given to all humankind:

> Is it not reasonable to grant that if our theory regarding the elite of nations is not sufficiently comprehensive to include a nation with such a creditable recommendation, that we should either enlarge our definition to harmonize with the facts or else treat the subject of Equality not as an

abstraction but as it manifests itself uniquely in Europe and in America?
A better hypothesis it seems to me, would be the postulate that progress
in the democratic sense is an inborn human endowment — a shadow
mark of the Creator's image, or if you will an urge-cell, the universal
and unmistakable hall-mark traceable to the Father of all.[4]

"Progress in the democratic sense," she hypothesized, was an
"inborn human endowment" and "a shadow mark of the Creator's image." Democratic progress could be traced right back to
God. It was an ordained, God-given reality in human history. Further, humankind was endowed with such principles. In this way
humanity is created in God's likeness. Democratic progress most
essentially had to do with freedom and equality. In a nutshell,
then, human beings were created fully equal and free by their
Creator, God.[5]

Moving beyond classical metaphors of "image," Dr. Cooper
further referred to humankind's likeness to God as a *"Singing*
Something." This *"Singing* Something" distinguishes humankind
from apes. Democratic principles in humankind are also like a
divine spark capable of awakening at any moment and "never
wholly smothered or stamped out." Democratic principles, like an
"urge-cell," a "divine spark," a *Singing* Something, surge forth
from era to era calling for reform.[6] Thus, Cooper argued, the
racial group or nation that supposes to play God by dominating
the earth takes on a terrible responsibility.[7] She warned of the
revolutions that met dominating governments in Russia, China,
Turkey, Egypt, and the Gandhi movement in India as examples of
the power of democratic principles of freedom and equality in the
human spirit.

Where is God's presence evident for Cooper? God is in the very
movement of reform. God is in this *Singing* Something in human
being that rises up against injustice and moves onward toward
a full realization of freedom. God is the power of freedom and
equality that moves them forward. What is striking about her
metaphor is that one can conceptualize God as a liberating voice
within human being. Such words are suggestive for contemporary
liberation theology. They suggest that something of the liberating voice of God rises up and speaks through those who resist
domination. It eventually flares, comes to voice, and rises up.

This has empowering implications for liberationist and womanist theologies. To conceive of God's message of freedom and equality as innate in the human spirit is empowering for the silenced and voiceless, for those whose knowledge has been trampled down to the underside of history, for those whose voices have been muted in the history of the Western Church with its distortions of the Gospel. If this divine message of freedom and equality that sparks and sings within humanity can never truly be suppressed by a dominating race or nation, then the proper role of the Church is to empower the politically powerless to find their voices. The movement toward freedom and equality is part of an unquenchable universal process. For Christians Jesus exemplified these principles in his work and teachings.

Jesus and Reform

Christ and Culture

Christ and the Church were "the source of the vitalizing principle of woman's development and amelioration" for Cooper.[8] Christianity, based on ideals given by Christ, was responsible for the ennoblement of women:

> Christ gave ideals not formulae. The Gospel is a germ requiring millennia for its growth and ripening. It needs and at the same time helps to form around itself a soil enriched in civilization, and perfected in culture and insight without which the embryo can neither be unfolded or comprehended.[9]

The development of civilization was necessary for the Gospel to unfold from a germ-like or embryonic state so that humankind, in turn, could develop and grow in its comprehension of the Gospel deposited by Christ. Christ deposited certain *ideals* that required the development of society to be comprehended. Without the enriching soil of civilization, culture, and insight the developing germ — now embryo — of the Gospel could not be comprehended. Likewise, without Christ's message of freedom and equality, human culture could not grow and mature. Christ and culture are interdependent in this system of thought. Christ's ideals are a source of life for human culture. They provide a kind of power of knowledge. But such knowledge is not simply given.

Human beings have a responsibility to develop Christ's ideals within self and society. Christ's ideals and civilization are deeply interdependent.[10]

There are elements of a liberal social evolutionary theory evident in Cooper's thinking, particularly in her presupposition that a fundamental characteristic of human nature and societies is that they continuously evolve or develop over millennia. Further, her presupposition that societies evolve toward a more perfect ideal of a Christian society with each new development shows she was influenced by optimistic nineteenth-century valuations of social progress.[11] And yet she was realistic in her assessment of human finitude, which was evident in men and women's stubborn thick-headedness when it came to fully appropriating Christ's principles of freedom and equality. This finitude meant that it would take millennia for Christ's principles to mature in civilization. For Cooper, the concepts of gender inequality and racial inequality were not inherent in the Gospels, but lay in humanity's miscomprehension of the Gospels. She saw her own era as one in which the truth of women's equality was beginning to unfold more clearly before heretofore unperceiving eyes. Her own era, she believed, was one in which the Church must recognize Christ's identification with women. She called for a Black feminist reading of scripture, employing the authority of Black women's experience in her biblical hermeneutics.

Christ and the Black Woman of the South

The contemporary womanist theologian Jacquelyn Grant, who in the tradition of Black liberation theology argues that Jesus is on the side of "the least of these," argues that for her Jesus today is "found in the experience of Black women, is a Black woman." That is, Jesus identifies with Black women who are among the least of "the least of these."[12] Because Christ is a "whole Savior" of all humanity, for Blacks as well as Whites, in the tradition of Black women's Christology, in which Grant places herself, then Christ is also a savior for women as well as men. Building on the work of James Cone, she explains that this Christ, who challenges oppression, who liberates the stranger, the outcast, the hungry, is concerned with particular peoples as part of God's universal will to liberate them from inhumanity.

There is a similar representation of Christ in "Womanhood a Vital Element in the Regeneration and Progress of a Race." Just as Christ identifies with the "least of these" in Black and womanist liberation theology, so for Cooper Christ identifies with the stranger, the outcast, the poor. Moreover, she employs literary techniques to draw parallel representations of Jesus and the Black woman of the South. The effect is that there is a strong similarity between her descriptions of Jesus and of the Black woman of the South.

Just as Cooper describes the Black woman of the South as mute, so she describes Christ as mute. Just as Christ is a vital element in the regeneration of civilization in a universal sense, so is the Black woman a vital element, in a particular sense, in the regeneration of a race. For example, in her introduction to *A Voice from the South,* she described the voice of the Black woman of the South as voiceless and as a "muted" note. Her symbolization of Christ is in some respects, then, a feminine one from a nineteenth-century perspective. His face is quiet. He "foreshadows" the perfection of civilization *mutely.* The image of Jesus as a *foreshadowing* and *mute* figure recalls the muted Black woman of the South. Both have a muted, liberating message that has been suppressed. Society can and must hear this liberating message.

The regeneration of the Negro race resided in the "Black woman of the South" in Cooper's thinking. The "vital agency of womanhood in the regeneration and progress of a race" was conceded on *a priori* grounds, because women formed and directed children of both genders from birth. Thus Cooper held that the position of women in a society "determines the vital elements of its regeneration and progress."[13] In the Black race, this must be the Black woman. She alone among humankind, Cooper wrote, is the fundamental element in the individual lives of her people quite literally from conception, to birth, toddlerhood, and beyond. Christ engages in a similar work on a universal level by leading the toddling child of civilization into regeneration and a greater comprehension of the ideals of the Gospel:

> The quiet face of the Nazarene is ever seen a little way ahead, never too far to come down to and touch the life of the lowest in days the darkest,

yet ever leading onward, still onward, the tottering childish feet of our
strangely boastful civilization.[14]

Like the Black woman of the South, Jesus is ever-present, leading society "mutely" onward to a fuller realization of ideals of
freedom and equality. On the other hand, the Black woman,
because she triply experienced oppression — sexually, racially,
and economically — suffered as Christ had suffered and had a
vital contribution to make in leading her race and civilization
toward a fuller realization of democratic principles. Cooper represented Christ as possessing a virtue that she and her auditors
would have associated with women: meekness. Moreover, like the
Black woman of the South, Jesus led a "lowly life." And yet this
meek, lowly figure "mutely" foreshadowed every progressive social force. She portrayed the life and story of Jesus as quiet and
humble in contrast to a boastful civilization:

> With all the strides our civilization has made from the first to the nine-
> teenth century, we can boast not an idea, not a principle of action, not a
> progressive social force but was already *mutely* foreshadowed, or directly
> enjoined in that simple tale of a meek and lowly life.[15]

The Black woman of the South is muted because she has been
dominated, because society has not given her an audience or requested her testimony on her own behalf regarding the problems
of racism and sexism in America. Christ, in this portrait, seems to
identify with the situation of the Black woman of the South, with
the dominated. Christ's muteness suggests that Christ lacks an audience. Further it is an indication that Cooper saw the world as
well aware of Christ's presence, but not of his message of freedom
for all. Cooper brought this message of freedom to the awareness
of her auditors and readers, articulating it from the perspective of
Black womanhood.

On the one hand, Cooper symbolized Jesus as being a figure of
the past who mutely foreshadows the development and perfection
of society. At the same time, Cooper portrayed the "quiet face"
of Jesus the "Nazarene" as being always slightly ahead, in the future, leading civilization onward the way a parent leads a toddling
child. Jesus is immanent in human history and also transcends it,
being ever ahead of civilization to lead it onward. The image of
Jesus leading civilization as a parent leads a toddling child reflects

Cooper's positive valuation of motherhood — a role for which she saw no comparison.

Christ was very much like a mother in Cooper's description. Cooper's feminine portrait of Christ is essential to understanding her concept of womanhood. Cooper's portrayal of Christ as having motherly and womanly virtues (tenderness, compassion)[16] lay the groundwork for Cooper's argument on the importance of women's voices as leaders in social reform. Because women embodied these virtues, they were natural leaders. On motherhood she wrote:

> Woman, Mother, — your responsibility is one that might make angels tremble and fear to take hold! To trifle with it, to ignore or misuse it, is to treat lightly the most sacred and solemn trust ever confided by God to humankind.[17]

Envisioning no higher responsibility than motherhood, she described motherhood as a sacred responsibility that made even angels tremble. While she did not come right out and say that for the Black race Jesus was like a Black mother, her use of metaphor suggests as much. She sacralized Black motherhood in her symbolization of Christ as mothering civilization into its development and progress to a perfected state. Such a strong association of motherhood with the work of God or Christ was not unusual during this period. The Methodist feminist preacher Anna Shaw, whose ideas were familiar to Cooper, saw the love of a true mother as analogous to God's love. Moreover, for both Anna Shaw and Elizabeth Cady Stanton, women inherently possessed the moral qualities that were required for a truly just social order. Stanton in contrast to Shaw saw God as the First Cause of the universe.[18] This universe required an eternal balance between masculine and feminine elements. Similarly, as we shall see later, Cooper places emphasis on a symmetry of male and female elements. What makes Cooper's representation of Jesus distinctive is that she identifies him with *Black womanhood* and *Black motherhood*. The portraits she painted of Jesus' role in civilization and Black women's role in the regeneration of a race were parallel in many respects. This is a powerful literary device that functions to persuade the reader to take Cooper's side regarding the development of Black womanhood and the importance of hearing women's voices along with the voice of Jesus.

Jesus and the Dominated

The historical Jesus, for Cooper, was concerned not only with the ennoblement of women, but of the weak and the dominated generally. Her foremost image of Jesus was that of the social reformer, leading humankind into freedom. She copied five pages of scripture passages that she found essential to the Christian message. The first page is missing. The text begins with page two, which instructs the reader to humble oneself as a little child and not to "offend one of these little ones which believe in me."[19] Such scripture was very likely important to Cooper because it supported her understanding of motherhood, the guardianship of children, as vital to the life of a civilization.

The second scripture passage is what Jesus cited as the greatest commandment in Matthew 22:37–39: "Thou shalt love the Lord thy God with all thy heart and with all thy strength and with all thy mind.... The second is.... Thou shalt love thy neighbor as thyself."[20] For Cooper, the most important question was, "Who is my neighbor?" Therefore she also recorded the parable of the Good Samaritan in Luke 10:29–37. The author of the Gospel of Luke records Jesus as asking the lawyer what the law says one must do in order to inherit eternal life. The commandments to love God and neighbor, in the Lukan account, are placed on the lawyer's lips and affirmed by Jesus. The Gospel of Matthew does not record the parable of the Good Samaritan. But in Matthew 22 the commandments to love God and neighbor are placed on Jesus' lips. Cooper preferred the Lukan account, which depicts the lawyer asking, "Who is my neighbor?" and Jesus presenting a parable in response. The question "Who is my neighbor?" is one that was particularly provocative for Cooper in terms of the movement toward social reform and amelioration.

The parable of the Good Samaritan was central to Cooper's understanding of the Christian message. Her question to the Church was: "Who is my neighbor?" She criticized American churches for looking only to the White poor as their neighbor, while leaving the Black poor on the side of the road. Cooper published a short story entitled "Christ's Church," in which she revised the Good Samaritan parable to address the race problem in the United States. As in classical Christian theology, Jesus in her interpretation of the parable identifies with the stranger, the out-cast, the dispossessed. But Cooper revises the parable to address the problem of racism in the modern period. In "Christ's Church," a poor Black man beset by thieves was refused entry into a White Church. As the poor Black man was made to understand he was not welcome, the preacher announced that he would be preaching on the text, "*I was a stranger and ye took me not in.*" "But you see, the stranger at the door was — Black!" Cooper wrote, "and, of course, that settles it."[21]

In this interpretation of the Good Samaritan parable, Cooper challenges White American churches to apply the Gospel to the color problem in America. She turned to an interpretation of the Synoptic Gospels based on a social hermeneutic that relied on Black women's traditional interpretation of the Bible and concur-rently on prevalent Social Gospel ideals that were finding a small but significant audience in the late nineteenth-century milieu in which Cooper was writing. The story had shock value. It directly enjoined White churches to treat Black Americans as their neigh-bors. The Christian ethical injunction to "love thy neighbor as thyself" was antithetical to racial prejudice. White Christians were not such "Good Samaritans" if they did good deeds only for their poor White neighbors.

Today, liberation theologians often cite Matthew 25 — which presents feeding the hungry, giving drink to the thirsty and visiting the sick and the imprisoned as a way of honoring Jesus — to argue that Christ is on the side of the oppressed. Since Cooper recorded the same set of scripture passages in her "Bible Quotations," one can gather that she held a similar perspective. Throughout her writings she is concerned with the well-being of the weak and the dominated. Matthew 25 would have supported her social under-standing of the Gospel just as it supports liberation theology's social interpretation of the Gospel today. She understood the ex-hortation to love one's neighbor as a call to give one's life in service to the needy across racial lines. This is what Cooper saw as the most significant message of the sayings of Jesus.

To supplement her reading of the Synoptic Gospels, Cooper turned to the Book of Acts and to several New Testament Epis-tles. She transcribed from James 2:3–10 the injunction that those in the faith of the Lord Jesus Christ should not be respecters of persons, that the poor must be treated with no less respect than the wealthy. From there she went on to transcribe into her notes Acts 10:34, in which Peter opened his mouth to say that he perceived that "God is no respecter of persons," perhaps feeling that this drove the point home. To be like God or in imitation of God required an impartial, unconditional love of all persons. Christian principles are not only antithetical to racism; they are also antithetical to classism.

The Social Gospel of Jesus

Anna Cooper read sermons and articles on the social teachings of Jesus with great interest. In an undated letter to the editor of the *Outlook,* she requested a sermon focusing on the problem of racism in America. She wrote that although she appreciated the *Outlook*'s teachings on the social teachings of Christ, particularly the work of Dr. Abbott, the editor needed to publish sermons that directly addressed the race problem. Arguing that Christ was concerned for the poor and oppressed regardless of race or nationality, she contended that the problem of racism ought to be addressed by American pulpits:

> I have read with deep interest the weekly talks in the Outlook on *Xt's Teachings on Social Topics* & there has come to me, as always from Dr. Abbott's unfolding of a truth, a quickening sense of the reality of Xt's hold on the everyday problems that vex and harass us.[22]

Cooper painted a socially concrete portrait of Jesus Christ meaningful to the everyday experiences of Black women and men in America. She explained in her letter to the editor of the *Outlook* that she had "often tried to imagine Xt (not a theological abstraction but the man Xt Jesus) living in our world of today." She asked: "What would he say, what would he scourge, with whom would he 'associate' — where would he feel at home?"[23] Employing her gifts of imagination and literary flair, she fleshed out a portrait of Jesus Christ as seeking a supportive, compassionate fellowship of followers who demonstrated their capacity of leadership by serving him in his oppression. Her image of Christ is of a man who preached to the poor and whose message contemporary churches need to hear with new ears:

...on whose breast could he lean with complacent love, whom would he choose to minister to him in tender sympathy & grateful affection, what pew would be assigned him in the Churches? The man whom Mary & Martha cheered & refreshed, whom Peter admired & John loved, who offended the upper crust of society by ignoring their shibboleths & receiving publicans & sinners & sitting at meat with them, the man who made it the climax of his peroration that "the poor have the Gospel preached to them," — what would be his sermon to the Churches of America today?[24]

"Dr. Abbott," to whom Cooper refers in her letter, was undoubtedly Lyman Abbott. Lyman Abbott, born in 1835, was a prominent Social Gospel leader. He became editor-in-chief of the *Christian Union,* a nondenominational religious weekly, in 1881. He was also the successor to Henry Ward Beecher's pulpit at Plymouth Congregational Church (Brooklyn, New York) in 1888. In his writings and sermons, Abbott, like Beecher, promulgated ideals of social reform that included a historical-critical analysis of the Bible and a liberal evolutionary theory influenced by the thought of Herbert Spencer and Charles Darwin.[25]

In 1893 the *Christian Union* became the *Outlook*. Initially, Abbot was liberal in his views regarding race and argued for equality. But by the 1890s he had adopted a position of gradualism. Abbott believed that he and many other White northerners had been overly enthusiastic about solving "the southern question." He came to maintain that the race problem should be worked out primarily by the Negroes and the White men of the South, with the North providing aid only under the supervision of the federal government. Abbott retreated from a position of reform to a position of accommodation.[26] From Cooper's letter, written in the spirit of a reformer, one can glean that she felt the accommodationist philosophy of the *Outlook,* as represented in Abbott's work, inadequately addressed the race problem in America.

Anna Cooper found the *Outlook* attractive because it emphasized Christ as a teacher of social ideals. She found Social Gospel teachings appealing because they emphasized a concrete, historical representation of "the man Xt Jesus," rather than an abstract concept of Christ. She found it appealing to imagine Christ in communion with the friends and disciples who loved, cheered, and refreshed him in the midst of his preaching among the poor, publicans, and sinners. She approved of a portrait of Christ who offended the upper crust of society by focusing his ministry on the

poor. But what, she asked rhetorically, would be Christ's sermon
to American churches today?

Would Christ find White American churches hypocritical, much
as certain Pharisees were portrayed in the Synoptic Gospels, in
their neglect of ministry to Black Americans? (Cooper was not
aware of the anti-Jewishness of such depictions of the Pharisees
among Christians.) In Cooper's opinion the answer was yes. She
saw the Social Gospel movement as needing to be more attentive
to the race problem in America, in order to be consistent with a
social gospel that was truly socially ameliorative. Her good friend
Francis Grimké made similar criticisms of White liberal Christian leaders who claimed a social gospel message. Both Grimké
and Cooper sought a logical consistency regarding Christian social
responsibility.

The sermons in the *Outlook,* Cooper wrote, more than in any
other series of sermons she had seen or heard in a long time
brought "this man-loving, practical, social teacher & reformer
in touch with our own daily life." Yet they failed to address
the race problem. For that reason, she explained, she was writing to request that the editor devote a sermon to the teaching of
Christ on "Race prejudice & proscription."[27] American preachers and Social Gospel leaders were remiss in sympathizing with
the grievances of the Irish, Hungarian, Bohemian, German, Ital-
ian, Norwegian, and other immigrant European labor populations
to the exclusion of the Black man:

> But in those sections of our country where the Black man is the laborer,
> poor, longsuffering, patient — oppressed — for the first time the pulpit
> becomes timid about "disturbing social conditions" & "antagonizing lo-
> cal prejudices." A great evangelist of the country preaching in the South
> & convicting many of sin of righteousness & of judgement — when told
> that this "common people" would hear him gladly, consented to set apart
> a day "to preach for colored people!" Has Xt no special message on this
> subject? Would he have ignored the sin of the Pharisees of this time who
> make broad their phylacteries but neglect the weightier matters of the
> law, who make long prayers but oppress God's poor & take comfort in
> being Abraham's seed & not as other men?[28]

White American churches were neglecting the weightier matters of the law, of Christian principles. Surely, Cooper exhorted,
Christ would have a special message to the conditions of colored
people in America. Christ would have a special word to the op-

pressed — not simply recent European immigrants, but to all of the oppressed, including the Black laborers of the South. Cooper's understanding of Christ as a social reformer was related to her understanding of God in relation to humankind. She saw God as the creator of all peoples across the globe. She suggested this pointedly in her doctoral defense, asking, "Must we blame God because He made of one blood all peoples that dwell on earth but went to sleep during the firing when some millions were tanned yellow, some brown and some even black."[29] Seeking a positive perspective on race, she contended that Whites in Europe and America must love "the least of these" of every color. Only by receiving the least of these, in every shade and hue, could one receive Jesus Christ. Eschewing the notion of blaming God for color difference as an absurdity, she asked:

> Or rather may we not rejoice that our civilization is to learn and finally apply this last and noblest lesson, the most difficult of all taught by the Master and so sacred that it should be studied, marked, learned and inwardly digested till graven on the hearts of men and emblazoned on the suffering pathway of the Cross: "By *this* shall men know that ye are my disciples, *that ye love one another*," and that so much the more because on receiving the least of my brethren ye are receiving Me.[30]

Here is the crux of Cooper's Christology. Christ received the least of these. Likewise, the Church must receive the least of these. Who were the least of these? Not just the poor of Western European descent, but the poor of every hue. Today, liberation, womanist, and *mujerista* (Hispanic feminist) theologians make a similar faith claim. The color line, the gender line, and class lines still plague a world dominated by Western culture. Christian Churches have yet to fulfill the call to "receive the least of these." There has been much trampling of this central message in the Gospel. Such trampling takes place whenever Christian theologians, clergy, and congregations dismiss the significance of the Church's role in social transformation around the problems of racism, classism, and sexism. Such trampling takes place when such problems are dismissed as "preliminary concerns," too "particular," not "universal." Racism, classism, and sexism are particular problems with universal effects. The Church universal cannot be whole until the "least of these" are received with the respect given those who are economically and politically powerful.

Church and Society

The work of the Church is not to emphasize a life of personal piety
alone. Personal piety apart from social transformation is sinful because it alienates self from society. It fails to consider the social
responsibility of individuals, who, after all, are dependent on society. The Church, then, is responsible for developing individuals
who are *socially* responsible. Sin and righteousness are concerned
with human relations in both the private and public spheres. Anna
Cooper argued that the Church's Christianizing influence requires
cultural and social activity.

The Church, in practicing Gospel principles, was called to ex-
ercise a *civilizing* influence, advancing the truth and ideals of the
Gospel. She used the term "civilizing" in a very qualified way, not
to refer to industrial or technological progress, but to refer to ethical progress. The Church must be a leader of the culture that it
nurtures and is nurtured by. Given Cooper's emphasis on freedom
and equality in her understanding of civilization, one might say
that civilization occurs when the Church produces a socially liberative effect in human culture. Civilization in this sense is a process
of moral transformation. The Church is, ideally, progressive. It
ought to be a civilizing influence. However, Cooper warned, it has
failed to live up to this calling many times in history. It too is in
the process of being civilized by the Christian principles it claims
to believe in.

In America, Cooper thought, the next triumph of civilization
would be the realization of equal rights between the races, an
equal hearing of women's voices, and the intellectual and moral
development of Black women. She was particularly concerned,
in the 1880s and 1890s, with gender equality. Critical of the
Church's subordination of women in certain historical periods,
particularly during the Middle Ages, Cooper made a distinction
between the Christianity of the Church and the teachings of
Christ.

The Church did not always act as a civilizing agent in human
culture. It was civilizing only in those contexts where its outlook
and practices were consistent with the principles of equality represented in the work and Gospel of Jesus Christ.[31] For Cooper,
the historical Jesus and his teachings were inseparable from the

development and role of the Church in Western social history and civilization. Casting an evaluative eye at the Church, she both praised and criticized it for its views and actions toward women. It was in tension in its attempt to comprehend the "spirit" and the "letter" of Christ's precepts, beset by incongruities and corruptions.[32]

By "incongruities," Cooper had in mind nineteenth-century scholarly interpretations of the development of the Church in the twelfth century, which held that marriage was relegated to an inferior position in relation to celibacy. This, Cooper criticized, resulted in hypocrisy on the part of clergy and in the discreditation of women.[33] She was critical of corruption in the history of the Church and charged it with committing "a double offense against woman in the middle ages":

> Making of marriage a sacrament and at the same time insisting on the celibacy of the clergy and other religious orders, she [the Church] gave an inferior if not an impure character to the marriage relation, especially fitted to reflect discredit on woman. Would this were all or the worst! but the Church by the licentiousness of its chosen servants invaded the household and established too often as vicious connections those relations which it forbade to assume openly and in good faith.[34]

While the facts of particular historical periods seemed to deny that the source of the vitalizing principle of woman's development and amelioration was the Christian Church, Cooper saw hope for the Church. Its problem was that it failed to practice the teachings of Jesus. To the extent that it was "coincident with Christianity," the Church was a positive, vitalizing influence. That is, when it exercised consistency in its interpretation and practice of a Gospel message of freedom, the Church was a positive, progressive social force. Cooper was well aware that the Church would continue to provide partial, incomplete, even outrageous interpretations of Christ's teachings. However, Christ, in her theological perspective, was in everlasting relationship to the Church with all of its flaws and ruthless misapplications of scripture. His precepts were more powerful than the Church with all its outrages against them:

> Individuals, organizations, whole sections of the Church militant may outrage the Christ whom they profess, may ruthlessly trample under foot both the spirit and the letter of his precepts, yet not till we hear the voices audibly saying "Come let us depart hence," shall we cease to believe and cling to the promise, "*I am with you to the end of the world.*"[35]

Christ and his precepts continued in history to the end of the world. Further, Christ transcended history in the sense that Christ transcended any given historical moment. He foreshadowed the future but also existed in the future, beckoning civilization forward. An anti-freedom, anti-equality stance, in Cooper's view, contradicted the Gospel. Those who professed Christ and who trampled underfoot the spirit and letter of Christ's precepts, which affirmed human equality across race and gender lines, were hypocrites. Asserting that the idea of "the radical amelioration of womankind" regardless of rank, wealth, or culture had come from and would continue to come from the Gospel of Jesus Christ, Cooper challenged the Church to grow in its noble ideals of womanhood.[36] Such growth required that the Church address the problem of gender equality, taking women's needs for equal economic and educational opportunities as seriously as men's.

That a high idea of womanhood was emerging in America was evidence of progress on the part of the Church and the nation. Further, the women's movement was an important development in the ever unfolding process of human history. It was one more reform toward the ideal of freedom for all. The very basis of the hope of America's reaching its ideal as a civilization lay in the germ deposited centuries past by the Christian Church and the feudal system:

> Now this high regard for woman, this germ of a prolific idea which in our own day is bearing such rich and varied fruit, was ingrafted into European civilization, we have said, from two sources, the Christian Church and the Feudal System. For although the Feudal System can in no sense be said to have originated the idea, yet there can be no doubt that the habits of life and modes of thought to which Feudalism gave rise, materially fostered and developed it; for they gave us chivalry.[37]

While on the face of it, Cooper seems to give too much credit for noble ideals of womanhood to American and Western European culture, she really sees both cultures as immature in their development. Their noblest ideals originated in the early Roman Catholic Church. Cooper's historical analysis, here, begs the question since orthodox early Church writers were not concerned with the equality of women. Of course her emphasis at this particular juncture is the "ennoblement" of women and not equality. This germ of an ideal was now bearing a "rich and varied fruit" in her own time. But this fruit did not indicate a perfection in European or American civilization. Modern civilization was yet in an embryonic state.

Critical of chivalry in the South, Cooper touches on the ennoblement of woman only briefly. Her real concern was not chivalry with its false, elitist, and racist standard of nobleness, where only middle-class White women are deemed to have worth. To the contrary, she envisioned true ennoblement as a high valuation of women's worth across racial, class, and gender lines. On the one hand, Cooper described modern civilization in Europe and America as "a society still fresh and vigorous, whose seed is in itself, and whose very name is synonymous with all that is progressive, elevating and inspiring." She referred to Europe and America respectively as the "bud" and "flower of modern civilization." But on the other hand, she was very careful to clarify that satisfaction in modern civilization, particularly in American institutions, "rests not on the fruition we now enjoy," but rather such satisfaction "springs from the possibilities and promise that are inherent in the system." The possibilities and promises were present because they had been grafted into civilization in the teachings of Christ. Moral perfection in Church and society, for Cooper, was a realm of infinite possibilities, not a finite, limited, and final *fait accompli.*

> Such conditions in embryo are all that we claim for the land of the West. We have not yet reached our ideal in American civilization.... But there can be no doubt that here in America is the arena in which the next triumph of civilization is to be won; and here too we find promise abundant and possibilities infinite.[38]

Her ultimate expectation was that civilization would move ever closer to a reflection of Godly, Christian principles. The Church was a continuously evolving, developing institution. God was calling it ever forward to correct its practices and outlook, advancing freedom and equality in American culture. To what extent has the Church met the challenges Cooper prophesied lay before it? Her words "We have not yet reached our ideal in American civilization" still ring true today. I suspect that they will continue to ring true for as long as American culture exists. Cooper did not envision a perfect society for her time or for ours, but rather she envisioned a perfected or ameliorated society. She died at the height of the Civil Rights movement. Born in freedom, a prophetic voice in a segregated world, she lived long enough to witness Martin Luther King's march on Washington and desegregation in America's public sphere. There is no written evidence to indicate she attended such events, but she would have known of them. She died one year before the voting rights bill was signed by President Lyndon Johnson. For a woman born in slavery, such events would have been triumphs in American civilization.

And yet there are other triumphs to be won. Desegregation has not produced a utopic world any more than the abolition of slavery did. What is the challenge to the Church today, one hundred years and more after *A Voice from the South* was published? It is to ask itself where it continues to trample on Christ's precepts of freedom and equality between women and men, Blacks and Whites. How does a nation empower people to live in freedom once it has freed them? Such was the question Cooper's generation brought to Church and society. How does a nation empower people to live in equality once it has desegregated them? Such is the question contemporary Americans must resolve.

Neither freedom nor equality can be fully realized unless Americans inside and outside the Church begin to realize that freedom and equality are not simply physical states, but political and spiritual realities. That is, freedom and equality cannot be limited to spatial movement — where one sits, lives, eats, or works. America will not be consistent in its principles of freedom and equality until it desegregates power relations between Blacks and Whites, women and men. America will not be free until there is a sharing of power among all peoples in Church and society. It is a more difficult task than dismantling physical barriers. The task of this generation is to dismantle barriers of socio-economic and political power, to bring about a desegregation of minds and hearts. Living into freedom and equality is no easy task. It is hard and it will become harder if America takes it seriously.

Reinhold Niebuhr argued that those in dominant positions of power do not easily or willingly give up that power but seek to maintain it out of self-interested greed.[39] "Sharing power" sounds warm, nice, fuzzy. But in reality, if America lives into the next stages of freedom and equality, the process will become increasingly painful for all as the masses of women, people of color, and poor Whites demand an equal voice, jobs, and education and the elite few are challenged to release their control of the world's socio-economic and political resources. The process will become increasingly painful as Americans are challenged to let go of inner prejudices. And yet such pain is part of the healing process required by true social transformation. If America covenants to withstand the painful but healing process of God's movement of reform, a social and spiritual revival is possible. But such possibility is dependent on commitment to change, a willingness to move beyond things as they are.

NOTES

1. Anna Julia Cooper, "Has America a Race Problem? If So, How Can It Best Be Solved?" in *A Voice from the South,* ed. Mary Helen Washington, Schomburg Library of Nineteenth-Century Black Women Writers (1892; New York: Oxford University Press, 1988), 168.

2. Ibid. Cooper used traditional, that is, masculine, language to describe humankind and God. She was in keeping with her social-historical context.

3. Ibid., 165.

4. Anna Julia Cooper, "Equality of Races and the Democratic Movement," privately printed pamphlet, Washington, D.C., 1945, 4–5.

5. See ibid., 4–9. Cooper refuted the notion of her examiner, Dr. Bougle of the Sorbonne, that there were certain "elite" nations and races who were "privileged as the most advanced to carry the torch of civilization for the enlightenment of the 'Backward races.'"

6. Ibid.

7. Ibid., 5.

8. Ibid., 16.

9. Ibid., 17.

10. Cooper's understanding of the development of truth in history is reminiscent of Hegel's idealistic concept of the infinite, unfolding process of history in which certain eternal truths unfold from era to era in human history. Cooper does not indicate that she read Hegel. Hegel's writings on the philosophy of art were translated into English and published as early as 1886, so it is possible that Cooper may have run across some of his ideas, at least indirectly.

11. The idea of happiness as related to progress reflects both Social Gospel and liberal evolutionary ideas. Henry Ward Beecher and Social Gospel leader Lyman Abbot, Beecher's successor at Plymouth Church, were influenced by Charles Darwin and Herbert Spencer. Beecher acknowledged Spencer, one of the fathers of evolutionary theory, as his intellectual foster father and was known for reconciling science with religion. Lyman Abbot proposed to replace the traditional notion of sin with an evolutionary view in which immoral

acts were viewed as a lapse into animality. Spencer claimed an evolutionary optimism in which "evolution can end only in the establishment of the
greatest perfection and the most complete happiness." See Richard Hofstadter,
Social Darwinism in American Thought (Philadelphia: University of Penn-
sylvania Press, 1944; London: Humphrey Milford, Oxford University Press,
1945; reprint, Boston: Beacon Press, 1955), 29–37. Some found an analogy
between Spencer's views of the transition from egoism to altruism and the
preachings of Christian ethics. Cooper suggests a similar analogy in her own
writings.

12. See Jacquelyn Grant, "Subjectification as a Requirement for Christological Construction," in *Lift Every Voice,* ed. Susan Brooks Thistlethwaite and
Mary Potter Engle (New York: Crossroad, 1990), 213.

13. Ibid., 21, 23–24, 28.

14. Ibid.

15. Cooper, "Womanhood a Vital Element in the Regeneration and Progress
of a Race," 17. The term "mute" refers not to a biological incapacity for
speech; rather it is a musical metaphor that refers to a muted note that sounds
suppressed and distant.

16. In nineteenth-century America, there was a growing trend towards the
feminization of Christ. He was popularly seen as being tender, compassionate,
merciful, sympathetic, peaceful — all virtues that were attributed to women.
Because these virtues were viewed as embodied both in women and in Jesus
Christ, women were then held to be naturally religious and to embody Christian virtues and principles. Both women and men were encouraged to adopt
these virtues and principles. Feminists went a step further to argue for women's
capacity for leadership based on their innate moral and religious feeling. Evelyn
Brooks explores this phenomenon as it occurred among Black Baptist feminists
in her article, "The Feminist Theology of the Black Baptist Church, 1880–
1900," in *Class, Race, and the Dynamics of Control* (Boston: G. K. Hall,
1983), 41–43.

17. Ibid., 22.

18. See Barbara Andolsen, *"Daughters of Jefferson, Daughters of Bootblacks": Racism and American Feminism* (Macon, Ga.: Mercer University Press,
1986), 57–59.

19. Cooper, "Bible Quotations," Anna Julia Cooper Papers, courtesy of the
Moorland-Spingarn Research Center.

20. Ibid.

21. Cooper, "Christ's Church," Anna Julia Cooper Papers, courtesy of the
Moorland-Spingarn Research Center.

22. "Letter to the Editor of the Outlook," Anna Julia Cooper Papers,
courtesy of the Moorland-Spingarn Research Center.

23. Ibid.

24. Ibid.

25. See Richard Hofstadter, *Social Darwinism in American Thought,* 13–
50, 29, 106–8; Charles Howard Hopkins, *The Rise of the Social Gospel* (New
Haven: Yale University Press, 1940), 130.

26. See Ronald C. White, Jr., *Liberty and Justice for All: Racial Reform and*

the Social Gospel (1877–1925), Rauschenbusch Lectures, new series 2 (New York: Harper & Row, 1990), 24–26.

27. Ibid.

28. Ibid.

29. Anna Julia Cooper, "Equality of Races and the Democratic Movement," 9–10.

30. Ibid.

31. Ibid., 14, 16–17.

32. Ibid., 16.

33. Ibid., 14–15. Actually, marriage was relegated to an inferior position with the establishment of Christian monasticism around the fourth century C.E. Marriage was officially recognized as a sacrament by the Church in the twelfth century. Cooper relied on secondary sources by nineteenth-century scholars, who looked at the history of the Church before the twelfth century as the mysterious "dark ages."

34. Ibid., 15.

35. Ibid.

36. Ibid., 14. Cooper wrote that "the idea of the radical amelioration of womankind, reverence for woman as woman regardless of rank, wealth, or culture, was to come from that rich and bounteous fountain from which flow all our liberal and universal ideas—the Gospel of Jesus Christ."

37. Cooper, "Womanhood a Vital Element in the Regeneration and Progress of a Race," 13.

38. Ibid., 12.

39. Reinhold Niebuhr, *Moral Man and Immoral Society* (1932; New York: Charles Scribner's Sons, 1960), 117–41.

3

The Power of Belief

C ONTEMPORARY AMERICANS live in a world where they are increasingly aware of a diversity of religious traditions among which Christianity is one of many. While the nineteenth century was not as pluralistic and global as we know the world to be today, there was a growing awareness of religious pluralism, as seen, for example, in the works of William James and Ralph Waldo Emerson. Americans began developing interests in various "major" world religions such as Buddhism, Hinduism, and Islam. Such an awareness is present in *A Voice from the South*, where Anna Cooper represents Buddha as challenging Hinduism with its caste system in India and appeals to the power of divine speech in the lives of the Prophet Mohammed, Buddha, Jesus, and St. Ignatius of Loyola. She concluded this collection of essays with a chapter entitled "The Gain from a Belief," which examined the power of religious belief.

Although Jesus remained the primary mediator of divine principles for Cooper, she appealed to the power of religious belief around the world and across the centuries. In "The Gain from a Belief," she made religious belief central to the concept of a progressive, developing world civilization. Arguing against the modern skepticism of David Hume and the agnosticism of Auguste Comte, she posited a belief in an "existence beyond our present experience" to drive home an overarching argument for a theology of universal human development.[1]

At Oberlin College, one of Anna Cooper's favorite professors, James H. Fairchild, president of the college and a scholar of natural theology and philosophy, lectured in the theology department on apologetics, with special reference to skepticism. He also lectured on moral philosophy. Cooper took Fairchild's philosophy courses in the Philosophy and Arts Department, where he also lectured. Cooper wrote that Fairchild was among the faculty members that proved most stimulating to her.[2] Philosophical and theological thinking, with some influence from her Oberlin years, is evident in *A Voice from the South*. Oberlin placed emphasis on the evidences of Christianity, the existence of God, and the nature of the soul. Students were exposed to Bible study, theological lectures, and prayer groups, where they received the Oberlin philosophy regarding religion.[3] Anna Cooper employed her Oberlin training in logic and mental philosophy in these essays along with the critical and constructive reasoning she undoubtedly learned in her home from her mother regarding the uniqueness of Black women's moral agency in relation to systemic evil in social structures like slavery and segregation. It is important to recognize that she had already received certain critical and analytical skills in her family, a point too often deemphasized in intellectual histories of African Americans. Oberlin simply provided Cooper with tools of formal education for a White-dominated social context in America, which she employed selectively with similar tools from St. Augustine's and the experiential wisdom of her mother.

The understanding of "life made true" as action, growth, and development in a never-ending process is a fundamental tenet of Cooper's concept of the meaning of "God," "Christ," and "Church" in human culture and development. It pervades the whole of *A Voice from the South,* although it is most consistently and explicitly discussed in the first and concluding chapters. Cooper saw human nature in relation to God as part of a concrete, historical, and eternal process of development of the human soul. She viewed Jesus as a historical figure who could not limit his own altruism or benevolence. Upon realizing the truth of an optimistic vision of the eternal development of the best in humankind, this Jesus began engaging in the activity of sharing this truth to build others up. She explained her understanding of Jesus, truth, belief, and faith in this way:

> To me, faith means *treating the truth as true.* Jesus *believed* in the infinite possibilities of an individual soul. His faith was a triumphant realization of the eternal development of *the best* in man — an optimistic vision of the human aptitude for endless expansion and perfectibility. This truth to him placed a sublime valuation on each individual sentiency — a value magnified infinitely by reason of its immortal destiny. He could not lay hold of this truth and let pass an opportunity to lift men into nobler

living and firmer building. He could not lay hold of this truth and allow his own benevolence to be narrowed and distorted by the trickeries of circumstance or the colorings of prejudice.[4]

Cooper portrayed truth as infinite and incapable of being "encompassed" by the narrow bounds of an age, nation, sect, or country. Human beings were creatures whose finite brains could not comprehend the infinite truth of their Creator.[5] Jesus' treatment of the truth as true, she claimed, is evidenced in his refusal to allow circumstance or prejudice to narrow his optimistic vision of the development of the human soul. For Cooper, religion must be *life made true;* life is growth:

> Life must be something more than dilettante speculation. And religion (ought to be if it isn't) a great deal more than mere gratification of the instinct for worship linked with the straight-teaching of irreproachabla [sic] credos. Religion must be *life made true;* and life is action, growth, development — begun now and ending never. And a life made true cannot confine itself — it must reach out and twine around every pulsing interest within reach of its uplifting tendrils.[6]

By "treating the truth as true," Cooper meant that human standards for apprehending infinite truth are very different from the empirical means by which one apprehends the finite. She defined truth as infinite, eternal, and as having to do with the perfectibility of human nature. She suggested that faith was the gain from a belief in this truth — the optimistic vision of the infinite possibilities of the human soul. Faith in practice is "hobbling," "blundering," "unscientific," but faith also works, however awkwardly, as humankind puts its beliefs in practice to work toward the larger goals of human progress.

To treat the truth as true would be to self-consciously consider the ways in which finite opinion or personal prejudice "distort" the truth of the perfectibility of the human soul across the ages and across the bounds of nation, sect, and culture. It requires a self-critical stance that questions one's biases and prejudices. One must recognize that one cannot fully and completely apprehend the truth by finite, empirical means. Rather, "truth must be infinite, and as incapable as infinite space, of being encompassed and confined by one age or nation, sect or country — much less by one little creature's finite brain."[7]

Against Skepticism and Agnosticism

Cooper argued against philosophical skepticism, which she suggested amounted to attempting to encompass the infinite in one's finite brain. She asserted that the radical empiricism of Hume, for example, was inadequate because it fostered skepticism of religious belief.[8] She was critical of "speculative unbelief," which she described as "curiously and sneeringly watching the humdrum, common-place, bread-and-butter toil of unspeculative belief."[9] In her view, faith — in spite of philosophical argumentation regarding its plausibility — worked: "Lofty, unimpassioned agnosticism, *that thinks* — face to face with hobbling, blundering, unscientific faith, *that works.*"[10]

Hume's argument that what one calls mind consists merely of successive perceptions and that we can have no knowledge of anything but phenomena was false in Cooper's thinking. Similarly, she criticized Comte's historical positivism for its agnostic conclusions and disagreed with Comte's claim that all facts that cannot be discerned through the senses are presumptuous and unwarrantable.[11] Comte replaced the idea of God with the idea of "Great Being," humanity in its collective sense, irreducible to individual women or men. Cooper found fault with his concept of worshiping Collective Humanity as symbolized by the loving sex — certain women who represent the present, past, and future of humanity (wife, mother, daughter).[12] An emphasis on humanity and a skeptical method for examining the idea of a God outside of human existence did not adequately address the concerns of everyday women and men. Comte's rejection of a traditional, theological metaphysics rendered him essentially agnostic, which Cooper criticized as leaving everyday women and men with no ground to stand on. Her concern was that it did not leave adequate room for hope in the infinite possibilities of human development. Agnosticism shut God and Love out and made merely formalistic ritual of religious practice. What happens to the precepts and sanctions of morality and the sense of responsibility? Cooper demanded. Concerned with the moral effects of agnosticism on society, she employed harsh rhetoric to describe its effects in relation to moral responsibility:

> For me it is enough to know that by this system God and Love are shut
> out; prayer becomes a mummery; the human will but fixed evolutions of
> law; the precepts and sanctions of morality a lie; the sense of responsibil-
> ity a disease. The desire for reformation and for propagating conviction
> is thus a fire consuming its tender. Agnosticism has nothing to impart.[13]

"Its sermons," she wrote, "are the exhortations of one who
convinces you he stands on nothing and urges you to stand there
too." Agnosticism took out "the vital principle" of all human endeavor. "All hopes in the grand possibilities of life," she wrote,
"are blasted." Agnosticism resulted in removing the inspiration
for beginning a growth that would mature in endless development
through eternity.[14] Agnosticism, then, could only have a fatalistic end, with humankind finding no real meaning in life. This was
not Comte's or Hume's intention, but it was, in Cooper's view, the
effect of such a system of thought. She put it this way:

> The sublime conception of life as the seed-time of character for the grow-
> ing of a congenial inner-self to be forever a constant conscious presence
> is changed into the base alternative conclusion, *Let us eat and drink for
> to-morrow we die.*[15]

Such thinking, she suggested, led to a fatalistic outlook on life.
Life became sapped of meaning, energy, and hope. It resulted in an
apathetic attitude about the possibilities of self-development. She
asserted the primacy of belief in the altruistic principles of the historical Jesus of the Synoptic Gospels, who was concerned with an
eternal principle of life and vitality in the inner-selves of all peoples. Belief in the power of some divine principle was essential
because it empowered people with faith to believe in their self-
development, which was a vital element for social development.
Social reform and inner development were interrelated in Cooper's
thought. Social reform was possible because God actively worked
in the inner lives of individuals in a transformative way.

With all her concern for social reform, it is interesting that
Cooper did not see some positive value to Comte's philosophy.
Comte, after all, developed a social philosophy and ethic. But
she opposed Comte's dismissal of feeling and his rejection of
theology, which she felt would be misconstrued and taken to
heart by lecture-goers. Lectures were a form of entertainment for
nineteenth-century middle-class people. Apparently, Cooper was
concerned that non-philosophically trained lecture-goers would

give an amoral interpretation to skepticism and agnosticism. Rather than work through the abstractions of conceiving God as a kind of projection of human consciousness, real, but a cultural product, she found it important to begin by presupposing God's existence rather than question it. What was most important was that God *worked* in human history.

The evidence of God's existence is not found in abstract, philosophical argumentation. God's existence cannot be proved by abstract reasoning. Rather, the proof of God's existence is evident in the fruits of placing one's faith in action. To look for evidence of God in the actual activity of faith is more viable, immediate, and available for most people. The metaphysical grounds for skepticism and agnosticism were not particularly harmful to the masses, she explained. Rather, the real reasons for and against agnosticism rested on "psychological and scientific facts too abstruse for the laity to appreciate" and genuinely understand. The danger was that there was "much subtle sophistry in the oracular utterances" of popular speakers like "Ingersoll" (possibly Robert Ingersoll, a popular lecturer) that appealed to the "fancy" and "imagination" of "the many."[16]

Feeling and Belief

Such philosophical speculation appealed neither to reason nor to feeling among the masses, the young reformer argued, but rather to the imagination. She did not define what she meant by imagination, but she did not have in mind the constructive, creative, symbolizing capacities of human beings in the positive sense that Samuel Taylor Coleridge or contemporary constructive theologians have employed the term. In this instance, she had in mind fancy, a more whimsical aspect of imagination. People attended lectures for entertainment in much the same way late-twentieth-century peoples watch television. Like many critics of television today, who lambast the media for its shallow representations of human relationships, Cooper was criticizing the quality of some of the lectures available to people. She felt they lacked substance and failed to challenge or motivate people to claim personal and social moral responsibility. In response to Ingersoll's remark that the average man "does not reason — he feels," Cooper rejoined, "For my part I am content to 'feel.' "[17] Cooper explained her position by presenting an example of a situation in which feeling is necessary:

> The brave Switzer who sees the mountain side threatening death and destruction to all he holds dear, hardly needs any very correct ratiocination on the mechanical and chemical properties of ice. He *feels* there is danger nigh and there is just time for him to sound the tocsin of alarm and shout tho his dear ones "fly!"[18]

In other words, a Swiss person when faced with an avalanche does not stop to engage in abstract speculation as to whether or not danger is present. He or she knows by feeling, gut feeling, that danger is present and that it's time to sound the alarm to warn all who are threatened. Cooper may have felt a similar feeling in her concern for social reform. The dangers women and people of color faced economically, socially, and politically were obvious. There was no need to make a scientific study of the detrimental effects of racism and sexism on the physical, spiritual, and intellectual well-being of women and people of color. Rather, it was time to sound the alarm and move into action. Thoughtful response, not abstract reason, was required. Feeling, an embodied way of knowing, would provide an appropriate response.

This idea of feeling is a pragmatic one based on a perception of danger.[19] Cooper's understanding of feeling was not one of sentimentalism or uncritical piety. Rather, she saw the "feeling" that has been attributed to women and to the average man as the most essential kind of thinking. Claiming neither to argue nor to refute skeptical and agnostic argumentation, she asserted, "I want to utter just this one truth":

> The great, the fundamental need of any nation, any race, is for heroism, devotion, sacrifice; and there cannot be heroism, devotion, or sacrifice in a primarily skeptical spirit. A great man said of France, when she was being lacerated with the frantic stripes of her hysterical children, — *France needs a religion!* ... At such times most of all, do men need to be anchored in eternal verities.[20]

Nothing except an anchorage in these felt eternal verities, Cooper explained, can propel humankind into "those sublime efforts of altruism which constitute the moral heroes of humanity."[21] There could be no altruism apart from feeling. Feeling, specifically feeling as compassion and mercy, was a form of thought. Thinking devoid of feeling is cold and non-altruistic. Self-sacrifice — in the sense of service and sharing one's talents with the community — is inconceivable without feeling.

From a late-twentieth-century perspective, "self-sacrifice" is a controversial ideal. There is more critical awareness of the problems involved in women's socialization into being self-sacrificial in ways that are literally destructive, i.e., in situations of domestic violence where bodily self-sacrifice is misnamed as redemptive by too many ministers. Late-twentieth-century theologians are more suspicious of the ethic of self-sacrifice. An "ethic of risk" best expresses contemporary feminist and womanist concepts of the real dangers involved in actively working for social reform. "Solidarity" best captures a contemporary concept of sharing one's gifts and talents with one another. But Cooper's concept of "feeling" offers some insights for a contemporary understanding of feeling in relation to solidarity and an ethic of risk.

Thinking apart from feeling was mere cold ratiocination for Cooper. In her argument against skepticism and agnosticism, she did not intend to disregard reason. Rather, she found fault with concepts of reason that were exclusive of the human capacity for feeling. She saw such concepts of reason as unbalanced and absurd. In part, Cooper was influenced by feminist conceptions of womanhood in her understanding of the importance of feeling as a part of the human reasoning process. Part of the liberal philosophy of the times was that humankind was bound together by fellow social feeling. Cooper was influenced by Social Gospel ideals regarding social feeling for one's neighbor. She held in common with Schleiermacher a positive valuation of feeling as part of the human thought process; her own ideas on the subject were in keeping with ideas that were becoming popular in the cultural context.

For Cooper, feeling was essential for discernment and decision-making. By feeling she did not mean an irrational, uncritical, thoughtless flux of moods or emotions. She did not move to the opposite extreme of abstracting reason from feeling; to the contrary, feeling was a form of thought, essential to moral decision-making. Reason without feeling for Cooper was inadequate and deprived persons of their full potential for development because it deprived humankind of its full capacity for moral decision-making.[22] Feeling was a form of reason that connected heart and mind, one might say.

Turning to "feeling," "tenderness," "sympathy," "mercy," and "compassion" as womanly virtues,[23] Cooper argued that such virtues were vital to social reform and were essential to women's contribution to the process of social amelioration. Such virtues were Christian virtues, as seen in the exemplar of Jesus and his ideals, and womanly virtues. These were not unusual ideas but were common among nineteenth-century women. Today, it is important to question such an analysis of "womanly virtues" and the "feminization" of Christ by considering that gender is a social-cultural construction. What people consider masculine or feminine varies across cultures. Compassion, feeling, and tenderness are not feminine in and of themselves. Rather in Western culture, women have been socialized to embody such values. But Cooper's discussion on the value of feeling in and of itself, as a form of moral reasoning and means of making faith commitments, is an important one. It challenges dichotomizations of mind and feeling, reason and belief.

Belief and feeling were interrelated for Cooper. Without belief and feeling there was no hope for the possibility of self-development and social amelioration — an eternal process. There was no possibility of thinking and moving beyond present existence and experience. There could be no moral improvement, no social amelioration without belief in an existence beyond the present one. One cannot come to religious belief, she suggested, through "cold" ratiocination. In other words, it is not ratiocination in and of itself that is problematic. Rather reason that abstracts itself from feeling is problematic and potentially leads to false, inadequate moral decisions that fail to meet the needs of everyday people in their everyday lives. Building on the information that Cooper presents her readers about feeling and pushing it a little further than she actually takes it, why not consider feeling as a form of "thoughtfulness" and thoughtfulness as a form of "compassion," an ethical practice that she writes about a great deal? In other words, reason without compassion cannot open out into belief in a God that wills personal and social transformation, actively moving in the hearts and minds of women and men who make a faith commitment to participate in God's movement of personal and social transformation. Compassion as a form of thoughtfulness is vital for creating capacity within the human spirit to believe in a God of personal and social change.

Faith as Empowerment

The gain from a belief in an existence beyond present existence was concrete and social in Cooper's thinking. As we have seen in *A Voice from the South,* Christ was first and foremost a historical figure. The perfection of Christ's ideals occurred in history, in culture, and in society. Cooper was far removed from any preachment on "sweet by and by religion." Her understanding of the "hereafter" was a belief in the development of the here and now by the present generation for the next generation:

> Yes, I believe there is existence beyond our present experience; that that existence is conscious and culturable; and that there is a noble work here and now in helping men to live *into* it.[24]

Humankind's relation to the infinite, here, is concrete and existential. All work concerning the infinite must be done in the here and now if humankind is going to be able to live into it. This next existence is not a dream-like state; it is conscious. It is not otherworldly; it is culturable and requires ethical transformation in the here and now. In an undated poem entitled "The Answer," Cooper wrote in the last verse:

> God — is not afar!
> The simple may know:
> The Hereafter is here;
> Eternity's now.
> And Myself am Heaven or Hell.[25]

Eternity, the hereafter, heaven, and hell were not outside of historical human existence. Heaven and hell were present in the inner-self. Cooper placed the responsibility of heavenly or hellish existence on her own shoulders, on the shoulders of human individuals. Heaven and hell were moral states of existence determined by concrete moral choices in everyday life. Humankind was responsible for creating heaven on earth by moving toward an ideal of the regenerated human self and society. Therefore, it was necessary for humankind to work nobly toward the goal of self-development and social amelioration. Progress and regeneration occurred in human history. Eternity was a reality to live into, not a reality to wait for.

Cooper ended her essay "The Gain from a Belief" with a ring of hope and optimism. She asserted that the world would move one generation forward. Progress, she suggested, is inevitable, and with belief all things are possible:

> There are nations still in darkness to whom we owe a light. The world is to be moved one generation forward — whether by us, by blind force, by fate, or by God! If thou believest, all things are possible; and *as* thou believest, so be it unto thee.[26]

In Cooper's thought, each race or nation has its own "particular keynote," which it must contribute to "the harmony of nations." If a race or nation is isolated from the "opposing ideas" and "conflicting tendencies" of other nations, it will develop abnormally.[27] Further, the abolition of race, caste, and national boundaries is supported by two great world religions. Although Cooper referred primarily to Christian symbolizations of God when arguing her understanding of human development, she found similarities in the figures of Buddha and Christ in that both "wrought to rend asunder the clamps and bands of caste."[28] Both Christ and Buddha were examples of religious figures who drew humankind into an awareness that the boundaries created by humankind are "imaginary."[29] Cooper explained it this way:

> I do not think it was all blasphemy in Renan when he said Jesus Christ was first of democrats, i.e., a believer in the royalty of the individual, a preacher of the brotherhood of man through the fatherhood of God, a teacher who proved that the lines on which worlds are said to revolve are *imaginary*, that for all the distinctions of blue blood and black blood and red blood — *a man's a man for a'that*. Buddha and the Christ, each in his own way, wrought to rend asunder the clamps and bands of caste, and to thaw out the ice of race tyranny and exclusiveness.[30]

Although Jesus was the dominant symbol of human salvation, wisdom, and perfection in Cooper's thinking, she saw the various religions of the world as forming the world's impulses to "higher growth." One needed to believe in a power greater than one's self that moves self and society forward to a more heavenly existence, that is, a more just existence, on earth. The faiths of the world moved people toward personal and social reformation. Moreover, by *faith* Cooper did not mean holding "correct" views on tradition and doctrine or reifying interpretations of Truth as Truth itself, but something deeper, something in process, something that could not be fully conceived and yet could be lived in the very hearts of the people of faith:

> It is the enthusiasms, the faiths of the world that have heated the crucibles in which were formed its reformations and its impulses toward a higher growth. And I do not mean by faith the holding of correct views and unimpeachable opinions on mooted questions, merely; nor do I understand it to be the ability to forge cast-iron formulas and dub them TRUTH. For while I do not deny that absolute and eternal truth *is,* — still truth must be infinite.[31]

Faith was a kind of power for Cooper. It was living and could not be contained in "cast-iron formulas." It was greater than the powers of human hearts and minds. Cooper did not make sharp distinctions between belief and faith but employed these terms interchangeably to assert that religious belief or faith had the power to unseal the lips of the dumb. The first act of faith is to say, "I believe." Cooper examines the power of religious belief around the world and across the centuries by asking: "Do you seek to know the secret charm of Ignatius Loyola, the hidden spring of the Jesuit's courage and unfaltering purpose? It is these magic words, '*I believe.*'" The words "I believe" are powerful. They are "the live coal from the altar which at once unseals the lips of the dumb." These words were "the strength and power to Paul, to Mohammed, to the Saxon Monk and the Spanish Zealot, — and they must be our strength if our lives are to be worth the living."[32]

Cooper saw religious belief around the world and across the centuries as foundational to the strength, power, and value of human life and existence. She makes an important contribution to a theological understanding of the empowering nature of faith and belief for personal and social change. In religious belief one finds strong principles regarding the value and worth of life. It is religious belief that gives humankind strength to speak and to live a life worth living. It empowers humankind to bring justice, freedom, and equality more fully into the world. Without religious belief people lose sight of the worth and value of their lives. Religious belief gives the power of speech, of voice, which is key to social reformation. Like a "live coal from the altar," belief empowers those who have been oppressed into silence to prophesy deliverance from injustice.

Just as great religious leaders like Mohammed, Buddha, Jesus, Paul, Luther, and Loyola were empowered with prophetic speech through belief in a power greater than themselves, now the voices of women — across lines of race and ethnicity — believed. They were the voices of a new era that would lift themselves up to be heard. She prophesied correctly to a degree. Through the efforts of the Black women's club movement more Black women certainly did gain access to educational institutions. But the socio-economic gains of women of color lagged far behind those of White women. Finally, it was the voices of White women who were heard on the right to vote. It would take another seventy years before Black people, male or female, would have that right and Jim Crow would be legally banned. Black women's voices still need to be heard and women across color lines still struggle against socio-economic disparities. Moreover, women of color, being female and colored in one body, continue to walk hand in hand with the men of their communities to fight socio-economic discriminations against peoples of color, just as women in the Black women's club movement did a century ago. Finally, within communities of color in Asia, Africa, Latin America, and among African Americans, women still resist the suppression of their voices by men who fail to recognize sexism as a real issue. The struggle for a wholistic fight for justice is far from over. The empowerment of the silenced is an ongoing battle. One of the tasks for contemporary theologians and ethicists is to ask: Whose voices are being silenced in our own time? The voices of women continue to be among the silenced. The voices of the economically poor are still not listened to as authoritative in their own right. There is a tendency to look to economically secure experts to analyze the problem of poverty. But who better understands the reality of poverty than the poor? The voices of gays and lesbians are just beginning to get a more open and serious hearing than in previous eras. But the steps toward a full hearing of gay and lesbian concerns are still in the stage of infancy. Too many would rather not hear and discuss questions regarding legislation allowing same-sex marriages, equal hiring practices, or the right for such women and men to adopt children. Finally, children are the voiceless of the voiceless, with the least access to a forum for their concerns in Church or legislative channels.

The power of speech is essential for human beings seeking meaning for life in a world of disproportionate socio-economic and political power. Also important is access to those arenas where decisions about the well-being of society are legislated. Given access to such arenas, not just any speech helps further the attainment of social and personal transformation. Rather, the power of speech that resonates with God's message of freedom, equality, and justice is vital for personal and social change. Such speech is not monolithic but requires a multiplicity of voices across race, gender, sexual preference, and religious lines from one era to the next.

NOTES

1. Anna Julia Cooper, "The Gain from a Belief," in *A Voice from the South,* ed. Mary Helen Washington, Schomburg Library of Nineteenth-Century Black Women Writers (1892; New York: Oxford University Press, 1988), 303–4. Cooper studied mental and moral philosophy at Oberlin College, where she was introduced to Comte and Hume. The Oberlin curriculum also included the study of philosophers such as Locke, Coleridge, Kant, and Cousin from 1835 on. See James H. Fairchild, *Oberlin: The Colony and the College, 1833–1883* (New York: Garland Publishing, 1984), 254–56.

2. Anna Cooper, "Negro College Graduates' Questionnaire," question no. 31, Anna Julia Cooper Papers, courtesy of the Moorland-Spingarn Research Center.

3. See *Catalogue of the Officers and Students of Oberlin College, 1883–84,* 58–67.

4. Cooper, "The Gain from a Belief," 298.

5. Ibid.

6. Ibid., 299.

7. Ibid., 298.

8. David Hume was an eighteenth-century Scottish empiricist (1711–76). For Hume, human beings know through the senses. There are two kinds of perception: (1) simple impressions and (2) complex impressions, which pertain both to the senses and ideas. Sense impressions precede ideas. All knowledge for Hume is based on the experience of sensory impressions. Reason cannot prove our beliefs or expectations about the future. But Hume did not discount belief, which he claimed can be described only in terms of feeling. Hume defined belief as an idea assented to. Beliefs must be tested by experience. See Frederick

Copleston, S.J., *A History of Philosophy*, book 2 (Garden City, N.Y.: Image Books, 1985), 258–92.

9. "The Gain from a Belief," 287.

10. Ibid.

11. Ibid., 291–93. The philosopher Auguste Comte (1798–1857) is known as the father of French positivism. He restricted positive knowledge to knowledge of observed facts or phenomena. Comte has often been interpreted as suggesting that there is no positive reason to believe in a transcendent God, since God's existence cannot be proved; the spread of atheism is an aspect of the mature development of the human mind. Comte did not assert atheism but rather asserted that both theism and atheism are concerned with problems that cannot be proved scientifically. There is no empirical proof of the existence or nonexistence of God. Cooper suggested that Comte was an agnostic in the sense that Comte proposed that God had become an unverified hypothesis in an increasingly scientific, rather than theological, world. He questioned the existence of God. But Comte did develop a metaphysics in which the object of worship was the "Great Being," or Humanity in a collective sense. For Comte, the basic social reality was humanity. Individuals could transcend egoism by devoting themselves to serve humanity. See Copleston, *A History of Philosophy*, book 3, 77–98.

12. "The Gain from a Belief," 292.

13. Ibid., 295.

14. Ibid.

15. Ibid.

16. Ibid., 296.

17. Ibid., 294.

18. Ibid., 294–95.

19. I am not suggesting that Cooper was familiar with Pragmatism. (William James had published *The Principles of Psychology* in 1890, which was not explicitly pragmatic). But Cooper shared with James something important to American intellectuals concerned with concrete and psychological human experience: an emphasis on recognizing human painfulness and suffering. Pragmatism recognized feeling as part of humankind's mental activity. Also like James, she shared a suspicion of merely formal mental logic. But her approach to the problem of apprehending reality placed far greater emphasis on social-historical analysis.

20. "The Gain from a Belief," 297.

21. Ibid.

22. One might draw on Cooper's work to suggest that feeling is a form of *moral thought*.

23. See chapter 4, "Womanhood." Also, Cooper's mentor at Oberlin, President Fairchild, was influenced by nineteenth-century notions of true womanhood. He wrote an article on womanhood in 1849, which argued that women's strength lay in their greater capacity for feeling and for dealing with concrete issues. He argued that feeling and intellect were equally important; neither was superior to the other. Women, he thought, were capable of scientific thought, but they did not prefer it. He did not see this as a result of a process

of socialization, but as the inherent nature of women as a species in contrast to men.

24. "The Gain from a Belief," 303.

25. "The Answer," Anna Julia Cooper Papers, Box 23–4, courtesy of the Moorland-Spingarn Research Center.

26. Cooper, "The Gain from a Belief," 304.

27. Ibid., 152.

28. Ibid., 154–55.

29. Ibid., 154.

30. Ibid. Joseph Ernest Renan was a nineteenth-century liberal French biblical scholar who sought to give both a historical-critical and poetic interpretation to New Testament literature, particularly the Synoptic Gospels. He was criticized for his poetic interpretations of the historical Jesus.

31. Ibid., 297–98.

32. Ibid., 302.

4

Womanhood

WOMEN'S ANONYMITY is one of the gravest sins of patriarchal systems of injustice. It is a form of violence. In traditional concepts of human being and womanhood, Black women have been rendered invisible. This is not simply a result of failing to write Black womanhood into concepts of womanhood and human being. That is, it is not simply an academic problem for writers and scholars. It is a social problem involving human relations on a wide scale. It is a result of the silence that has surrounded Black women's dehumanization and subjugation during slavery and beyond. To include Black womanhood in concepts of womanhood and human being requires a continual breaking of the silence that surrounds the violation of Black women's bodily and parental rights. To illustrate the tragedy of the separation of Black women from their families during the era of American slavery, I will share a story from my maternal family's narrative tradition.

My maternal family's narrative tradition tells of a woman by the name of "Dilcey," who was of Black and Dutch ancestry. Her son, Steve McBeth, was fathered by a Scotch-Irish man, probably a slave master. In my great-grandmother Desiree McBeth Harris's written narrative, "Our Family Tree — As I Know It," she explains:

> My Father's Mother [Dilcey] is reported as being Dutch. She had a brother, who after they were separated by slave trades received the name Dave Moffett. I never heard of her family name. My Father was an infant in her arms when he was taken from her and given to the family of Gen. Robert Lowery; there he was reared as one of the family. They all loved him until his death. He followed Gen. Lowery in the Civil War and there he received the title "Major Mcbeth." He was said to be "Scotch Irish." He was never able to see his Mother again nor her brother. But after his passing and I had married [and] had five children and moved from Brandon, Miss. my birthplace to Meridian Miss., one day this Brother, my

[great] uncle, found me; He told me of my father being separated from his mother and of his being sold to some other section of the world.

Their native home I don't know of, but they at one time lived in Raleigh, Smith Co.

My mother was born to Jane Finch of an Indian tribe. My Mother's Father was a white man named Fox. She had one real brother whose Father was the same man Fox. Other sisters and brothers were born after Grandma Finch married an Indian man named Jack Finch. My mother married Steve McBeth and nine children were born all looked like white children. I am the darkest one and the only one living today in fact.

The McAllister family is closely related to our family. I am not able to explain just how. Most of them have now passed on. Some of their children still live. Dr. R. G. Johnson Dentist in Chicago. Florice in Durham, N.C. Dr. Jane McAllister teacher at Jackson College–Miss. Dorothy and Dixie of Washington, D.C.

Uncle Jack Finch's family (our cousins) are living in Chicago.

Your father (my husband) was the Son of a white man, His mother part Indian. I do not know more of them.

According to slave law, the children of slave women followed the condition of the mother. This meant that the children whom White men fathered through rape and forced concubinage followed the slave condition of their mother, regardless of their paternity. As a child, I found my great-grandmother's references to Dutch and Scotch-Irish ancestry perplexing. As an adult, I see a certain spirit of defiance in her naming European ancestry as well as Black ancestry in the person of the long-lost slave woman Dilcey, who was a product of the same violent system of slavery as her son, Steve McBeth. My grandmother, Kathryn Harris Jett, once referred to Dilcey as "an anonymous Black woman." By naming what they knew of the family's entire ancestry (Black, White, and Indian), Desiree McBeth Harris and her daughter, Kathryn, defied the system of denial that slave law had required.

To fully claim my maternal great-great-great-grandmother, it would be inauthentic for me to refer to her simply as "Dilcey," which is the way slaveholders would have addressed her. In African American culture we honor our elders with titles fitting their age, experience, and wisdom. So I shall refer to her as Mama Dilcey. In my maternal family's tradition, we generally refer to our women elders by their last name: "Mama Jett," "Mama Harris." But Mama Dilcey's full, true name was stolen by the same unjust system that stole her child from her arms. My mother, belonging to a younger generation of grandmothers, prefers to be called "Mama Kay" or "Mommy Kay," so while "Mama Dilcey" isn't quite in keeping with the tradition of past generations at least it has some resonance with our changing family tradition.

Mama Dilcey and her sons had lived in Raleigh, Smith County, in Mississippi — near Brandon, according to my grandmother Kathryn Jett. Mama Dilcey's baby boy, later known as Major Steve McBeth, was taken from her arms and, according to family accounts, raised in General Robert Lowery's home in Meridian, Mississippi, "as if he were one of the family." His paternity, at present, remains shrouded in mystery and silence. Such mystery and silence surround stories of the pain and wrenching violence that accompanied mixed-race children like Steve McBeth. In my great-grandmother's telling of the story, the euphemism of being raised as "one of the family" veils some of the pain and horror of being sold away from one's mother. Apparently Steve McBeth found relative privilege in his role as house servant and as servant to General Lowery during the war. But the pain, violence, and betrayal of slavery emerges very clearly in Desiree McBeth Harris's narrative in the references to lost names, nameless fathers, sold children, lost mothers and brothers, and found uncles. Perhaps to soften the blow of the actual pain of slavery for her children and grandchildren, Mama Harris chose to emphasize the fact that the "sold" child was treated as one of the family. My family was able to employ the Lowery-McBeth connection with political astuteness to gain relative economic and educational privilege after the war. This was not unusual for house servants and their descendants, especially if they may have been related to the master's family. The full story of the Lowerys, McBeths, Moffetts, and Mama Dilcey may never be known.[1]

Sadly, Steve McBeth's descendants know very little about his mother. Nor do we know much more about his uncle, Dave Moffett. It is ironic, but not unusual, that Steve McBeth ended up following the man to whom he was sold in the Civil War. It is ironic because it demonstrates a perpetuation of a cycle of violence and distortion in which slaves were forced to follow and serve masters of the very system that kept them in bondage in a war that would eventually lead to its abolition. It is an ultimate form of violence to the mother of Steve McBeth that he should be raised to serve his master in such a war.

Such is the legacy of many a son and daughter of slavery. The family histories become fragmented. The full names and histories of too many Black women and their children have passed into anonymity. Their faces have not been remembered. Steve McBeth's picture has been preserved, though fading, and remains in family albums. Not so his descendants' vaguely remembered maternal ancestor. She has all but disappeared into the underside of history. The most vivid memory is of her once full, then empty arms. Like the character Beloved, in Toni Morrison's novel *Beloved,* nobody knows her true and full name. No one knows who she was. And yet somewhere she exists in all of her descendants. We are bone of her bones and flesh of her flesh. Her blood has given life to many. Her arms and the arms of all Black women like her reach out from history and into the future to reclaim and be reclaimed in the arms of new generations. Womanists must reclaim those whose womanhood and very humanity have been dishonored. We must recover them, layer by layer, from the dust that forms the graves of anonymity. In West African worldviews, the ancestors are considered part of the community. Many African American families have continued this tradition in various ways — through memorial services in some churches, through family stories, and in the last twenty years through Kwanzaa ceremonies. By doing so African Americans reclaim the ancient ontological and cultural heritage of their forbears. In part, the question of what it means to be a human being is shaped by one's knowledge of the struggle for dignity, freedom, and survival among one's ancestors.

Traditionally, classical and liberal Christian theologians have presented an analytical discussion on human nature, asking what the nature of human being is in relation to God or Being. In past and recent history, from Augustine to Tillich, the nature of human being was universalized as the understanding of "man," without attention to the practical exclusion of women. If women have been envisioned as less than human, Black women have been considered less than women. During slavery they were considered "breeders," "broodsows," and "chattel."[2] The very humanity of Africans brought to America by the slave trade was questioned. In order to justify slavery slavetraders and owners determined that

Black people were inferior to White people, not quite human, closer to the animals. How else could they argue that an unjust institution was just, that to treat humans as animals was God-ordained? In the midst of such absurdity and insanity, Africans in America and their descendants subverted dehumanizing characterizations and the brutal practices they were meant to support. In the midst of inhumanity they created a humane, life-affirming, dignity-bearing culture.

Negative stereotypes of Blackness and Black womanhood did not cease with slavery. The Reconstruction period, with all the new opportunities for education and Black community development that came with it, was not a utopian period in any sense for anyone, let alone the masses of Black women and men. A new slavery system was created in which the masses of African Americans, still dependent on White employment and a White economic power base, continued to be economically, physically, and mentally exploited. Most Black women in the hierarchy of the new hiring system were employed as domestic servants in White homes for meager salaries. Some were able to work independently as laundresses. Black women continued to be stereotyped negatively as lazy, promiscuous, immoral, unchaste, ignorant, and coarse, or as all-nurturing, all-giving mammies, who were wise in matters of home-keeping and childrearing. Such stereotypes continue today. Historically, Black women in America have challenged such stereotypes, insisting on naming their humanity, their womanhood, in their own ways. "Arn't I a woman?" proclaimed Sojourner Truth, when her womanhood was questioned by a White male heckler. Contemporary Black women continue to praise and celebrate their God-created womanhood today.

Little attention has been given women's nature in Eurocentric ontologies of human being, and Black women have been excluded most of all. If humankind has been conceived of as "man," to the exclusion of women, woman has been conceived of as "White" women to the exclusion of women of African descent. What it means to be Black and female is an ontological question: What does it mean to be human in relation to God and the world when one is Black and female?

In 1983, many Black women seminarians, religious scholars, and clergy found in Alice Walker's *In Search of Our Mothers' Gar-*

dens a unique name (*nommo*) to describe the distinctiveness of Black womanhood. For Walker, a womanist is a Black feminist or feminist of color who passes on the wisdom of Black women's cultural heritage from mother to daughter. Walker derives the term "womanist" from the Black folk expression "womanish," which means to act "grown up, be grown up, in charge, responsible."[3] A womanist prefers women's culture but she is not a separatist.[4] A womanist is concerned with issues of both racism and sexism. Cheryl Sanders has observed in her article "Afrocentrism and Womanism in the Seminary" that for Walker womanists "name ourselves after our own fashion" and that similarly Molefi K. Asante emphasizes "the presence of *nommo* in African discourse," which resists dominant ideology. *Nommo* is the generative and productive power of the spoken word. Black feminists who call themselves womanists participate in naming.[5]

Black women theologians in recent discussions on womanism have begun to reflect on the meaning of "womanist," which is a way of talking about Black womanhood.[6] One important task of womanism is to debunk negative stereotypes and to replace them with positive namings. Naming Black womanhood is important not simply as a reactive measure to correct negative stereotypes, but it is also important for proactive reasons. Positive symbolizations of Black womanhood are necessary for developing positive self-images among Black women and girls. Great women of the past and present serve as exemplars of Black womanhood who point to the truth of Black women's being. They suggest possibilities of who Black women are and who they can become in relation to God and the world. In the Black community there is a frequent cry for positive "role models." Looking at others who embody qualities of strength, courage, creativity, dignity, beauty, and liberation is a way of reviewing or reimaging oneself. Contemporary Black women, for example, might look to Cooper as an example of what Cornel West, influenced by Antonio Gramsci, refers to as an organic intellectual — an intellectual who is actively engaged in counterhegemonic activity.[7] Cooper, like many women today, looked to certain women as models of the depth and breadth of women's potential. She referred to Charlotte Forten Grimké, Sojourner Truth, and Frances Ellen Watkins Harper, for example, as influential "chieftains of service."[8] These were all women who did not despair of the reality of social injustice, but believed enough in God, self, and others in their community to fight for freedom and equality. They believed enough in their capacity to make good things happen, with faith in a God who was on the side of the weak and the dominated, that they built up themselves and their communities. They "made a way out of no way."

Great women of the past and the present, along with their communities, offer important information about the possibilities of becoming, of moving into a fuller realization or development of human potential. The process of becoming whole brings women into a fuller realization of the potential of human being as they live in the present and move into the future. Who women (as well as men and children) can become today depends on a social-historical process. Models are not important for the purpose of outright, uncritical interpretation. The word "model" is rather limited, because it refers to real ancestors who lived and breathed. Moreover, it refers to real people today, prominent and anonymous, whose moral values and practices offer helpful guidelines for women, men, and children.

As Sanders has noted, womanists like Asante look to the witness of African American history to argue for excellence and efficiency in African American culture.[9] Womanists turn to historical Black women as exemplars of liberating and survival practices. Walker describes Harriet Tubman and Rebecca Cox Jackson as exemplars of womanist practice and values. Jacquelyn Grant names Sojourner Truth, Jarena Lee, and Amanda Berry Smith as historical examples of a womanist tradition.[10] Delores Williams looks to biblical women like the African slave Hagar, who liberated herself on one occasion and later found a God of survival in the wilderness; she looks to historical women like Harriet Tubman, who possessed gifts of survival on the dangerous route of the Underground Railroad and gifts of liberation in bringing over three hundred slaves safely to freedom; and she looks to twentieth-century women like Fannie Lou Hamer, Rosa Parks, and others who have continued a tradition of survival and liberation practices.

Williams emphasizes Black women's "survival and quality-of-life struggle," best represented by the "art of connecting" among women like Tubman, Milla Granson, and Mammy Pleasant, who knew "with whom and how to connect in order to liberate slaves."[11] She seeks to balance Black liberation theology's emphasis on a God of liberation with Black women's everyday experience of a God of liberation. "God liberates and God does not always liberate all the oppressed," she argues.[12] In the interim, *survival,* making "a way out of no way," is a divine gift in itself. Grant similarly defines a womanist as "one who has developed survival strategies in spite of the oppression of her race and sex in order to save her family and her people.... Black women speak out for themselves."[13] Grant's emphasis on speaking out is in harmony with the Afrocentric idea and practice of *nommo,* the generating word, the power of naming.

"Womanist" is a contemporary term, not employed by historical Black women. But contemporary Black women who have named themselves "womanist" build on a tradition of Black women freedom fighters, as Delores Williams calls them, in their theological and ethical construction. Williams turns to women of the past whose "voices, actions, opinions, experience, and faith" the womanist theologian must search. Williams further observes that Walker points us to a historical tradition of Black mothering and nurturing whether in respect to bearers of children or to community freedom fighters who strategized to liberate themselves and others.[14] A womanist Afrocentric concept of mothering and nurture envisions nurture as a liberating activity whether practiced by biological mothers or not.

Again, while persons who offer a positive vision of the embodiment of principles of survival and liberation are commonly referred to as "role models," it is important not to develop a rigid, static ideal of Black womanhood. To do so would be to create a false sense of the norm, to create a monolithic symbolization of Black womanhood. The term "model" is a noun and contradicts the feminist emphasis on God and human being as a verb — becoming and Be-ing. Process theology offers a similar non-static concept of both humankind, as part of creation, and God. If one uses the terms "model" or "role model," it is important to redefine the terms to envision womanhood as involving continuous growth. There are lives worth studying, learning from, hearing about. But feminist and womanist individuals and communities must enter their own growth process, their unique understanding of who they are becoming. Hazel Carby calls this process "reconstructing womanhood."

Reconstructing Womanhood

Hazel Carby explains that in nineteenth-century ideologies of womanhood, "black womanhood was polarized against white womanhood." Thus, Black women writers "had to define a discourse of black womanhood that addressed their exclusion and rescued their very bodies from a persistent association with illicit sexuality."[15] Black women reconstructed womanhood to mean something different from the dominant ideal in American culture. African American women are still engaged in this process today. Anna Julia Cooper engaged in such a reconstruction of womanhood.

I turn to her work for a moment to consider the significance of her concept of freedom and equality. Like womanist theologians today, Cooper was concerned with the "survival and wholeness of entire people, male *and* female," across class lines. She was one of the founding members of the National Association of Colored Women's Clubs, which addressed human rights issues for both Black women and men. There are certain eternal verities, she argued, that are essential to human life and that are found in all religions.[16] Cooper interpreted the Gospel as revealing a universal principle of human freedom. The birthright of freedom, Cooper argued, transcends race and sex even as it belongs to and is the concern of each one.[17]

Women today, like Cooper, find it important to demythologize popular conceptions of women's existence and potential by pointing to women who have dared to live lives and think thoughts outside the conventional molds society casts for women. It is important to engage in this process of demythologization (1) to expose the truth of women's nature and potential and (2) to prove false the illusion of isolation and singularity cast on women who break with conventional ideals regarding women's roles.

By looking to one another womanists and feminists find that they are "in good company." By looking to the past, they again find that they are often in good company. That is, they are not the first to address particular problems regarding womanhood and women's experience, even if their methods and historical contexts are quite different.

Problems and Questions

There are two problems that I would like to introduce at this point. First, it is important to remember the contributions of anonymous Black women. Theological ethicists like Katie Cannon and Delores Williams and novelists like Alice Walker have written about the contributions of anonymous, ordinary working women. Cooper made little reference to such women, except her mother, to whom she was deeply grateful for encouraging her education. Whereas theologians and writers today celebrate the lives, folk wisdom, and creativity of everyday Black women, Cooper spoke primarily of the oppression of such women. She spent little time celebrating their enormous creativity and wisdom.

There are hints of Cooper's appreciation of the masses of Black women in her praise of the political savvy of Black women in the South who questioned their husbands' race loyalty. But she referred to this savvy as a "blind instinct" among "ignorant" Black women.[18] She did not refer to it as folk wisdom. Cooper did not escape being elitist in her views on the importance of education, although her intention was to be altruistic. She reflected some ambivalence about folk culture. For example, she defended Paul Robeson's folk lyrics as rich and representative of Black culture. At the same time, she wrote with pride of her educational activities with an illiterate Black family in Indiana, whose colloquial speech she could barely understand. To a large degree, this ambivalence reflects her emphasis on survival skills in a predominantly White culture. It was one thing to know both the folk language and the language of the dominant White culture. It was another thing not to be able to communicate with those of privileged social-economic status. To do the latter provided a measure of potential to move beyond the unskilled labor positions that Whites thought most suitable for Black women and men. Still, Cooper tended to emphasize what the formally educated could teach the less liter-ate masses, rather than what the masses could teach the formally educated. She did not escape an attitude of condescension. Today, womanists emphasize the importance of moving beyond this kind of unbalanced relationship.

Second, Cooper presupposed that it is possible to speak of womanhood in an idealistic sense. Like many nineteenth-century Black and White feminists, she appealed to a model of True Womanhood, which she reshaped to argue for Black women's education. One might argue that Cooper was essentialist in her thinking, because she presumed to speak on behalf of "the Black Woman" and presupposed that it is possible to identify the essential nature of an ideal of Black womanhood.[19] Cooper spoke of *woman* rather than *women*. One might ask, How could Cooper presume to speak on behalf of all Black women? Is there such a thing as "The Black Woman"? Did Cooper reify womanhood? Before moving further into a womanist criticism of this aspect of Cooper's thought, it is important to ask why Cooper found it necessary to construct an ideal of womanhood and woman's voice. I will explore the social climate and religious perspective from which Cooper shaped her understanding of womanhood.

A Voice from the South as a Call for Reform

Cooper found it necessary to criticize ideologies of womanhood that had their sources in chivalry, particularly in the South. Hazel Carby, author of *Reconstructing Womanhood,* presents a compelling historical literary analysis of the ways in which African American women have revised dominant conceptions of womanhood to fit the concerns and experiences of African American women. She cites Cooper as a fine example of an early Black feminist thinker on Black womanhood and suggests that she was a critic of popular conceptions of womanhood. She explains that "Cooper's initial argument was based on the assumption that a civilization should be measured by the way its women are treated." She further describes Cooper as dismissing "ideologies of womanhood that had their source in codes of chivalry (as in the Southern states) as being elitist, applying only to an elect few."[20] Moreover, Carby astutely observes that she interpreted the Gospel of Christ as social and liberating for women and as in frequent conflict with the organized Church:

> Cooper's apparent reference to the Middle Ages and feudalism in Europe was but a metaphorical disguise for the vaunted ideals of chivalry and elevated notions of womanhood of the South. She situated the possibilities for the "radical amelioration of womankind, reverence for woman as woman regardless of rank, wealth, or culture," in relation to the Gospel of Christ but was careful to separate what she regarded to be the radical potential of the Gospel from the actual achievement of the organized Church that had done "less to protect and elevate woman than the little done by secular society."[21]

Cooper dismissed chivalry, the Middle Ages, and the feudal system to criticize ideals of womanhood in Southern culture.[22] Her discussion of feudalism and the Middle Ages was a literary device that allowed her to levy a harsh but subtle critique of ideals of womanhood in the South. At the same time, she was able to show a profound intellectual awareness of the history of the issues of womanhood. Knowledgeable about the South and Euro-American history, she was ever conscious of her role as intellectual and educator. The Social Gospel understanding of Christianity that she participated in and helped shape resonates, in some respects, with late-twentieth-century liberation theology in its argument for the equal rights of women and the dominated.

As Hazel Carby describes Cooper's work, she "interpreted the Gospel as a liberation theology, a set of ideals which argued for equality not only for women but also for the poor, the weak, the starving and the dispossessed." She further observes that Cooper's optimism that these ideals could become the practices of American institutions "stemmed not from current social conditions but from the 'possibilities and promise that are inherent in the system, though as yet, perhaps, far in the future.'"[23] Although Cooper was not a liberation theologian, there are strong parallels between liberation theologies of the contemporary world and her social interpretation of the Gospel. Cooper emphasized a portrait of Christ as concerned with social salvation, but not to the exclusion of people of color, a point she felt White Social Gospelers missed.

Carby describes Cooper's Christianity as "radical Christianity." From the perspective of people today, Cooper was moderate in her views. Although she was social-democratic in her perspective, for example, she did not entertain a strong critique of capitalism as

Du Bois eventually did. She was not critical of America's socio-political system to the point where she left the United States to live as an exile in Africa, as Du Bois also did. Nor did she entertain the idea of a separate nation for Black people, as did Marcus Garvey. In her dissertation, although she lamented that violent revolution was inevitable when a nation failed to live according to democratic principles, Cooper focused on "the Friends of the Blacks" in Haiti to argue for cooperative liberative action between the races. Moreover, legislation, in her view, was the ideal means for bringing about social change. Some of the ideas that do not seem so radical from a twentieth-century perspective, however, were radical for her own time.

In her call for the amelioration of social conditions, Cooper saw the Declaration of Independence and the U.S. constitution as basically good and founded on biblical principles. But she, like her contemporaries, interpreted these documents in ways that their writers never considered, namely, to include Black people and people of every color in their understanding of freedom. Moreover, democracy was a biblical concept in her perspective, a universal principle innate to all humankind. She synthesized Christian and democratic principles to argue for the development of Black womanhood as an aspect of human rights.

In Cooper's view, Christianity and democratic government simply had not been clearly understood or logically adhered to in the past. This was due not to a fault in Christian or constitutional ideals, but to a weakness in human nature. Women and men are in a never-ending process of development in their understanding of freedom — a basic principle of the Gospel — and are in need of growth and correction from one age to the next. Cooper's interpretations of these ideals were controversial for her time, an era when America was intransigent about giving people of color and women a right to vote. Mary Helen Washington refers to Cooper as "progressive" in her ideas on womanhood.[24] Indeed, Cooper was progressive both in her ideas on womanhood and on Christianity. If we were to have asked Cooper to describe herself, she would probably have used the word "reformer." It is a word she used a great deal to describe her concerns for social change. Further, the idea of reform was very current in her social-historical context.

Cooper's work is a fascinating source because of her self-conscious reflections on womanhood. In a time when women were fighting for their right to participate in the public sphere, Cooper linked her voice with the women's movement. She argued for equal rights in government and education. In the process of pleading women's cause, she invited her readers and auditors to reflect on one aspect of human being, one half of the human race. What is the value of womanhood? What is the meaning of womanhood? Why is the education and development of womanhood necessary for the fulfillment of humanity? And, in responding to these questions, Cooper revealed to the reader her understanding of the value and meaning of womanhood. Further, she demanded that her readers reflect specifically on the meaning of womanhood from a Black woman's perspective.

In the very act of writing *A Voice from the South,* Cooper's intention was one of reform. She appealed to her readers' basic Christian and democratic sensibilities as she presented her argument for a reformation of ideas, attitudes, and actions regarding the Black woman of the South. Carby captures well the spirit in which Black women intellectuals wrote during the post-Reconstruction period: "In the black women's movement at the turn of the century, organizing to fight also meant writing to organize."[25]

Women like Cooper, Frances Ellen Watkins Harper, Josephine St. Pierre Ruffin, Ida B. Wells-Barnett, and Mary Church Terrell were part of a forum in what eventually became the National Association of Colored Women. Their writings, nationally disseminated, were part of an organized effort among Black women in America to fight racism and sexism. Through speaking and writing, they called for reform.

Cooper and Nineteenth-Century Feminism

When Anna Cooper published *A Voice from the South* in 1892, women did not have the right to vote, and for a woman to speak in the public sphere to mixed-sex audiences was considered unladylike. Women's proper place was seen as the domestic sphere, and women had few property rights. African Americans did not have the right to vote and were denied equal opportunities in the economic and educational spheres.

Because women in the Black women's club movement were both Black and female, they were sympathetic to human rights issues for both women and for the Black community. Similarly, White feminists had compared the lot of White women in America to slavery. Mid-century, many had been abolitionists. Early White feminism emerged in part out of sexist reactions to White women abolitionists. But by the end of the nineteenth century, White feminists such as Carrie Chapman Catt and Elizabeth Cady Stanton had taken on a White supremacist ideology in order to argue for White women's qualifications to vote over and against those of Blacks, European immigrants, and Native Americans. Stanton argued that White women were more qualified to vote than illiterate Black men. Black women found themselves excluded from the White women's movement, particularly in the South. Afraid that Southern women would be offended by Black women's presence at conventions, Northern White women discouraged and often barred Black women from attending meetings.[26]

"There is no grander and surer prophecy of the new era and of woman's place in it, than the work already begun ... by the Women's Christian Temperance Union (WCTU) in America," Cooper asserted.[27] She saw the WCTU as prefiguring women's increasing power as a moral factor. As for Black women, she argued that in such a transitional, unsettled period, their status seemed "one of the least ascertainable and definitive of all the forces which make for our civilization."[28] Colored women, "confronted by both a woman question and a race problem," were "an unknown or unacknowledged factor in both." All the same, she argued, colored women should not be ignored. White feminists ought to include Black women's rights in the women's movement.

Black women's opinion was valuable, Cooper explained, as demonstrated by the writer and lecturer Frances Ellen Watkins Harper, by preachers Sojourner Truth and Amanda Berry Smith, and by the poet/reformer Charlotte Forten Grimké. Their analysis and possible solutions for the problems of racism and sexism were invaluable. Cooper asserted that Negro women were "able to grasp the deep significance of the possibilities of the crisis," a unique heritage in human history.[29] Her most famous statement on Black womanhood is still quoted today:

> Only the Black woman can say, "When and where I enter, in the quiet, undisputed dignity of my womanhood, without violence and without suing or special patronage, then and there the whole *Negro race enters with me.*"[30]

In the thought of Anna Cooper, the Black woman was the vital and essential element in the regeneration of the race. Similarly for Cooper women worldwide across races and culture were the fundamental agents in the development of a race or culture. Why? Because women as mothers were the trainers, teachers, and educators from the moment they educated young children at their feet. Thus, they were the earliest influence for all those who would become women and men. In her chapter on "The Higher Education of Women," Cooper suggested that even silent, educated Christian women had influence and power, as did vocal women who taught:

> The earnest well trained Christian young woman, as a teacher, as a home-maker, as wife, mother, or silent influence even, is as potent a missionary agency among our people as is the theologian; and I claim that at the present stage of our development in the South she is even more important and necessary.[31]

Christian faith and intellectual development in Cooper's view made for a woman who would be foundational in the regeneration of a race or a society. Cooper's understanding of the nobility of womanhood, particularly of women as mothers, was characteristic of the era in which she wrote. In popular literature and in early women's movement circles there was a strong ideal of true womanhood, particularly of motherhood. The more conservative view was that women's sphere was domestic, man's sphere public.[32]

Women influenced men and children morally in the domestic sphere, passing on in subtle, gentle ways their civilizing influence. Early feminists did not reject the ideal of the true woman as being endowed with greater moral wisdom and strength. Rather, they employed the ideal of true womanhood, reforming it like remoldable clay, to further their arguments for the women's movement. Precisely because women were endowed with greater moral feeling they should be involved in the public sphere. Women's powers of moral persuasion, early feminists argued, were greatly needed in government and in education.

There was tension between early White and Black feminists, because White feminists found it to their political advantage to adopt racist and supremacist rhetoric to further their cause. Barbara Andolsen points out that race and class prejudice underlay White feminist appropriation of the myth of True Womanhood. White suffragists chose to manipulate the belief that Anglo-Saxons were uniquely qualified to create good governments to advance the case for women's voting rights.[33] White supremacist and classist ideologies were implicit in much of the White feminists' appropriation of the myth of True Womanhood:

> White feminists openly manipulated white supremacist ideology in order to persuade Anglo-Saxon men to share political power with Anglo-Saxon women. They appealed to a more subtle form of race and class prejudice when they invoked the American myth of True Womanhood.... The True Woman was almost certainly the wife of a well-to-do male (usually white and native-born) whose economic success made it possible for her to reign as queen of the home. Poor women, Black women, and immigrant women often led lives that precluded the development of a "refined," "feminine" character.[34]

Cooper's *A Voice from the South* was all the more significant as a feminist text because it sought to address the feminist concerns of Black women in a social environment in which White feminists on the whole found the inclusion of Black women problematic to the furtherance of their cause. Cooper employed the Myth of True Womanhood to meet the needs and experience of her ideal of the Black woman. Her voice was that of a Black feminist. She took a model of womanhood originally meant to be descriptive of conservative White middle-class womanhood and reshaped it to her perception of Black women's needs and experiences. Cooper chided Black men, White men, and White women for presuming to speak *for* Black women. She published *A Voice from the South* to present the concerns of Black womanhood in the voice of a Black woman from the South. Anna Cooper's voice was unique (1) because she presented an early feminist perspective on race and gender and (2) because she demanded an inclusive conceptualization of women's issues as universal issues in the movement for human freedom.

On the one hand, Cooper, like liberation theologians today, argued from the standpoint of particularity. She spoke with great strength and consciousness from the standpoint of Black womanhood, aware of her particular dignity in the midst of race and gender oppression. She was aware of Christianity as her particular religious framework and focus. On the other hand, she was conscious of the interrelationship of the problems of Black Christian women and women of diverse cultures and religions.[35] She found it essential to return to a universal standpoint. There are certain universal truths, eternal verities, she argued, that are essential to human life in all religions — like freedom and benevolence.

Freedom: A Universal Birthright

In her essay "Woman versus the Indian," Cooper set forth some of her most acerbic criticisms of racism in the White feminist movement. But Cooper was not simply critical. She wanted to get on with a fuller vision of the task at hand — the task of human freedom. Therefore she presented constructive ideas on Christ and freedom from a Black, feminist perspective.

The context for Cooper's critique and constructive analysis of the problem of racism in the women's movement is her response to a speech presented by Methodist preacher Anna Howard Shaw. Cooper inveighed a harsh critique against Shaw's speech "Indians versus Woman," charging that the topic was indicative of a more general "caste" mentality in America.[36] She first expressed admiration for Shaw and applauded her for her attitude toward Black women. She recognized, for example, Shaw's and Susan B. Anthony's efforts on one occasion to include Cooper in a meeting of Wimodaughsis (a women's club for women, mothers, daughters, and sisters) despite racial opposition:

> In the National Woman's Council convened at Washington in February 1891, among a number of thoughtful and suggestive papers read by eminent women, was one by the Rev. Anna Shaw, bearing the above title [Woman versus the Indian]. That Miss Shaw is broad and just in principal [sic] is proved beyond contradiction. Her noble generosity and womanly firmness are unimpeachable. The unwavering stand taken by herself and Miss [Susan B.] Anthony in the subsequent color ripple in Wimodaughsis

ought to be sufficient to allay forever any doubts as to the pure gold of these two women.[37]

But Cooper's expression of admiration for Shaw serves as a basis for expressing profound disappointment in the racist overtones of Shaw's speech.[38] Shaw argued that women's ability to vote had been overlooked, while a share in government had been granted to Native American men — who in her view were less civilized and less capable of government. Although elsewhere Shaw applauded the innate moral character of Native Americans, Cooper was offended by the racism of Shaw's views on Native American men's ability to vote.[39] Cooper paraphrased the racist arguments White women used to plea for suffrage:

> The great burly black man, ignorant and gross and depraved, is allowed to vote; while the franchise is withheld from the intelligent and refined, the pure-minded and lofty souled white woman. Even the untamed and untamable Indian of the prairie, who can answer nothing but "ugh" to great economic and civic questions is thought by some worthy to wield the ballot which is still denied the Puritan maid and the first lady of Virginia.[40]

In Cooper's judgment, such argumentation amounted to a suit of *"Eye vs. Foot,"* each of which is a vital, necessary part of one body, one organism. She argued that women should not be plaintiff in a suit versus the Indian, Negro, or any other race or class "crushed under the iron heel of Anglo-Saxon power and selfishness."[41] Her interpretation of the Gospel as revealing a universal principle of human freedom is central to her argument for social justice across racial and gender lines. This birthright, she argued, belongs to women and men of every race. And to the extent that it belongs to each gender and to every race of human being, this birthright of freedom transcends race and gender even as it belongs to and is the concern of each one.

Cooper called attention to the need for White women to apply the Golden Rule by recognizing that freedom is not the exclusive right of an individual group or person. While she was aware of the needs of particular groups, she saw herself as engaged in a universal cause for freedom: "The philosophic mind sees that its own 'rights' are the rights of humanity. That in the universe of God...the recognition it seeks is...through the universal application ultimately of the Golden Rule."[42]

Women, men, and persons across color lines, Cooper argued, are created sacred, in the image of God.[43] With a keen sense of the rights and dignity of the individual, she challenged White women to recognize individual human rights across racial lines. "Let her [woman] try to teach her country that every interest in this world is entitled at least to a respectful hearing, that every sentiency is worthy of its own gratification," she prophetically proclaimed. Believing that people of all races are created in the image of God, Cooper further argued for the sacredness of the rights of individuals, proclaiming that:

> when the image of God in human form, whether in marble or in clay, whether in alabaster or in ebony, is consecrated and inviolable, when men have been taught to look beneath the rags and grime, the pomp and pageantry of mere circumstance and have regard unto the celestial kernel uncontaminated at the core...then is mastered the science of politeness, the art of courteous contact, which is naught but the application of the principal [*sic*] of benevolence, the back bone and marrow of all religion; then woman's lesson is taught and woman's cause is won.[44]

All, she argued, are worthy of a hearing. All are created in the image of God and are sacred. Thus women must extend benevolence — the backbone and marrow of all religion — to persons of every race and class. Cooper saw the women's movement as a continuation of a never-ending reform. She suggested that reform in each age is embodied in a different movement. White women, she argued, must recognize their continuity with a larger movement than the one they were most immediately aware of. This movement that courses throughout the ages, in Cooper's thinking, was the movement of freedom — the very birthright of humanity:

> The cause of freedom is not the cause of a race or a sect, a party or a class, — it is the cause of human kind, the very birthright of humanity. Now unless we are greatly mistaken the Reform of our day, known as the Woman's Movement, is essentially such an embodiment, if its pioneers could only realize it, of the universal good. And specially important is it that there be no confusion of ideas among its leaders as to its scope and universality.[45]

Cooper saw the women's movement as a particular embodiment of a universal good. In the process it was necessary to remember one's interconnectedness with the good of others across race, class, and gender.[46] Cooper made reference to the parable of the Good Samaritan in her argument for universal human rights. She demanded that White suffragists ask, "Who is my neighbor?" Cooper agreed with Shaw's and Anthony's concerns for women's suffrage, as long as they affirmed a Christian theology that emphasized universal principles and a "love of neighbor," regardless of class, race, or sex. White women, she argued, must be inclusive in their understanding of who the right of freedom belonged to. They needed to recognize "the red woman" and "the black woman" as their neighbors. Cooper contended that "it is important and fundamental that there be no chromatic or other aberration when the teacher is settling the point, 'Who is my neighbor?' "[47]

Cooper argued that a woman who claimed or desired to be a teacher of morals must clear her eyes of "all mists" in order to see clearly "Who is my neighbor?"[48] She portrayed White women as having their vision blurred by mists. She saw their failure to see the humanity of Black women and other women of color as a problem of vision, which needed correction. White women, she suggested, had misperceived the Gospel. Only with corrected vision could they fully see their neighbors and the Gospel's message of freedom.

Further, Cooper asserted that women must understand that the world needs to hear their voice on social issues, specifically in the realm of morals. The world must hear not only the voice of White women on moral and social reform, however, but the voices of women of color in America and around the globe:

> It is not the intelligent woman vs. the ignorant woman; nor the white woman vs. the black, the brown, and the red, — it is not even the cause of woman vs. man. Nay, 'tis woman's strongest vindication for speaking that *the world needs to hear her voice.*[49]

As for Black women, only Black women themselves, Cooper argued, are able to speak on behalf of Black women. She criticized White women, White men, and Black men who would attempt to speak for Black women. I would like to introduce here some of the possible reasons for the use of the word "voice" in the singular. Feminist and womanist theologians today are conscious of religious and cultural pluralism. To speak of the "voice of the Black woman" sounds odd to our ears, because we are aware of the multiplicity of women's voices across and within different cultures.

Cooper lived in a world in which there was an organized group of Black women, many of whom were well-educated, who traveled on the lecture circuit to speak out on issues of racism and sexism. Whether or not participants in the Black women's club movement agreed on every method for attaining racial uplift, they agreed on common issues and goals. These women spoke, wrote, and acted on social issues in "solidarity." And, to the extent that they spoke, wrote, and acted on issues of racism and sexism in solidarity, it is understandable that Cooper saw herself as being part of one voice, one movement, one cause. She was part of a minority group of educated, outspoken women who found it necessary to speak in relative unity on social issues in order to be heard.

Cooper's intention was to speak in solidarity with other Black women as a representative voice. What is problematic is that her audience is a middle-class audience. While she claims to speak on *behalf* of Black women, including the masses, she rarely appears to speak *with* or *to* them. While she was aware that there were many voices among Black women, she tended to speak *for* them. Why? She probably considered it an act of altruism and benevolence. Undoubtedly she felt that since she was in a position to gain an audience it was her responsibility to speak for those who did not have the opportunities for publishing and speaking that were available to her and her peers. Today, womanists must seek ways of standing in solidarity with an entire people across class lines by insisting on an audience for a diversity of voices.

Gender Roles

Cooper's conception of woman as the essential element in the progress and regeneration of a race rests on two presuppositions: (1) women are the earliest educators of women and men — the world's future leaders, and (2) women as the dominated sex across race and culture have a stronger moral sensitivity, are more greatly endowed in feeling, and because of their own domination ought to have greater sympathy for the weak and the dominated. She further believed that women should extend their sympathy to all the world's dominated by working against socio-economic and political inequality.

I have discussed Cooper's concept of Christ as a depositor of ideals, in the form of the Gospel, which requires millennia for its growth and ripening in human civilization and culture. As for women, Cooper saw the historical Jesus as laying down a code of morality equal for men and women. She interpreted the life and death of Christ as giving men a guide for the estimation of women as equals and friends as well as helpers:

> By laying down for woman the same code of morality, the same standard of purity, as for man; by refusing to countenance the shameless and equally guilty monsters who were gloating over her fall, — graciously stooping in all the majesty of his own spotlessness to wipe away the filth and grime of her guilty past and bid her go in peace and sin no more... throughout his life and in his death he has given to men a rule and guide for the estimation of woman as an equal, as a helper, as a friend, and as a sacred charge to be sheltered and cared for with a brother's love and sympathy, lessons which nineteen centuries' gigantic strides in knowledge, arts, and sciences, in social and ethical principles have not been able to probe to their depth or to exhaust in practice.[50]

This syncretism of (1) a concept of equality between men and women on the one hand and (2) traditional models of women as helper and men as protectors on the other hand were characteristic of nineteenth-century feminist argumentation.[51] In Cooper's case, her emphasis on women's need for protection, care, and shelter was meant to counter the overriding abuse of Black women in the South.[52]

Black women were not accorded the same rights over their bodies as middle-class White women. To the contrary, they were stereotyped as having no sexual morals and therefore as unworthy of respect.[53] So Cooper presented Christ's formula and example for relations between the sexes as one in which women were treated and respected as equals, friends, and helpers and as worthy of respect and protection.

For Cooper, equality between men and women did not abolish gender distinctions in terms of attributes or roles. She described "man" as physically superior and more cooly rational. But, she clarified, man had abused his physical strength and rationalism to coldly dominate the "weaker" sex and weaker cultures. Woman, on the other hand, stood for the preservation of the deep, moral forces of social righteousness. Therefore, Cooper asserted, "In the era now about to dawn, her sentiments must strike the keynote and give the dominant tone. And this because of the nature of her contribution to the world."[54] Cooper portrayed this "dominant tone" as different from male political domination:

> Her kingdom is not over physical forces. Not by might, nor by power can she prevail. Her position must ever be inferior where strength of muscle creates leadership. If she follows the instincts of her nature, however, she must always stand for the conservation of those deeper moral forces which make for the happiness of homes and the righteousness of the country. In a reign of moral ideas she is easily queen.[55]

The language of "dominant tone" to describe the potential compassion in women's leadership is problematic in moving away from systems of domination. What is most helpful is Cooper's concept of a society that realizes social, political, economic, and ontological equality among human beings with compassion. Essentially Cooper accepted the ideal of woman as the conservator of deep moral forces that made for the happiness of homes and the righteousness of American government and culture. She described women as inferior in areas where leadership depended on "strength of muscle." But here Cooper's wit was at play once again. Cooper decried leadership created by strength of muscle. For Cooper, "woman's cause is the cause of the weak." Cooper criticized Anna Howard Shaw for the disparagement of the weak implied in her speech "Indians versus Women" by arguing that "woman should not, even by inference, or for the sake of argument, seem to disparage what is weak. For woman's cause is the cause of the weak."[56]

By "the weak," Cooper meant those who did not strive to attain greatness and power through physical domination. She meant all those who are dominated by patriarchal, imperialistic, and racist rule, including women. The weak included White women, Native American women and men, people of African descent around the globe, and Asians. She had in mind persons who were lacking physical strength and military power. Today, liberation theologians would refer to these various groups as "the oppressed." Cooper's critique of domination was a critique of European and American imperialism. She opposed the subjugation of women and people of color around the globe.

Cooper based her argument against women's disparagement of the weak on the premise that the rights of all the weak are inter-

related. She chided Shaw, explaining that "when all the weak shall
have received their due consideration, then woman will have her
'rights,' and the Indian will have his rights, and the Negro will
have his rights, and all the strong will have learned at last to deal
justly, to love mercy, and to walk humbly."[57]

Moreover, Cooper reminded her White feminist audience of the
principle of neighborliness in a truly Christian society. When all
have learned the universal principles of justice, mercy, and hu-
mility, she argued, then, "our fair land will have been taught the
secret of universal courtesy which is after all nothing but the art,
the science, and the religion of regarding one's neighbor as one's
self, and to do for him as we would, were conditions swapped,
that he do for us."[58] Critical of militarism and conquest of one
nation by another, she decried "brute force" against Black Americans, Africans, Native Americans, and the Chinese. Even in her
dissertation, she described the Haitian military revolt as a necessary but unfortunate response to France's militaristic, imperialistic
failure to follow its own democratic principles.

Inner, moral strength was preferable to physical strength,
Cooper thought — it belongs to the order of justice. The weak, she
asserted, are more merciful than the strong. They have a greater
understanding of mercy. The strong, that is those who historically
have been oppressive, must learn to be merciful from the weak.
Cooper suggested that woman's lesson of mercy could work in
symmetry with man's task of truth and that man's ideal of right-
ness together with woman's ideal of peace would result in a more
just world.[59]

Anna Cooper saw the nineteenth-century women's movement
as the beginning of a new era in which civilization would realize
positive social developments. She gave a long but eloquent description of the variety of social injustices women's contributions
would correct in the twentieth century. "Religion, science, art,
economics, have all needed the feminine flavor; and literature, the
expression of what is permanent and best in all of these, may be
gauged at any time to measure the strength of the feminine ingredient,"[60] she argued. Envisioning a world that included women's
leadership, she sharply contrasted such a world against a male-
dominated society and challenged theological, social, economic,
and political absurdities such as infant damnation, an impersonal

God, economic inequality in marriage, and supply and demand economics. She put it this way:

> You will not find theology consigning infants to lakes of unquench-able fire long after women have had a chance to grasp, master, and wield its dogmas. You will not find science annihilating personality from the government of the Universe and making of God an ungovernable, unintelligible, blind, often destructive physical force; you will not find ju-risprudence formulating as an axiom the absurdity that man and wife are one, and that one the man — that the married woman may not hold or bequeath her own property save as subject to her husband's direction; you will not find political economists declaring that the only possible adjustment between laborers and capitalists is that of selfishness and ra-pacity — that each must get all he can and keep all that he gets, while the world cries *laissez faire* and the lawyers explain, "it is the beautiful working of the law of supply and demand"; in fine, you will not find the law of love shut out from the affairs of men after the feminine half of the world's truth is completed.[61]

Women's half of the world's truth would balance the scales of justice. Cooper asserted that it is "transmitting the potential forces of her [woman's] soul into dynamic factors that has given symme-try and completeness to the world's agencies."[62] She challenged women to generate a new kind of civilization. Women must de-mand that principles of peace and mercy work together with ideals of truth and righteousness to generate a society that is merciful in its attitudes toward children, believes in a God of peace rather than of physical force, gives equal property rights to women, and declares economic justice for working people. The feminine principles of love, peace, and mercy would complete the world's truth. There would be sympathy for the weak. There would be an amelioration of social situations, compassion for human suffering:

> Nay, put your ear now close to the pulse of the time. What is the key-note of the literature of these days? What is the banner cry of all the activities of the last half decade? What is the dominant seventh which is to add richness and tone to the final cadences of this century and lead by a grand modulation into the triumphant harmonies of the next? Is it not compassion for the poor and unfortunate, and as Bellamy has expressed it, "indignant outcry against the failure of the social machinery as it is, to ameliorate the miseries of men"?[63]

In Cooper's writings, compassion for the poor and unfortunate is a standard of justice, the dominant seventh that adds richness and tone. Women, because of their own domination, have no ex-cuse for a lack of sympathy. The very value of women is their ability to sympathize with the rest of the world's weak, that is, the rest of the world's oppressed peoples. Women, from their own experience Cooper suggested, understand the problem of domination. Their experiential understanding of the failure of domination and of the call for compassion as a standard of justice is a vital element in the regeneration of a society.

Although Cooper claimed that neither women nor men were superior to the other, she portrayed women as the best potential leaders of a new era. She conceded that there are compassionate, feeling, sympathetic men but clarified that such men learn these virtues at some mother's feet. The masculine virtue of intellect and the feminine virtue of sympathy emerge as most vividly embodied in women in her early essays. Educated women, in her view, were the future leaders of the new era. She employed gender-typing as a literary device to argue for women's leadership.

Women would herald in a more compassionate social order. Cooper suggested that women are a vital element of the reign of God, because she went on to state that Christianity is part and parcel of the social amelioration she envisioned. True Christianity is on the side of the poor and the weak. It too is "brought to the bar of humanity and tried by the standard of its ability to alleviate the world's suffering and lighten and brighten its woe."[64] In other words, Christianity is not exempt from God's judgment. It is a religion among religions. It is not sacred in and of itself. It is a human cultural institution that seeks to attain knowledge of who God is.

Christians are imperfect in their understanding of who God is and the meaning of God's revelation in history. They participate in God's activity of alleviating the world's suffering imperfectly and with great difficulty. Cooper asks, "What else can be the meaning of Matthew Arnold's saddening protest, 'We cannot do without Christianity, . . . and we cannot endure it as it is'? "

NOTES

1. From the family papers of the descendants of T. J. Harris and Desiree McBeth Harris, edited by Arthur Victor Jett, Jr. The family history merits much more archival research than I can provide here.

2. See Katie Cannon, *Black Womanist Ethics* (Atlanta: Scholars Press, 1987), 31–38.

3. Alice Walker, *In Search of Our Mothers' Gardens* (New York: Harcourt Brace Jovanovich, 1983), xi–xii.

4. See Alice Walker's definition of womanism in the preface to her book, ibid., xi–xii. Most simply a womanist is a Black feminist or feminist of color.

5. See Cheryl J. Sanders, "Afrocentrism and Womanism in the Seminary," *Christianity and Crisis,* April 13, 1992, 123–24.

6. Walker, *In Search of Our Mothers' Gardens,* xi–xii.

7. See Cornel West, *Prophesy Deliverance!* (Philadelphia: Westminster Press, 1982).

8. Anna Julia Cooper, "The Status of Woman in America," in *A Voice from the South,* ed. Mary Helen Washington, Schomburg Library of Nineteenth-Century Black Women Writers (1892; New York: Oxford University Press, 1988), 140–41.

9. Sanders, "Afrocentrism and Womanism in Seminary," 125.

10. Jacquelyn Grant, *White Women's Christ and Black Women's Jesus* (Atlanta: Scholars Press, 1988).

11. Delores Williams, *Sisters in the Wilderness* (Maryknoll, N.Y.: Orbis Books, 1993), 121, 238, and 199.

12. Ibid., 197.

13. Delores Williams, "Womanist Theology: Black Women's Voices," *Christianity and Crisis,* March 2, 1987, 67–68.

14. Ibid.

15. Hazel Carby, *Reconstructing Womanhood* (New York: Oxford University Press, 1987), 32–36.

16. See Cooper, "The Gain from a Belief," in *A Voice from the South.*

17. Cooper, "Woman versus the Indian," in *A Voice from the South,* 120–21.

18. Cooper, "The Status of Woman in America," 139.

19. I am thankful to Debra Haynes for raising the question of essentialism in a conversation, Spring 1990.

20. Carby, *Reconstructing Womanhood,* 97–98.

21. Ibid.

22. Ibid.

23. Carby, *Reconstructing Womanhood,* 98.

24. See Washington, introduction to *A Voice from the South,* xxx–xxxi.

25. Carby, *Reconstructing Womanhood,* 97.

26. See Barbara Andolsen, *"Daughters of Jefferson, Daughters of Bootblacks": Racism and American Feminism* (Macon, Ga.: Mercer University Press, 1986), 31–35. She quotes Stanton: "American women of wealth, virtue and refinement, if you do not wish the lower orders of Chinese, Africans, Germans and Irish, with their low ideas of womanhood to make laws for you...demand that woman, too, shall be represented in the government."

27. Ibid., 134. The Women's Christian Temperance Union, founded in 1874, developed into a major movement within the nineteenth-century women's movement. Under Frances Willard's leadership, it became one of the greatest women's organizations in the United States. The WCTU endorsed suffrage

as early as 1887. See Paula Giddings, *When and Where I Enter* (New York: William Morrow, 1984), 91.

28. Ibid.

29. Ibid., 144.

30. Cooper, "Womanhood a Vital Element in the Regeneration and Progress of a Race," in *A Voice from the South,* 31.

31. Cooper, "The Higher Education of Women," in *A Voice from the South,* 79.

32. See Barbara Welter, *Dimity Convictions: The American Woman in the Nineteenth Century* (Athens: Ohio University Press, 1976), 21–41. Early to mid-nineteenth-century women's magazines and religious literature (1820–60) presented ideals of True Womanhood: women's purity, piety, submissiveness, and domesticity. Feminists used the ideal of women's piety and purity to argue for women's natural abilities as leaders in society as well as in the home.

33. See Barbara Andolsen, *"Daughters of Jefferson, Daughters of Boot-blacks,"* 21. Andolsen has written an incisive study of racism and sexism in the nineteenth-century women's movement.

34. Ibid., 45.

35. In "Womanhood a Vital Element in the Regeneration and Progress of a Race," 9–11, Cooper was critical of Islam's subjugation of women. Later, in "The Gain from a Belief," 301–2, she positively cited Mohammed as an example of the power of religious belief. Cooper compared Christ and Buddha as breaking caste systems in "Has America a Race Problem? If So How Can It Be Solved?" in *A Voice from the South,* 154–55. Cooper held that religion, in all its diversity, was the source of all ideas on the fulfillment of human potential.

36. For information on Anna Shaw's attitude toward Native Americans, see Barbara Andolsen, "Racism and Nativism," in *"Daughters of Jefferson, Daughters of Bootblacks,"* 31–33. Andolsen notes that in their descriptions of Native Americans they observed in South Dakota in 1890, White women suffragists Anna Shaw and Carrie Chapman Catt perpetuated the notion that Indians were less capable of self-government than White women, dwelling on details that made Native Americans seem less civilized. Although she claimed no moral superiority, Shaw found it repulsive that Native American men — far less civilized than White women according to the Euro-American standard — were granted a share in government, while White women were disfranchised.

37. Cooper, "Woman versus the Indian," 80.

38. See Andolsen, *"Daughters of Jefferson, Daughters of Bootblacks,"* 33–34; from Anna Howard Shaw, "Indians versus Women," *Woman's Tribune,* May 9, 1891.

39. Ibid.

40. Cooper, "Woman versus the Indian," 123. See also Andolsen on Cooper, *"Daughters of Jefferson, Daughters of Bootblacks,"* 41–42.

41. Cooper, "Woman versus the Indian," 123.

42. Ibid., 118.

43. Ibid., 120–22.

44. Ibid., 124–25.

45. Ibid., 120–21.

46. Cooper's rhetoric is similar to that of the Social Gospel, which emphasized the Fatherhood of God and the brotherhood of man to call attention to the significance of human interconnectedness and social feeling.

47. Cooper, "Woman versus the Indian," 121.

48. Ibid.

49. Ibid.

50. Cooper, "Womanhood a Vital Element in the Regeneration and Progress of a Race," 17–18.

51. See Andolsen, *"Daughters of Jefferson, Daughters of Bootblacks,"* 44ff.

52. Ibid. See also p. 62.

53. Ibid.

54. Cooper, "The Status of Woman in America," 133.

55. Ibid.

56. Cooper, "Woman versus the Indian," 117.

57. Ibid.

58. Ibid.

59. Cooper, "The Higher Education of Women," in *A Voice from the South,* 57.

60. Ibid., 57–58.

61. Ibid.

62. Ibid.

63. Ibid., 58–59.

64. Ibid.

5

Coming to Voice

NNA COOPER wrote during a period in American history when Black women were organizing to raise their voices. During the early and mid-nineteenth century, Black women like Maria Stewart, America's first Black woman political speaker and writer; Harriet Tubman, leader of the Underground Railroad; Sojourner Truth, a feminist, abolitionist, and voting rights activist for Black women and men demanded that Black women be heard on the issues of racism and sexism. At a women's convention in Akron, Ohio, where Truth delivered her famous "Arn't I a Woman" speech in 1859, she boldly asserted Black women's humanity and womanhood.

Sometimes by applying formal educations wrested from hardship, sometimes by self-education (Stewart or Rebecca Cox Jackson), sometimes by skillfully using the force of their great intellects to work biblical knowledge and folk wisdom into eloquent arguments for justice (in the case of Tubman and Truth), such women challenged oppressive institutions in America without the privilege of sustained formal education. Such women were known for their audacious and courageous oratory and laid the groundwork for turn-of-the-century women leaders like Cooper.

In the 1830s, more than fifty years before Cooper would do the same, Maria Stewart made a plea for equal educational and economic opportunities for Black women before Black and White audiences in Boston.[1] Marilyn Richardson describes Stewart as doing "what no American-born woman, black or white, before her is recorded as having done. She mounted a lecture platform and raised a political argument before a 'promiscuous audience,'" an audience composed of both women and men.[2] Her "bold and militant" work as an orator, as Richardson describes it, predates the careers of Sojourner Truth, Ida B. Wells-Barnett, Mary Church

132

Terrell, and Anna J. Cooper. A child during the Reconstruction period in the South, Cooper received the kind of education Stewart had demanded for Black women some thirty years earlier. Sojourner Truth, like Cooper and her contemporaries, had argued for equal opportunities for Black women, challenging Black men and White women to look beyond their self-interested perspectives on equality to demand equality for all. By the end of the century, Black women employed their educations not only to teach at schools for the newly freed slaves, but also to organize a national network to address their concerns from public lecterns. Tired of the silencing lash of slavery, threatened by White backlash through the establishment of the Ku Klux Klan, and humiliated by Jim Crow codes in the South, Black women organized in unprecedented numbers to write and speak out against segregation.

The South was in the throes of trying to maintain the semblance of a feudal order, to use Cooper's description. It remained grossly and violently segregated. Few escaped the new slavery to become economically independent. House slaves became house servants, field slaves became sharecroppers who were still tied to overseers and a landowner. Southern chivalry — the protection of feminine honor — was, as in slavery, reserved for elite White women. Black women were still being raped. Black men were being lynched. Some Black women were lynched as well. The masses of Black women were not educators or lecturers. To the contrary, the masses of Black women labored for long, hard hours at the tasks considered the most menial — work that was considered too harsh for poor and immigrant White women, who were lowest in the hierarchy of White laborers. They toiled as domestic servants, charwomen, washerwomen. This was true not only in the regions of the deepest South, but in the nation's capital, where Cooper lived and taught.

The District of Columbia had maintained slavery for nearly as long as the rest of the South. Slavery was not abolished there until 1862, one year before the General Emancipation.[3] While there were no lynchings in the nation's capital, segregation prevailed in restaurants, theaters, department stores, and hiring practices. Also, when Black women were hired as low-level government clerks, employers preferred light-skinned Black women. Black men were preferred to Black women for clerical positions — after White men and White women. Black women were on the lowest tier. The percentage of clerical positions that went to Black women and men varied with changing presidential administrations. Under Woodrow Wilson's administration segregation increased in government agencies, and there was a substantial loss in the number of presidential appointments given to Black men. Clerical positions for Black men and women decreased. By World War I fewer such positions were available for Black Americans, male or female.

Most Black women in the nation's capital hired by the government between 1890 and 1920 worked in menial, unskilled positions as charwomen, janitors, or elevator operators. Sharon Harley explains that "since few white women or black and white men competed for char or cleaning positions in the federal government, an applicant's race and gender were not major factors in determining success in obtaining such employment." Rather, physical strength was the most important qualification. Similarly, Black women seeking nongovernment jobs were also discriminated against. Most worked, again, in menial, unskilled positions for very low wages. The majority of Black female workers were not government workers, but were employed in domestic and personal service occupations.[4]

In the mid-twentieth-century women's rights movement, much was made of women's right to move out of the home and into the job market, largely for the purpose of self-fulfillment. The discussion tended to be cast in middle-class career-oriented terms. For poor Black women in America, however, as well as for poor and working White women, historically the right to work has been a matter of survival rather than a matter of personal fulfillment. This has been particularly true for Black women. Historically a greater proportion of Black families than White families have not found it possible to live on one salary. This was true long before the inflation periods of the early 1970s and late 1980s. During the late nineteenth and early twentieth centuries a good one-half of the Black married female population in Washington, D.C., worked. Black married women found it impossible to live on their husbands' salary alone, especially since Black working men were paid lower wages than White working men. While educated

Black men received higher salaries from professional jobs than either educated White or Black women, the masses of Black men received substandard wages. Although wages for Black women were even more substandard, it was easier to live on two incomes than one. While 49.7 percent of married Black women, aged fifteen and above, worked, only 17.1 percent of the White female population worked.[5] Work for Black women with families was not a matter of choice; it was a necessity. They worked for survival — to feed, clothe, and shelter themselves and their families.

In her descriptions of her travels back to the South, Cooper commented on the inadequacy of toilet facilities for Black women and men under Jim Crow. She cited an incident in which she approached facilities labeled "Women" and "Colored" and pondered which heading she came under. This was a gross indignity, but a relatively minor irritation compared to the risks to their physical safety that Black women and men experienced on the job. In response to the gross discrimination she and other Black women had experienced, Cooper raised her voice. In the preface to *A Voice from the South,* entitled "Our Raison d'Être," she described the South as "silent" in "the clash and clatter of our American Conflict." "Like the Sphinx, she inspires vociferous disputation, but herself takes little part in the noisy controversy." Most concerned with the silencing of Black folk, Cooper described the voice of the Negro as "one muffled strain" in the midst of "the Silent South" and as "a jarring cadenza." But Black women were the most oppressed of the oppressed in the South. The "one mute and voiceless note has been the sadly expectant Black Woman," Cooper observed.[6] She and her contemporaries, in the tradition of others before them, rose collectively to thwart the obdurately repressive expectation that Black women and men could be coerced into silence by White backlash.

Translating her love and knowledge of music into metaphors for the voices of a diversity of people, Anna Cooper used musical terms to poetically describe the significance of the speech of Black and White women as well as of the Black community. Her metaphors represent the subjugation of a people and the suppression of their collective voice, which strained to be heard in the American controversy. The South preferred to withdraw from the controversy altogether and employed violent, coercive measures to silence the newly freed slaves.

When the voice of the Negro was heard, it was a jarring cadenza, a flourish, one might say, that startled those who heard it. Within this chord — the voices that made up the "voice of the Negro" — the Black Woman was a voiceless note, the most suppressed of all. The image recalls more violent images than Cooper presents, images that she would have been loathe to describe, given her interest in being viewed as an embodiment of ideal womanhood. Her metaphor recalls the binding, whipping, rape, and gagging of Black women who dared to assert their innate human liberty under slavery and Jim Crow. "Mute" is not simply a referent to Black women's silence. It refers to their *subjugation*. It is a signifier for the multiplicity of oppressive acts employed to silence them. The muffled strain of the Negro, startling to Euro-American ears with its cry for justice, was and still is an incompletely heard chord without the voices of Black women. The full cry for liberty, justice, and equality, the assertion of the innate freedom of voice, is a jarring sound to those whose will for power is based in selfish greed and a desire for dominance. Prophetic, it shakes the foundations of self-interested rationalizations for the maintenance of structures of evil. It cuts to the quick of false justifications for systemic sin. Perhaps this is why the very tongues of runaway slaves were sometimes cut out when the slaves were recovered by their masters.

A Voice from the South is divided into two parts. "Part First," which is comprised of essays on womanhood, is entitled "Soprano Obligato." "Part Second," which deals with the question of the problem of race in American culture, literature, and economics, is entitled "Tutti Ad Libitum." The first title describes the voice of the Black woman as a counter-melody that stands out in the listener's ear and is used to add drama.[7] The metaphor also suggests the separateness, the isolation of the voices of such women. In contrast, the second title describes the Black community as a whole, its men and women, as an improvisational movement. There is no set plan, no set ending. Rather they are in the process of a creative event even as they are heard by their listeners.

Sensitive to the problems of voice and audience for both Black women and men, Anna Cooper described the "colored man's in-heritage and apportionment" as "the sombre crux" or "*cul de sac*" of the nation, like "a dumb skeleton in the closet." Critical of America's bungled understanding of the plea Black men had brought before the bar, she contended that despite their ceaseless harangues, they were "little understood" and "seldom consulted."[8]

If Black men were not understood or consulted, Black women were virtually invisible. Appalled at the absurdity of making judgments about systemic injustice in the South without hearing all witnesses, Cooper chastised America for not consulting Black women for their testimony in the nation's consideration of the race problem:

> Attorneys for the plaintiff and attorneys for the defendant, with bungling *gaucherie* have analyzed and dissected, theorized and synthesized with sublime ignorance or pathetic misapprehension of counsel from the black client. One important witness has not yet been heard from. The summing up of the evidence deposed, and the charge to the jury have been made— but no word from the Black Woman.[9]

America's attempts to analyze the race problem were coarse, gauche. The nation failed to comprehend the scope and depth of the issues. Not only did Cooper describe America's understanding of the race problem as misapprehended, but she also asserted that the problem was incompletely understood without the testimony of Black women. Optimistic, she expressed faith in America's conscientious commitment to a fair trial. Mixing musical and legal metaphors, she described the voice of the Black woman as the voice of a witness in a trial on the race problem:

> It is because I believe the American people to be conscientiously committed to a fair trial and ungarbled evidence, and because I feel it essential to a perfect understanding and an equitable verdict that truth from *each* standpoint be presented at the bar,—that this little Voice has been added to the already full chorus. The "other side" has not been represented by one who "lives there." And not many can more sensibly realize and more accurately tell the weight and the fret of the "long dull pain" than the open-eyed but hitherto voiceless Black Woman of America.[10]

The Black woman as described here, hitherto voiceless but open-eyed, was the personification of Black women in the South. She had seen the evils of slavery, segregation, and discrimination, particularly in the South, and could give testimony. Very few besides the Black Woman, Cooper asserted, could more sensibly realize or give a more accurate account of the pain of oppression in the South. No one could voice an analysis of America's race problem as Black women could, and no one could reproduce that voice:

> At any rate, as our Caucasian barristers are not to blame if they cannot *quite* put themselves in the dark man's place, neither should the dark man be wholly expected fully and adequately to reproduce the exact Voice of the Black Woman.[11]

Like her colleagues in the NACW, Cooper was ever conscious of the middle-class Black and White male and White female audience from which she sought support for developmental programs. Therefore she presented what she and the NACW considered an ideal of Black womanhood in her writings. By referring to "the Black Woman" in this fashion, she sought to thrust Black womanhood from the bare periphery of America's consciousness into full view. To move Black women from virtual invisibility to visibility she rendered them larger than life, like blasphemed and abused goddesses clothed in the garb of true womanhood, to draw on the sympathies of her audience. This is sometimes irritating to readers today, but it was effective for the context in which she wrote. *A Voice from the South* was a great success when it was reviewed in 1892. It received numerous positive reviews, particularly among reviewers for Black newspapers.

While on the one hand Cooper's description of the voice of the Black woman as "this little Voice" betrays the sense of isolation Cooper must have felt, it also belies her true feelings about that voice. Spelling the "word" voice with a capital "V" reveals a spirit of defiance. To call her own voice or the voice of Black women "little" is a rhetorical gesture. There is a sense of ambiguity in the phrase "this little Voice." The capital "V" signifies Cooper's deepest feelings about the importance of Black women's voices. Her reference to "Voice" as little does not refer to the actual significance of Black women's voices. Rather, it signifies the expectations of her audience, particularly middle-class men, Black and White. She was able to reach an audience that was conservative in its attitudes toward women by appearing to be diminutive, which as she proceeds further we see is clearly not the case. Once she brings her audience into her confidence, she unabashedly criticizes those whose minds she seeks to change. She proceeds forthrightly to name her Black male audience, for example, as inattentive to the social development of the women of the race and chastises White women for failing to see their darker sisters as equal.

Cooper personified the voice of Black women as "the Voice of the Black Woman of the South." Such personification is often used in literature to designate divinities, goddesses, mythological figures, and the power of specific characteristics of human nature or the natural world. Through literary style, she asserted the strength of the physical, vocal presence of Black women. Cooper described the initial vocalization among Black women as being "with no language but a cry."[12] This initial cry was a primary sound of pain, outrage, and longing for freedom shared by Black women in America. The feeling of outrage at America's social injustices regarding Black women and men was and is a shared feeling. Cooper's words suggest that Black women in post-Reconstruction America were essentially unified in their feelings of pain and suffering and in their cry for freedom and deliverance. On the title page for the section of *A Voice* entitled "Soprano Obligato," she quoted George Eliot to capture her feeling that there were sufferings whose pain no words could articulate:

> For they the *Royal-hearted Women* are
> Who nobly love the noblest, yet have grace
> For needy, suffering lives in lowliest place;
> Carrying a choicer sunlight in their smile,
> The heavenliest ray that pitieth the vile.
> Though I were happy, throned beside the king,
> I should be tender to each little thing
> With hurt warm breast, that had no speech to tell
> Its inward pangs; and I would sooth it well
> With tender touch and with a low, soft moan
> For company.[13]

Those who suffer socio-economic justice and/or physical illness need more than words. They need feeling hearts and tender, working hands to actively seek improvement for their condition. The practice of helping the needy was central to Cooper's understanding of altruism and benevolence. Here, by quoting Eliot, Cooper suggested that royal-hearted women are those who have grace for needy, suffering lives. Moreover, those with socio-economic privilege and eloquent speech derived from formal educations must speak on behalf of those who are not so advantaged. Years later

W. E. B. Du Bois articulated this as a need for a talented tenth who would lead Black Americans. The problem that emerges with such an ideal is that of elitism. On the other hand, this is a view that challenges those who are even remotely on top to take social responsibility. That is the significance of Cooper's words.

Cooper concluded her preface, "Our Raison d'Être," by portraying the Black woman as a calorimeter, sensitive at every pore to America's social climate. She described her own speech, surprisingly, as "broken utterances." Perhaps this description is, in part, rhetoric meant to foil the defenses of sexist and racist readers who would resist the idea of a Black woman educating them on the problems of sexism and racism. But this is also more than rhetoric. Cooper's words suggest that despite her own privileged educational background, her speech, too, has been crippled by the devastating effects of racism:

> Delicately sensitive at every pore to social atmospheric conditions, her calorimeter may well be studied in the interest of accuracy and fairness in diagnosing what is often conceded to be a "puzzling" case. If these broken utterances can in any way help to a clearer vision and a truer pulse-beat in studying our Nation's Problem, this Voice by a Black Woman of the South will not have been raised in vain.[14]

The above passage demonstrates Cooper's awareness of the singularity of her own voice as the author of *A Voice from the South*. She referred to her own voice as "by" that of "a" Black Woman of the South, rather than by "the" Black Woman of the South. Moreover, the use of the preposition "by" suggests that she was aware that she was self-consciously constructing a voice of "the Black Woman of the South." As an author, she carefully crafted every aspect of the text, including its narrative voice. This voice was Cooper's literary construction of her own voice as narrator, her representation of the collective voices of her peers in the NACW, and her ideal of Black womanhood. Conscious of both her uniqueness and her identification with a unified effort among Black women in America, she entitled her volume *"A" Voice from the South* rather than *"The" Voice from the South*.

But overall, Cooper's language suggests that she saw herself as representing the views of the majority of Black women. Cooper was representative of the spheres in which she circulated — a group of mostly elite, educated Black women. She essayed to speak not only on the behalf of educated Black women, but on the behalf of uneducated Black women as well. Her primary concern was for their education and development. Why did Cooper think it important to lend her voice to speak and write on their behalf?

Literary eloquence was an important criterion in Black Americans' efforts to be heard. Education was a means of developing eloquent speech that would belie stereotypes regarding the intellectual capacity for Black Americans to analyze their own situation. As a formally educated, eloquent Black woman, Cooper undoubtedly expected that her voice would be given a more serious audience than the voices of less literate Black women. For those who were doubtful about Black women's capacity for learning, she was an example of what Black women could attain and thus was living proof of her own arguments for the education and development of Black women and the protection of their honor. This sounds patronizing to contemporary ears. But for Cooper, the carefully crafted prose of *A Voice from the South* was in itself evidence of the intellectual equality and potential for the development of Black womanhood.

The Value and Significance of Woman's Voice

Why was the vocalization of woman's voice so important to Cooper? For some of the same reasons it is important to feminist and womanist theologians today. The recognition of women's right to speak in traditionally male-dominated spheres was a problem in the nineteenth century, and in many respects it is still a problem for women today. In nineteenth-century America, for women to speak on public platforms to mixed-sex audiences was considered unladylike. Women who ventured to do so defied a model of subjugation and silence allowing at most sweet, subtle whisperings to spouse or father in the domestic sphere.

In Cooper's view, it was subversive of every human interest that one-half of the human family be stifled. That is, to stifle women's perspective is counterproductive to the establishment of a good society. The world only half-perceives truth. The presence of women's voices is necessary to complete the world's vision. Further, women's speech is of value and importance because women are linked with the world's wronged and suffering, for whom they must serve as interpreter and defender:

> It would be subversive of every human interest that the cry of one-half the human family be stifled. Woman in stepping from the pedestal of statue-like inactivity in the domestic shrine, and daring to think and move and speak, — to undertake to help shape, mold, and direct the thought of her age, is merely completing the circle of the world's vision. Hers is every interest that has lacked an interpreter and a defender. Her cause is linked with that of every agony that has been dumb — every wrong that needs a voice.[15]

Like feminist scholars today, Anna Cooper argued that women make up one-half of the world's population. Stifling women's voices incorrectly alters the world's vision so that the world limps along with a "darkened eye," she lamented. It undermines the best interests of everyone, male and female. Describing women as stepping down from the pedestal of statue-like inactivity in the domestic sphere to dare to think, move, and speak, she presented women as leaders in molding and directing the thought and practice of a new era.

Cooper referred to a model of womanhood intended to represent White middle-class women, who were expected to remain in the domestic sphere. It is a model that she herself, dependent on her employment as a teacher, could hardly have fully identified with. But she adopted it to make her argument for women's daring to speak on political affairs. Her purpose was to argue for women's speech, an activity in which she was already engaged, as a morally and philosophically essential human activity.

Unlike White feminists, Black feminists like Anna Cooper, Ida B. Wells-Barnett, Mary Church Terrell, and Sojourner Truth do not express the dichotomy between public activity and motherhood that is evident in works by White feminists. Susan B. Anthony, for example, became angry and disappointed when her friend Ida B. Wells-Barnett decided to marry and have children. Convinced that this would be the end of Wells-Barnett's activism, she thought it a regretfully unwise decision.[16] A captivating speaker in great demand who took her babies to meetings across the country, Wells-Barnett, like most Black women writers, speakers, and evangelists, did not see her roles of activist and mother as oppositional.

Likewise Cooper combined mothering with scholarship, teaching, and activism. She presented women's purpose as familial, not to the exclusion of social activism, but as concomitant. Some have interpreted her as emphasizing women's roles as mothers and their responsibility to children to the exclusion of taking on activist and/or professional roles. Delores Williams points out that Cooper inadvertently used language of true womanhood, which could be construed by conservative, middle-class Black men as condoning women's relegation to home and family.[17] It is true that such a reader who was careless and inattentive could misread Cooper's thinking in this way. But such an interpretation would be an incorrect evaluation of the author's intent and meaning, crediting her with beliefs diametrically opposed to her argument. Like her contemporaries in the Black women's club movement, for whom it was not unusual to combine social activism with family concerns, she had a wholistic view of women's roles.

Cooper extended the concept of family from the domestic sphere to the public sphere. Women, in her thinking, were not simply one-half of a privatized, nuclear, or extended family in the domestic sphere. Rather, women represented one-half of the world's voice. In other words, they formed one half of the social sphere in every way — domestically and publicly. Cooper took women's rights very seriously. She did not see women as responsible only to other women. Nor did she see women as responsible only to immediate family or kin. It was also women's responsibility to interpret and voice the concerns of all the world's dominated who had not been privileged a hearing.

Today feminist theologians like Mary Daly have argued that the oppression of women is the most profound and elemental of oppressions, that all other forms of oppression proceed from this one form of oppression. Cooper, although she took a much less radical stance than Daly, suggested something similar. For Cooper, women's issues were linked with the issues of oppressed peoples generally. Sexism for Cooper was a fundamental form of oppression. She presented women as the most dominated group of human beings. Further, she presented Black women as the most dominated women among women in the Western sphere.

Arguing that women were the most dominated group of human beings across cultures, Cooper linked women's issues with every wrong that needed a voice. The domination of women, she argued, because of its depth and its worldwide effects, afforded women the ability to interpret the interests of the weak generally. Women's power, as she described it, included the ability to interpret and defend from experiential understanding the plight of the weak, the oppressed everywhere. Women, Cooper's words suggest, have a distinctive and powerful ability to interpret truth — to interpret every wrong and agony that has lacked a defender.

Can women really interpret the interests of every oppressed group? Does this afford women too much power? Perhaps. Contemporary feminist theologian Sharon Welch warns that the temptation to define others' hopes for liberation must be avoided. "It is oppressive to 'free' people," Welch writes, "if their own history and culture do not serve as the primary sources of the definition of their freedom."[18] The question arises: Which women will engage in shaping, molding, and directing the thought of their age? Highly educated White women and women of color? Where are the voices of the poor, the illiterate, of laboring women and men?

Cooper's intention was not to establish a new imperialism. The value of her thought is that she recognized the interrelationship between various forms of oppression: sexism, racism, cultural imperialism. She purposed to raise women's consciousness, White and Black, to an awareness of the interrelated nature of the problem of oppression. And yet Cooper wrote with a measure of elitism. Her audience was highly educated and middle-class. Her language was inaccessible to the masses of Black women.

In order to effect social change, it was necessary to appeal to the sensibilities of those who had some level of power to effect such change. Thus Cooper particularly addressed middle-class White and Black Americans. In order to be heard and to be taken seriously it was necessary to speak in the highly educated, sophisticated language of those who held some degree of political power. In order to argue for the uplift of Black women through education in a racist society, Cooper and her peers demonstrated that Black women could be educated in part by conforming to an Anglo-American model of the educated lady. They made the model their own, although imbuing it with their own interests and concerns. They made the language of the culture that had been used to oppress them their own, shaping it and nuancing it to paint the atrocities of racial and gender discrimination. They used the rhetoric of "uplift" and "true womanhood" persuasively to demand dramatic shifts in the treatment of African American women and men. At the same time, they were confined to some extent by the very language they shaped to address their needs.

Black middle-class women were only narrowly free to move within the very bounds that afforded them a voice in post-Reconstruction American society.[19] Mary Helen Washington, literary critic and editor, expounds on this dilemma:

> As a middle-class black woman, Cooper, like all of her contemporaries—Fannie Jackson Coppin, Frances Harper, Mary Church Terrell, Ida B. Wells-Barnett, Josephine St. Pierre Ruffin—had a great stake in the prestige, the respectability, and the gentility guaranteed by the politics of true womanhood. To identify with the issues and interests of poor and uneducated black women entailed a great risk. Cooper and her intellectual contemporaries would have to deal with their own class privilege and would undoubtedly alienate the very white women they felt they needed as allies. Burdened by the race's morality, black women could not be as free as white women or black men to think outside of these boundaries of "uplift"; every choice they made had tremendous repercussions for an entire race of women already under the stigma of inferiority and immorality.[20]

Perhaps it was because she perceived that close identification with the issues and interests of poor and uneducated Black women entailed a great risk that Cooper presumed to speak *for* them rather than *with* them or *beside* them. Within her social-historical context, the very language that distanced her from the masses of Black women made her more acceptable to an educational system dominated by Whites who believed that Black women and men were intellectually inferior and incapable of learning. She and her contemporaries believed that it was the safest way they could get a fair hearing.

Women's Voices and the One-Eyed Man

The exclusion of women's voices from the public sphere, in Cooper's thought, resulted in a crippled society. Without women's voice the world is half-blind. One eye darkened, it hobbles along with a limping gait. Again, the problem is one of vision. For men to see clearly without women was an impossibility. Thus it was not their fault that their vision was faulty. Without women's voice, that was the only logical possibility. The darkness of men's vision was inevitable.

Cooper was harshly critical of the privilege of White women, which she saw as including the leisure to engage in frivolous, worthless pursuits. Seeing them as abusive of what little power they did possess, she held them accountable for their own domination and for the world's insensitivity to the domination of the weak. Thus, she challenged them to speak out so that men could wake up to their faulty perception of the world:

> It is no fault of man's that he has not been able to see truth from her standpoint. It does credit both to his head and heart that no greater mistakes have been committed or even wrongs perpetrated while she was making tatting and snipping paper flowers. Man's own innate chivalry and the mutual interdependence of their interests have insured his treating her cause, in the main at least as his own. And he is pardonably surprised and even a little chagrined, perhaps, to find his legislation not considered "perfectly lovely" in every respect. But in any case his work is only impoverished by her remaining dumb. The world has had to limp along with the wobbling gait and one-sided hesitancy of a man with one eye. Suddenly the bandage is removed from the other eye and the whole body is filled with light. It sees a circle where before it saw a segment. The darkened eye restored, every member rejoices with it.[21]

The harsh criticism of White middle-class womanhood and the apparently lighter criticism of men, in this instance, is complex. One might ask how Cooper perceived White women's experience of domination by White men. She did not acknowledge that White women may have experienced tatting and snipping as an activity of women's subjugation, for example. But as the daughter of a slave woman, it is not surprising that she would see the time to engage in such activity as a leisurely privilege of elite, White women. She wrote this in "Woman versus the Indian," which was a critique of White women's racism addressed to White women. It is important to remember Andolsen's observation that Cooper gave White women responsibility for having more power to step outside established roles than perhaps they had. But it is even more important to remember the sense of outrage Cooper and other Black women felt at White women's participation in the oppression of Black women and men while they turned their eyes to their snipping and tatting.

During slavery and after their emancipation, Black women experienced gross oppression at the hands of White Southern women. As domestics in the post-Reconstruction era, many Black women worked under the rule of White women for substandard wages. In contrast, the lifestyle of the White middle-class woman was privileged. While White middle-class women were encouraged to stay in their own homes and spend time with their children, Black women domestics were denied the opportunity to tend their own homes and family.[22]

One might argue that White middle-class women, in turn, lived in subjugation to White men. Their roles were dictated for them. But that does not excuse the appropriation of White supremacist ideology on the part of White women. It certainly does not excuse mental and physical abuse exacted on Black women and men by many White Southern women. Cooper chose to criticize White middle-class women for remaining silent, for accepting the roles dictated to them, and for appropriating White supremacist language. She chastised them for their moral insensitivity. The purpose of her rhetoric functionally was to shock White women into self-awareness and self-criticism: "Why not dare to speak out?"

Cooper was also critical of the role of men in women's oppression. She described man as dominating by brute, physical force and by cold, unfeeling reason. Although she never used the term "patriarchy," her criticism of White male domination in particular and male domination generally, as central to the world's problems of inequality and injustice, is a criticism of patriarchy and its hierarchical system of oppression. Here we see that women's voices serve as the much-needed corrective for a one-eyed perspective. Women complete the world's vision. Without women's voices, there is no hope for a perception of full truth. Without women, men can see only an arc of the full circle of truth.

Optimistic that the world's vision could be made complete, Cooper was a meliorist who believed that society could be reformed to include just relations between women and men. This is evidence of a hope and belief, on her part, that she was on the threshold of an era of social change for women. She had faith in the women's movement. She believed herself to be at the beginning of a new era of women's reform, which should have progressed much further than it has in the one hundred years since *A Voice* was written.

Cooper did not naively expect that there would be no future need for reform. Rather, she thought that the concerns for reform of the next generation would be far different from her own in their specificity. She saw reform as part of life and as the natural pulse of the revelation of the Gospel in human culture. But she hoped that her concerns would not be the immediate concerns of the next generation:

> "Isms" have their day and pass away. New necessities arise with new conditions and the emphasis has to be shifted to suit the times. No finite mind can grasp and give out the whole circle of truth. We do well if we can illuminate just the tiny arc which we occupy and should be glad that the next generation will not need the lessons we try so assiduously to hammer into this.[23]

Placing the source of humanity's power for reform in God, Cooper claimed that reformers think God's thought after God. Limited by their human finitude, they are part of a process that they cannot fully perceive. Weak in vision, distorted in their interpretations of God's revelation, reformers in even their greatest moments just barely grasp God's vision of freedom. Reform for Cooper was the activity of God within humankind. It transcends the immediacy of particular problems, while at the same time giving strength, vim, and verve to call for social transformation. But the problems of a particular age are themselves limited aspects of a whole. They form part of a larger universal human problem that pervades history:

> Not unfrequently has it happened that the impetus of a mighty thought wave has done the execution meant by its Creator in spite of the weak and distorted perception of its human embodiment. It is not strange if reformers, who, after all, but think God's thoughts after him, have often "builded more wisely than they knew"; and while fighting consciously for only a narrow gateway for themselves, have been driven forward by that irresistible "Power not ourselves which makes for righteousness" to open a high road for humanity. It was so with our sixteenth century reformers. The fathers of the Reformation had no idea that they were inciting an insurrection of the human mind against all domination.[24]

For Cooper, God is not separate from human culture, society, and history. God is transcendent and immanent. Her concept of

God in relation to humankind has some parallels with process thought, in which culture is the creative work of God. This does not mean that it is not also the work of humanity. Rather, humanity and God, who are of the same substance, perform different functions, with God's activity preceding human activity and lasting for eternity. In this temporal realm, we have the freedom to choose to participate in God's initial aim for freedom, justice, and equality. But even as one fights for reform, one has only a narrow view of the larger idea one is fighting for. Humanity, thinking God's thoughts after God, is in effect an instrument of a larger power, a greater thought, a grander concept of reform.[25] In any given era, the reformers of that age voice one small aspect of the fight for freedom. The larger fight for freedom is a fight against all forms and systems of domination.

Womanist theologians and ethicists today, highly educated at elite institutions, must work in concert with the masses of Black women to fight against racism, sexism, classism, and imperialism. Black women leaders today require a language that moves beyond the rhetoric of uplift with its exclusive, classist overtones. Rather than employ the language of uplift, it is more appropriate to turn to the language of Black folk church tradition and "lift one another up." Social reform requires that Black women "Lift Every Voice"[26] to create a symphony that truly blends the voices of a diversity of Black women, standing in solidarity to resist oppression of every form. Black communities, male and female, must lift every voice with a wholistic vision of freedom and equality. To do this, Black men must join in to challenge not only racism, but sexism. The middle class must join in to address not only racism and sexism, but classism. Heterosexuals must take seriously the human dignity and rights of Black gays and lesbians, whom all too many would like to silence. If the masses of Black heterosexual women are triply oppressed, Black lesbians are four times removed from so-called normative culture and the seats of power that come along with that culture. They face a quadruple jeopardy. Moreover, the symbolization of white maleness as the *norm* of human virtue subverts the possibilities for full humanity for *all* women of color — and men.

If, as Cooper claims, there is a Singing Something within all of humankind, Black women included, that rises up against systems of domination, then Black women, in their diversity, like every other people are created in the voice of God. History bears Cooper's claim out. Black women have not sat silent in face of oppression. There are numerous examples of Black women who have risen up to speak out in bold, sometimes progressive, sometimes militant speech. Black women of every class, status, and hue are called to rise up in the midst of oppression to participate in ushering in God's liberating message.

NOTES

1. See Marilyn Richardson, *Maria W. Stewart, America's First Black Woman Political Writer* (Bloomington: Indiana University Press, 1987), xiii–xvii, 3–27.

2. Ibid.

3. See Sharon Harley, "Black Women in a Southern City: Washington, D.C., 1890–1920," in Darlene Clark Hine, ed., *Black Women in United States History* (New York: Carlson Publishing Co., 1990), 144–45.

4. Ibid.

5. Ibid.

6. Anna J. Cooper, "Our Raison d'Être," in *A Voice from the South*, ed. Mary Helen Washington, Schomburg Library of Nineteenth-Century Black Women Writers (1892; New York: Oxford University Press, 1988), i.

7. Definition from Garth Baker-Fletcher, conversation December 19, 1989.

8. Cooper, "Our Raison d'Être," i.

9. Ibid., ii.

10. Ibid.

11. Ibid., iii.

12. Ibid., i.

13. Cooper, opening for "Part First," in *A Voice from the South*.

14. Ibid., "Our Raison d'Être," iii.

15. Cooper, "Woman versus the Indian," in *A Voice from the South*, 121–22.

16. See Alfreda B. Duster, ed., *Crusade for Justice: The Autobiography of Ida B. Wells* (Chicago: University of Chicago Press, 1970), for a fuller discussion of Wells-Barnett's work as activist and mother.

17. See Delores Williams, *Sisters in the Wilderness* (Maryknoll, N.Y.: Orbis Books, 1993), 222–30.

18. Sharon Welch, *Communities of Resistance and Solidarity* (Maryknoll, N.Y.: Orbis Books, 1985), 83.

19. See chapter 7 for a discussion of how Black middle-class women might best address this problem today.

20. Mary Helen Washington, introduction to *A Voice from the South*, xlvii.

21. Cooper, "Woman versus the Indian," 122–23.

22. See Jacqueline Jones, *Labor of Love, Labor of Sorrow: Black Women, Work and the Family, from Slavery to the Present* (New York: Vintage Books, 1985), 127ff., for a full discussion of problems faced by Black domestics in the post–Civil War South.

23. Cooper, "One Phase of American Literature," in *A Voice from the South,* 183.

24. Ibid., 118–19.

25. My understanding of process theology has been influenced by Marjorie Suchocki, *God, Christ, Church,* rev. ed. (New York: Crossroad, 1992), and Henry James Young, *Hope in Process* (Minneapolis: Fortress Press, 1990). These authors apply process philosophy to a relational and social understanding of pluralism in American culture.

26. "Lift Every Voice," commonly known as the Negro National Anthem, was written by James Weldon Johnson.

6

A Womanist Critique of
Anna Cooper's Life
and Thought

L IKE CONTEMPORARY WOMANISTS, historical African American women have often demanded racial *and* gender equality in American social reform. The masses of Black women in America have faced a triple jeopardy of racism, sexism, and classism, which form the context in which Black women in America practice faith in a God of freedom and equality and ethics of survival, resistance, and liberation.[1] By employing historical materials as resources for contemporary theology and ethics, womanists contextualize Black women's ethical practices, norms, and values culturally and historically.

Theologians and ethicists have traditionally written from and for a particular social-historical context and culture, whether self-consciously or not. Womanist ethicists engage in an ongoing process of "dusting off" neglected resources by and about Black women that have been pushed to the underside of history. By examining similarities, differences, and paradigmatic shifts in the ways Black women have addressed various issues historically and the ways in which they address similar issues today, one can gain a clearer understanding of Black women's theological and ethical concerns.

Anna Cooper's work offers several insights for the contemporary world. Moreover, the religious values that undergird her philosophy of social reform can make a valuable contribution to womanist theology. She identified certain issues regarding racism, sexism, and classism that have been problematic in American culture. In particular, her identification of Black women as being plagued by two problems — a race problem and a gender problem—continues today. Her emphasis on ensuring greater educational and economic opportunity for Black women shows her concern for greater economic freedom and movement, an ongoing problem in America and around the globe.

The similarity of Cooper's concerns for social reform to concerns for social transformation among contemporary womanist theologians like Jacquelyn Grant and Delores Williams demonstrates the historical depth of the problems of racism and sexism African American women face in America. Her appeal to Christian principles is also familiar. The historical Jesus, with his concerns for the weak and the dominated, is essentially a Jesus who is on the side of the oppressed. Cooper's thought has much in common with that of late-twentieth-century womanist and liberation theologians. Jacquelyn Grant writes:

> Black feminism grows out of Black women's tridimensional reality of race/sex/class. It holds that full human liberation cannot be achieved simply by the elimination of any one form of oppression. Consequently, real liberation must be "broad in the concrete"; it must be based upon a multidimensional analysis.[2]

Like Cooper a century ago, Grant points out that liberation from the perspective of Black feminists must seek the elimination of all forms of oppression. It must be broad, concerning itself with the varieties of forms in which oppression manifests itself and concrete in its efforts at the elimination of oppression. Grant goes on to indicate that with this in mind Black feminists have challenged White feminists and Black race analysis by introducing data from Black women's experience that White feminists and Black liberationists have too often ignored.[3] Like Cooper and her contemporaries, she challenges the exclusive nature of Black men's and White women's efforts at reform.[4]

Jacquelyn Grant further suggests that the possibly irreparable nature of the tension between White women and Black women and between Black men and Black women necessitates a completely different word to describe the liberative efforts of Black women: "womanist."[5] She builds on Alice Walker's definition and moves beyond it to describe womanism as "being and acting out who you are and interpreting the reality for yourself."[6] She emphasizes the importance of Black women's autonomy and suggests that speech is an essential aspect of womanism. For Grant, an essential aspect of womanism is simply this: "Black women speak out for themselves."[7] The possession of one's own voice is an important aspect of womanism.

Was Anna Cooper a womanist? Is it appropriate to so name her? The term was not in use during her lifetime. It is probably more accurate to call her a Black feminist. But Cooper's work shares something in common with contemporary womanist interpretations of reality. Although Walker describes Harriet Tubman and Rebecca Cox Jackson as historical Black women who practiced womanist values, "womanist" is a contemporary term, not employed by historical African American women. It is difficult to say whether, given the choice that Black women and women of color have today, they would have chosen to name themselves "womanist."

One might begin considering the significance of historical materials as a resource for womanist ethics by recalling that Alice Walker coined the term "womanist" with a description of both historical and contemporary African American women in mind. In her collection of essays, *In Search of Our Mothers' Gardens,* Walker cites historical African American women as illustrations of womanist thought and practice. In her definition of "womanist," Walker refers to Black women's commitment to freedom by alluding to Harriet Tubman (1820–1913), who led more than three hundred slaves out of slavery on the Underground Railroad. Sarah Bradford, in her 1886 edition of *Harriet: The Moses of Her People,*[8] emphasizes Tubman's religious faith, her commitment to freedom, her wisdom in employing coded spirituals to communicate with slaves seeking freedom, her modesty, and her *human* capacity for *feeling* during a period when White people questioned Black peoples' full humanity. While the work is written in the genre of the romantic novel and somewhat dependent on stereotypes of Black Southern dialect, the words and thought ascribed to Tubman ring true. The text reveals an ethic of courage, survival, and resistance against social injustice.

Moreover, as Cheryl Sanders has suggested, the writings of Rebecca Cox Jackson (1795–1871) are a foundational resource for womanist thought because much of Walker's definition of "womanist" emerges from her reflections on Jackson.[9] On the basis of religious experiences of a Mother God and life in a Shaker community, Jackson founded a Black, female Shaker Community with Rebecca Perot. Jean Humez edited Jackson's writings in *Gifts of Power: The Writings of Rebecca Jackson*.[10] Walker, who appreciates Humez's editing, disagrees with her on one point. Humez notes in her introduction that since Jackson lived "in close relationship with a single cherished, intimate woman friend who shared her religious ideas," today she may have been "an open lesbian." Jackson, however, described herself as dead to sexuality or "lust." Walker questions "a nonblack scholar's attempt to label something lesbian that the black woman in question has not." She argues that "If Rebecca Jackson and Rebecca Perot *were* erotically bound," they would have had their own word for it. Why, Walker asks, did they not accept the name "lesbian" from male clergy in reference to the religious settlement of women and children they founded? Walker proposes that such woman-bonding among Black women, sexual or not, might best be called "womanist."

Walker coined the term "womanist" to define the diverse ways in which Black women have bonded. She questions the cultural accuracy of tying Black women's sexuality and culture to the Isle of Lesbos, arguing that woman-bonding among Black women is more ancient than Greek culture. Moreover, it is not separatist but seeks liberation for the entire community in a culture that "oppresses all Black people." The heart of the issue for Walker is self-naming from within one's cultural context. The term "womanist" affirms woman-bonding, sexual and non-sexual, from a distinctive Black feminist perspective. Walker seeks a term that is spiritual, concrete, "organic and characteristic not simply applied"[11] to describe Black women's bonding.

Although historical Black women did not employ the term "womanist" themselves, it is descriptive of the attitudes and practices of certain historical Black women. Womanist theologians, ethicists, and clergy build on a tradition of Black women freedom fighters, as Delores Williams calls them in an early essay.[12] Many of the principles of womanism have emerged from Black women's history and culture; that is, womanism embodies many of the concerns, ideas, and principles that Black women have held historically. Thus, womanist theologians like Delores Williams and Jacquelyn Grant have chosen the name "womanism" as descriptive of Black women freedom fighters' historical and traditional values, ideas, self-understanding, and social outlook.

Self-Naming

Black women, whether reformist and liberationist or radical and revolutionary in their theological and christological constructions, must be revolutionary in their theological anthropologies of Black womanhood. It is important for communities and individuals to name themselves and their experience in their own words.

Black women who choose the name "womanist" first presuppose the right of self-naming. Naming oneself from within oneself, refusing categorizations of self and community that come from outside dominant groups and persons, is the first and most basic step in coming to voice. Second, Black women who choose the name "womanist" indicate that they stand in solidarity with other Black women who have chosen to name themselves womanist. Black feminists or feminists of color who name themselves womanist stand in solidarity with Black women who honor Walker's understanding of the term "womanist" as formally and substantively emerging from Black women's culture. Moreover, it is important to support and affirm the processual nature of Black women naming themselves, defining womanism, creatively expanding on the meaning of womanism, and developing womanist literature and theology.

Cheryl Sanders astutely observes similarities between the significance of naming in Afrocentrism (*nommo*), commenting that the "self-affirmation and self-assertiveness of womanism and Afrocentrism should be regarded not in individualistic terms but as indicative of the self finding expression in harmony with others."[13] By coining the name "womanist," Alice Walker participates in the power of self-definition. Black feminists who call themselves womanists participate in naming, which in both womanism and Afrocentrism is the generative, productive power of the spoken word.[14] To name is to give rise to speech, which is to participate in the power of creating one's context. Different historical periods and different social circumstances may require different names.

Historical Black women who engaged in social reform around race and gender issues chose methods of self-naming different from contemporary Black women. But contemporary Black women share with their historical predecessors a concern for correcting conventional descriptions of Black womanhood. Cooper, for example, named herself and named Black women by redefining Black womanhood. This new definition of Black womanhood and bold vocalization went hand in hand. Language is oppressive or freeing. The words we use to describe ourselves and one another are as oppressive or freeing as our attitudes, which are shaped by language and the words we choose to articulate experience.

Black women determined to name themselves "womanists" are questioned about the viability and meaning of the term and discouraged from using it. But the power of the term is precisely in its usage and in the ongoing process of elaborating its definition. If there is one thing that Black women theologians can find of value in the works of Mary Daly, it is her revolutionary and rebellious commitment to self-naming, an elemental form of giving voice.

Because of racism within White feminist structures, many Black women have wrestled with the term "feminist," finding it inadequate as a name with liberating power for their context. Jacquelyn Grant makes distinctions between feminist theological discourse and womanist theological discourse. Grant understands "feminist" to mean "White feminist," because all too often the concerns of feminists of color are an afterthought. Grant describes the social-historical experiences and responses of Black women and White women in relation to oppression as radically different:

> Feminist theologians are White in terms of their race and in terms of the *nature of the sources* they use for the development of their theological perspectives. Although there are sharp differences among feminist theologians, as we have seen, they are *all* of the *same* race and the influence of their race has led them to similar sources for the definition of their perspectives on the faith. Of course, chief among the sources is women's experience. However, what is often unmentioned is that feminist theologians' sources for women's experience refer almost exclusively to White women's experience. White women's experience and Black women's experience are not the same.[15]

Grant explains that she does not mean to assert that "because feminist theology is White it is also racist."[16] Nor are all White feminists racist in some simplistic sense simply because their skin is White. Rather, the feminist movement has been structured so that it has taken on and continues to take on a racist character. Grant argues that White feminist theologians have misnamed themselves. Misnaming themselves as "feminists" who appeal to "women's experience," Grant contends, is no different from what oppressors have always done, which is to define the rules of the game and then solicit others to play it. As a result, many Black women are suspicious of feminism and "believe that Black feminism is a contradiction in terms."[17] Thus, Grant chooses to claim Alice Walker's term "womanist" to describe Black women's experience and concerns.

Walker describes a womanist as a Black woman or woman of color who wants to know more than is good for her.[18] The heights of Cooper's academic achievements are evidence of her quest for knowledge. As an educator, she wanted her students to know more than was good for them. She insisted that Black people ought to have far higher educations than the dominant society thought they should have. In this respect Cooper embodied and expressed certain qualities that are currently attributed to womanism.

The context that Walker identifies as important is the context of nonbourgeois Black folk culture.[19] Delores Williams explains that within this context there were great freedom fighters — folk heroines like Harriet Tubman. This leads a womanist theologian's memory to a liberation tradition of Black women leaders who acted as catalysts for revolutionary action and social change.[20] According to Williams: "The womanist theologian must search for the voices, actions, opinions, experience, and faith of women whose names sometimes slip into the male-centered rendering of black history, but whose actual stories remain remote."[21]

Although Cooper was not an anonymous Black woman from nonbourgeois Black folk culture, her slave birth gave her a sensitivity to the anonymous Black woman. In fragments of unpublished autobiographical manuscripts, Cooper wrote with pain and sensitivity in praise and defense of her mother — the victim of the violent abuse of slavery. Her life's work was affected by her birth. She described her mother as too shamefaced to discuss the events surrounding young Annie's conception. Anna Cooper's general silence on the subject suggests that she shared her mother's feelings of anger and shame. She was deeply aware of the horror, injustice, and outrage surrounding the conditions of her own origins. Overcoming these conditions lay at the heart of Cooper's motivation as an educator and a leader.

Delores Williams suggests that two of the principal concerns of womanist theology ought to be "survival and community building and maintenance" to establish a positive economic, spiritual, and educational quality of life "for black women, men, and children."[22] To the extent that she worked toward these goals Cooper shared some of the principal concerns of womanist theology as described by Williams. Moreover, a freedom fighter in her own right, Cooper fought for the equality of women with men, Black people with White people, nation with nation. She made an appeal for women's full participation in social reform. In particular, she argued for the importance of Black women's leadership before Black Episcopal clergy. She supported the women's movement with its appeal for women's equality and challenged the women's movement to work for reform of all forms of domination.

Recognizing the anonymity of Black women's thoughts, feelings, and voices in America, Anna Cooper attempted in a way that she best understood to bring these voices out of anonymity. She did not speak with "the exact voice" of Black women in the sense of representing every particular viewpoint possible, but she did speak with the exact dignity of Black women for freedom and against social, economic, and educational injustice.

Cooper was an early Black feminist, evidenced by her support of the women's movement and the Black women's club movement and her identification of problems related to gender oppression. There are certain parallels between her thought and contemporary womanist thought. She was outspoken, conscious of her own voice and the need for it to be heard in the chorus of Black women's voices that were speaking out for the uplift of women and the race. She was "womanish" in the sense that she was self-motivated, "in charge,"[23] a leader. It is viable for womanist theologians to build on her work.

Anna Cooper and Liberation Theology

Anna Cooper's writings are eloquent and sophisticated. She wrote with grace and dignity about the horrifying realities of educational and economic disparity between Black and White Americans and between Black women and men, and about the alienation of Black women from White women in the post-Reconstruction world she lived in. Black women today, living in the post–civil rights era, can resonate with many of the problems, feelings, and solutions Cooper identified. But her work does more than resonate with our own interests, our contemporary needs and concerns. To use her metaphor of music, *A Voice from the South* strikes a repetitive note in our ears. Its repetitiveness ought to create a sense of discomfort. It ought to evoke an awareness of the discordance in the world, an awareness that something is wrong. That is part of the value of Cooper's writings — not simply the solutions she has presented, but her identification of the gross discordance in the human network of communities and relationships. The problem of attaining acceptance of the interrelatedness of diverse communities and of establishing harmonious relations remains today.

The problems of racism and sexism in America are not a Black problem or a woman problem; they are America's problem. Cooper's thought indicates very carefully the interrelatedness of communities in America and across the globe. And, more than that, she envisions the problem of the domination of the physically and militaristically weak by the strong — imperialism — as not simply an American problem but a world problem. Such problems, I agree, are of global import and significance.

Contemporary theologians and ethicists can build on Cooper's thought. In particular, womanist, feminist, and liberation theologians can build on Cooper's thought. She, like contemporary feminist, womanist, and liberation theologians, analyzed particular forms of oppression and challenged specific structures of oppression. Her appeal to Christian principles in resolving this problem has something in common with contemporary liberation theology. For liberation theologians, the historical Jesus, with his concerns for the weak and the dominated, is essentially a Jesus who is on the side of the oppressed. Similarly, Cooper portrays Jesus as being concerned with the plight of the weak and the dominated.

Womanist thought has emerged independently out of Black women's culture and experience. It has also emerged in relationship with and in the gap between Black theology and Feminist theology. It challenges Black male theologians and White feminist theologians to be more inclusive in their understanding of freedom and equality, liberation and wholeness. At the same time, it shares mutual concerns and stands in solidarity with both.

Feminist theologian Sharon Welch presents an apt and inclusive definition of interpretations of sin in various forms of liberation theology that has some parallel's with Cooper's Social Gospel concerns.[24] Welch argues, for example, that in liberation theologies the analysis of sin is concrete, historical, and political:

> These analyses of sin and redemption are historical and political, not ontological. Rather than examine the structure of the human will and its potential for sin or describe the sociality of human existence and the possibility for social deformation of individual lives (thus delineating the ontological roots of complicity in institutional evil), liberation theologians analyze particular forms of oppression. They do not address oppression as such, but challenge specific structures of oppression.[25]

Similarly, womanism recognizes that a major contribution of liberation theology is its analysis of concrete historical and political systems of oppression. In Cooper's thought we see both an ontological and a concrete, historical analysis. She discussed social problems around the world — racism, sexism, imperialism, general domination of the "weak" by the strong. Unlike liberation theologians, she presented no explicit definition of domination or oppression as "sin" or "evil." But she viewed these problems as acting against the principles of Christ as represented in the Synoptic Gospels and other New Testament literature. We can build on her analysis of the social problems and identify them as institutional sin.

Anna Cooper recognized that communities of a diversity of races, cultures, genders, and nationalities shared a responsibility for working towards freedom and questioning their own complicity in domination. She identified oppression as a problem for which women and men are responsible universally. Implicitly, she suggested that these problems were part of an ontological problem and here her thought is different from Welch's definition of liberation theologians. She presupposed that humankind is created in the image of God and that God is the creator of human beings. It is the divine spark in human nature that makes women and men in God's own image across race, gender, and culture. Her concept of God suggests a universal ontology of freedom and equality. It is in freedom and equality that human being is created in God's image. Likewise, it is in freedom and equality that human being is created in the voice of God. She envisioned a reality in which humankind would exist in harmony under the principles of equality, freedom, and democracy. An ontology of freedom and equality was of universal application:

> The concept of Equality as it is the genuine product of the idea of inherent value in the individual derived from the essential worth of humanity must be before all else unquestionably of universal application. It operates not between such and such races, — such or such shape of the cranium, such or such theories of civilization. In my opinion, which makes no pretensions to scientific sanctions on either sociological or psychological grounds, instead of being the Special product of any unique cult, the idea of human equality is the result of the final equilibrium of all the human forces of the entire world.[26]

Equality, freedom, and even democratic principles in an ideal sense were ontological, universal aspects of human nature. There was something — a Singing Something — in human being that transcended the social reality of injustice. It was this Singing Something that rose up in human beings across nations and continents to call out for justice. Unlike Welch, however, Cooper presupposed an ontological ideal of freedom and equality. The Singing Something within human being was part of the very voice of God in human being. She described freedom as an inherent universal aspect of human being from creation. Her presupposition of an ontology of freedom and equality has been of value historically for Black women and men. Black leaders such as Frederick Douglass and Martin Luther King, Jr., presupposed that an inner, psychological freedom was necessary for oppressed persons to rise up against injustice and call out for freedom. Cooper made a similar kind of presupposition. She presupposed that if human beings held an ideal of freedom, then they must hold an inherent, in-born knowledge of freedom.[27]

Like liberation theologians today, Cooper used her theological imagination to construct a concrete understanding of Christian ideals in relation to human being and social change. Like James Cone and Jacquelyn Grant, her Christian perspective was concrete and historical. The hereafter in her view was something to be lived into in human history. Cooper's writings suggest that salvation and redemption occur in the here and now. Heaven was on earth in present, living individuals who participated in its creation by altruistically working and living into it. Hell was the failure to work toward reform.

Practical in her understanding of the Christian life, Cooper was ever the teacher as missionary — concerned with touching people concretely in this life. There are several examples of her commitment to this vocation. There is her overarching appeal for women's full participation in social reform. In particular, she argued for the importance of Black women's leadership before Black Episcopal clergy. She supported the women's movement with its appeal for women's equality and challenged the women's movement to work for reform of *all* forms of domination. She further lived what she spoke by participating in the founding and supervision of a Colored Settlement House, teaching the needy during several of her summers, devoting her life from childhood to educating Black women and men, taking in orphaned children during two periods of her long life, serving as a member of the National Council of Christians and Jews, participating in the life of the Church, and lecturing nationally and in Europe.

As Mary Helen Washington points out, Cooper never wrote another explicitly feminist book after *A Voice from the South,* probably because of professional insecurity and financial difficulty. Moreover, the 1890s were a conservative period for African Americans, with Black men dominating intellectually and politically.[28] But she continued to exemplify feminist ideals. Throughout her life, Cooper fully believed in women's leadership. Identifying women as the world's most oppressed group of people, one full half of the human race, Cooper described Black women as the most dominated women in America. Today, feminists like Mary Daly have echoed that women are the most oppressed group in the world and that men are the primary perpetrators of oppression. For contemporary feminists, however, the degree to which men are morally able to participate in correcting the problem is a matter of controversy. On the most radical end of the spectrum, feminists like Mary Daly reject the Church and its Christocentrism. There is a great deal of skepticism about men's capacity for full commitment to moving beyond patriarchy to an inclusive vision of humanity and the planet. Feminists who have chosen to remain within the Church, like Rosemary Radford Ruether, seek women's space within the traditional Church with hope for eventual reform. African American womanists, whether Christian or Muslim, in keeping with the wholistic emphasis of womanism continue to emphasize the importance of Black women and men engaging in social reform together. At the same time they acknowledge the difficulties involved, given the problem of sexism, as Cooper and her contemporaries did a century ago.

Historical women in the Black women's club movement and contemporary womanists have both emphasized the significance of context and experience in their arguments for Black women's participation in social reform. Cooper's epistemological basis for her arguments for social reform, like Grant's, was experiential and contextual. She argued that Black women were particularly able to sympathize with and articulate the problem of domination and were important to social reform because of the depth of their experience of domination. Just as Cooper a century ago assessed Black women as the most oppressed group in America so today theologians like Grant have observed that the experience of Black women is "at least three time removed from the so-called normative culture, placing them on the underside of history."[29] Grant describes Black women in today's nuclear age as being "among the poorest of the poor and among the most oppressed of the oppressed." Therefore, they bring a unique contribution to America's analysis of the problems of domination. Grant, like Cooper, calls for a movement inclusive of women and men rather than a separatist movement. This emphasis on the liberation of entire people, male and female, is in keeping with Alice Walker's definition of "womanist."

The context of Cooper's discussion of Black women as the *most* oppressed women in America is that of *Black/White* relations and her discussion is meant for the ears of White women and men. Both Cooper and Grant move further to consider the oppression of women of color generally for some very important reasons. In reference to oppression among a diversity of women of color in America, the assertion that Black women are the most oppressed women in America (which is statistically true in relation to the socio-economic, political, and educational opportunities of White women) becomes more complex. Native American women, for example, stripped of their rights to their original lands and marginalized to reservations can easily argue that *they* are the most oppressed group of women in America. Globally, Haitian Black women in many respects suffer poverty at a more profound level than Black American women. Once one focuses on women of color rather than Black women in relation to White women, it is not so clear who is *most* oppressed, since women of color across the board have fewer socio-economic, political, and educational opportunities than White women in America and abroad. The effort to engage in such discussion would evade the reality that *socio-economic, political, and educational poverty needs to be eradicated wherever it exists.* The variety of forms that injustice takes on among women of color is a manifestation of the same evil: the evil of the triple jeopardy of racial, gender, and class oppression.

Cooper moves beyond Black women's experience to consider the ways in which others are affected by the experience of domination. In the end domination of one group by another brutalizes *all* of humanity in her view. To enter into the question of who is most oppressed among women of color results in a morbid and oppressive form of competition between the oppressed. It is counterproductive. It buys into the racial hierarchies of an insidious White supremacist mentality that has been internalized. This is perhaps the negative side of being able finally to name one's own victimization, a life-saving step. But it is a life-saving step only when counterbalanced with the vision and practice of continued survival practices and the hope of eventually overcoming oppression. To sink into a morass of arguments about who is *most* victimized evades the larger issue of working together to realize social justice. Pain is pain. Moreover, oppression is like a cancer that if left untreated in one part of the body will destroy the whole. People of color cannot transform the false hierarchies that have created the oppressions they seek to eradicate if they give in to racialized competition.

Martin Luther King, Jr., insisted that a threat to justice anywhere is a threat to justice everywhere. Crises of socio-economic and political injustice must be recognized wherever they exist. One of the dangers of suggesting a hierarchy of oppression in the form of a kind of triage system is that people of color will not be able to work effectively together. It begs the old question of "Who is more important: the many or the one?" If the one and the many are interrelated, then even to ask the question creates a false dualism. The survival of one group is interdependent with the survival of all. Since a womanist is a Black feminist *or* feminist of color, it is important to consider what such an interdependent view of the reality of oppression means in terms of praxis in the movement toward greater freedom and equality for all.

As Katie Cannon has so often said, womanists move beyond either/or thinking to proclaim both/and thinking.[30] It is important to note that this does not mean that womanists or any other group must divert attention away from their particular concerns, neglecting their own healing to attend solely to the healing of others. Global solidarity *begins* with attention to the issues of a *particular* community. Only by carefully examining and taking care of the concerns of Black women can Black women be adequately empowered to stand in solidarity with others. Strengthened, it is then *possible* to share in mutual support and listening with others. Further, by hearing similar, though different, stories of oppression, survival, and liberation from other women of color, all become strengthened. Finally, by taking the same care to engage in self-naming among themselves *and* careful listening to the theological and social-ethical concerns of women of color, it is possible for White women and women of color to move more fully toward mutual cooperation and solidarity with one another. This is evident, for example, in the collective work of Letty Russell, Kwok Pui-Lan, Chung Hyun Kyung, Katie Cannon, and Ada Maria Isasi-Diaz: *Inheriting Our Mothers' Gardens*.[31] Such collective work requires a painful disarming and continuous healing of racial prejudices, moving beyond initial defensiveness, guilt, and shame to true release from the illusions of racial privilege or superiority and the establishment of relationships of equality. Isasi-Diaz refers to those who are able to make this move as "friends of the oppressed."[32] True friendship can occur only between those who understand themselves to be equal to one another.

For Cooper, reform was necessary not only for the regeneration of Black women and men, but for a regeneration of the larger society and world. The present generation in this system must work toward the amelioration of society for the next generation, who will continue the development. Contemporary womanists are part of that next generation. Theologians across the board, whether they realize it or not, are part of that generation. Anna Cooper implied a universal accountability for freedom and justice, arguing for freedom and equality as universally inherent rights. She claimed that Black women possessed inherent worth and value.

While Cooper's life and thought shares much in common with the work of contemporary womanist, feminist, Black, and liberation theologians, she placed a stronger and more explicit emphasis on a universal ontology of the worth, value, and freedom of human being than liberation theologians. Like many Black Americans historically (Frederick Douglass, Henry Highland Garnett, Frances Ellen Watkins Harper), she sometimes purposefully conflated democratic principles with Christian principles in order to argue for human rights. The social-political structure was seen as having its creation, development, and origins in a universal ontology. God was ever at the head of reform urging humanity forward.

Scripture and Black Womanhood

Part of Black women's language about their experience and their belief in freedom is informed by biblical narrative. It is important, therefore, that we look at what Grant refers to as "the use of the Bible in the Womanist Tradition."[33] Grant explains that though Black women historically were politically powerless, they were able to appropriate themes from the Bible that spoke to the reality of their experience.[34] We have seen Cooper engaged in this kind of appropriation.

Cooper interpreted Christian scriptures from a perspective similar to liberationist interpretations. She used scripture to speak to the social situation of Black women and men and to criticize dominant, privileged White Americans. Jacquelyn Grant writes that this is characteristic of Christian Black women in African American history. There are two sources, she observes, for Black women's understanding of God:

> ... first, God's revelation directly to them, and secondly, God's revelation as witnessed in the Bible and as read and heard in the context of their experience.[35]

Grant notes that an interplay of scripture and experience has been exercised by many Black women historically. She cites, for example, Jarena Lee's sermons on the theme of "Life and Liberty," a common theme for Black women generally. Similarly, we see someone as different from Jarena Lee as Anna Cooper employing the theme of liberty and human life. Grant's inclusion of God's direct revelation to Black women in her analysis of Black women's religious experience is in reference to many of the historical African American women she mentions. She discusses, for example, the role of Jesus in the life of Sojourner Truth, an illiterate but powerful spokeswoman and preacher who had a mystical experience of Jesus. Grant refers to Black women's mystical experiences of the divine, particularly experiences that have given great assurance of God's empowerment and that have encouraged faith, courage, and strength to fight against the odds. There are many such accounts in extant slave narratives, biographies, and autobiographies.

For Sojourner Truth, who could not read but heard about Jesus, Jesus was directly revealed and experienced.[36] The evangelist Jarena Lee referred to a revelation of God's voice in her life. Cooper similarly alluded to a sense of God's voice within the self but not in the strongly enthusiastic, mystical, strict Christocentric sense of a Jarena Lee. For Cooper, this voice was an indelible part of the natural order of things, present in peoples of all religious faiths. It is a Singing Something that breaks forth in all human beings across the bounds of religions, cultures, and nations. It is the Singing Something within that makes women, men, and children *anthropos,* human.

Cooper was highly literate and turned to an interpretation of the Synoptic Gospels based on a social hermeneutic that relied in part on Black women's traditional interpretation of the Bible, as defined by Grant above, and concurrently on prevalent Social Gospel ideals that were finding a small but significant audience in the late nineteenth-century milieu in which Cooper was writing. While she believed in the power of God in a diversity of religious traditions, she was a Christian who emphasized the life and work of Jesus. She made little reference to the God of the Hebrew Bible. She was interested primarily in Christian scriptures. She selected scripture passages that affirmed a symbolization of

Christ as redemptive, salvific. Further, she portrayed Jesus Christ as preceding and leading human being in its development and social amelioration. Symbolizing Christ as a salvific figure in history and in the future, she did not emphasize the divinity of Jesus explicitly. She referred to a Jesus who deposited ideals and who was a great reformer. But her symbolization of Christ as a salvific figure of the future suggests that Christ is also a Christ of eternity for Cooper. Christ was represented in his actions and ideals, which she presented as having a divine, eternal effect on human being. An essential aspect of human amelioration, for Cooper, was the comprehension of Christ's actions and principles. Such actions and principles, Cooper's words suggest, require millennia for their development.

Moreover, Cooper transcribed Galatians 3:28, which enjoins that in Christ "there is neither Jew nor Greek...bond nor free ...male nor female." This verse affirms the equality of the races and nations and of women with men. Historically this verse has been popular among Black women, and women generally, especially those claiming a call to preach. This is scripture that Christian womanist theologians can still appeal to today. Cooper also recorded the verses from Matthew 25 regarding feeding the hungry, giving drink to the thirsty, visiting the sick and the imprisoned as a way of honoring Jesus, which supported her concept of altruism. For Cooper, altruism — active compassion for the suffering of one's neighbors — was the starting point of a philosophy of freedom and equality. Her selection of scripture reveals a social interpretation of the Gospel. For Cooper, one might say, the voice of God wills healing and wholeness for the weak, the oppressed, the downtrodden, the dispossessed. With them, all of humanity is called forth by the Singing Something within into healing and wholeness in antiphony with God. As in the tradition of Black folk churches, we are called to participate in call and response with God, giving voice to a Gospel message of freedom. Herein lies one's humanity. It is found in setting forth the Singing Something within the human soul that resonates with a Gospel message of freedom and equality for all.

Criticisms of Cooper's Life and Thought

Anna Cooper came close to suggesting what Sharon Welch refers to as "universal accountability and the integrity of the particular."[37] While arguing against the construction of universal ontologies, Welch argues for a universal accountability for freedom and justice. She argues that one can and must respect the integrity of the particular while holding oneself universally accountable for the effects of our particular actions on other individuals and communities. Given Cooper's training and identification with Euro-American culture from her formative years on, one might ask if her concern for freedom was limited by class and cultural elitism. Did Cooper neglect to see her own complicity in classism and cultural elitism? Welch asks:

> If my definition of freedom is based on the experience of liberation from sexism, how can I address other forms of domination such as racism and capitalism? Concerns such as these seem to indicate the value of universally applicable definitions of freedom and justice.[38]

Euro-Americans cannot define freedom and justice for African Americans, men cannot define freedom and justice for women, Americans cannot define freedom and justice for Third World nations, but each individual, each community, each nation is responsible universally for respecting the integrity of the other. One must always be aware of one's own complicity in oppression. It is in this respect that Cooper's thought resonates most closely with liberationist understandings of the relation between particular experience and certain universal truths or values.

As a feminist liberation theologian who is Euro-American, middle-class, and academically trained, Welch finds universal accountability vital to the task of liberation. She admits that as a woman she is oppressed by structures of patriarchy, but as White she benefits from the oppression of people of other races.[39] She emphasizes the necessity of being aware of the degree to which one is a participant in "structures of oppression, structures of race, class, and national identity."[40] Similarly, womanist theologian Jacquelyn Grant urges Black women today to "explore more deeply the question of what Christ means in a society in which class distinctions are increasing."

With the growing Black middle class, classism is a more pressing problem than it was for historical African Americans who, Grant notes incisively, "were essentially poor by virtue of their race."[41] In her essay on womanist Christology, Grant briefly quotes Cooper to support her own argument that "the daily struggles of poor Black women must serve as the gauge for the verification of the claims of womanist theology." She sees that Cooper includes the problem of class when Cooper says: "Women's wrongs are thus indissolubly linked with all undefended woes, and the acquirement of her 'rights' will mean the supremacy of triumph of all right over the might, the supremacy of the moral forces of reason, and justice and love in the government of the nations of the earth" as including problems of class.[42] Cooper sought to improve the conditions of Black women in America by providing alternatives to the demeaning work conditions they were subjected to. At the same time, it is important to acknowledge a certain level of condescension in the NACW regarding their relationship to the masses.

Cooper was part of a small but elite class of highly trained Black Americans. What is problematic in her work is the lack of self-criticism regarding the degree to which the Black middle class can speak on behalf of working-class and poor Black people. On the one hand, women who share a passion for justice and an outrage at domination can resonate with Cooper's words and thought. On the other hand, her voice was and is most easily accessible to the educationally privileged in its tone, choice of vocabulary, method, and style. Womanist and feminist theologians today, trained and working in academic institutions, share this problem. Moving beyond Cooper's understanding of voice and of humankind's likeness in God's voice, I recommend that contemporary womanists consider the multiplicity of Black women's voices. Whereas Cooper sought to speak *on behalf* of the Black Woman of the South, contemporary womanists must seek to speak *with* a multiplicity of Black women across class lines.

Although Cooper aptly identified the problem of Black women and men's social-economic oppression, she was not as critical of her middle-class, educated perspective as Black women need to be today. Jacquelyn Grant, Delores Williams, and Katie Cannon expand Cooper's description of racism and sexism with their efforts at an explicit and consistent recognition of a triple oppression: racism, sexism, and classism. The voice we hear in *A Voice from the South* is undeniably the voice of a highly trained Black middle-class woman. Cooper's training and background meant that it would have been virtually impossible for her to write in any other voice. To write in one's own voice is to be true to one's self and is necessary for honest reflection. But that does not mean one cannot address multiple audiences, difficult though it may be. Nor does addressing multiple audiences mean that one must do it all in one book, essay, lecture, or sermon. One of the most important arguments of liberation theologies is that the particular experiences of various communities and individuals shape their varied and particular perspectives of God, life, humankind, and the world. But given the complexity of oppression, Welch is astute to underscore the importance of recognizing one's own complicity in oppression.

As Mary Helen Washington has noted, Cooper participated in classist ideology by speaking for the masses of poor and working Black women rather than with them. Her florid speech distances her from the masses of Black women. Moreover, she fails to really include them as the basis of her feminist arguments for reform. She writes for them, on behalf of them, but not with their words as they emerge from their own experience. Her audience was primarily middle class. She sought financial support for programs from the White and Black middle class and inclusion in Black intellectual circles.[43] Washington offers a helpful analysis of classism in the Black women's club movement.[44] It is important, however, to note further distinctions between Anna Cooper and Mary Church Terrell, with whom she has been compared.

While Washington is careful to note contrasts between Terrell's open condescension and Cooper's discreet distancing from the masses, some distinctions between Terrell and Cooper have not been made clear.[45] In her speech about the "lifting as we climb" motto of the NACW, Terrell, president of the NACW, argued for support of the masses of Black women by saying: "Even though we wish to shun them, and hold ourselves entirely aloof from them, we cannot escape the consequences of their acts."[46] She called them "lowly," "illiterate," "vicious." While Washington notes this is not characteristic of Cooper's speech, it is important to observe the ways in which her speech is different. The patronizing, class-tolerant attitude of such statements is not reflected in Cooper's writings. Her classism emerges in other ways: in speaking for the masses of Black women rather than with them; in her adulation of high, Anglican liturgy and her criticism of ecstatic religious worship; in focusing on a highly literate audience as did her contemporaries; by moving primarily (although not exclusively) in literate circles. But Cooper also remembered where she came from. She identified herself as a Black woman from the South, one who came up from the masses of Black women. Washington insightfully notes Cooper's discreet distancing from the masses, but she also discreetly identified with the masses. The problem is that she failed to question the class ideology she grew into as she moved up the socio-economic ladder.

Although Terrell and Cooper graduated together from Oberlin College and were founding members of the NACW, there was great social distance between them. The reasons for this distance are something of a mystery. I suspect that part of it has to do with the classism within the ranks of the Black elite during that time, which continues today. Terrell was wealthy and grew up with economic privileges few Black women enjoyed then or enjoy now. She belonged to the highest tier of the Black elite and was connected with powerful political and social figures in Washington, D.C., through her husband, Robert Terrell, who was a federal judge. Cooper, who did not share Terrell's truly upper-class economic status, did not belong to this inner circle. Terrell does not name Cooper in her autobiography, *White Woman in a Colored World*, referring to her merely as one of "three colored women" graduates from Oberlin and "the third" Black woman from the class of 1884 who taught at the Dunbar High School.[47]

Cooper paid her way through school throughout her life. Terrell's father paid for her education. Cooper was born of a union of sexual violence, the rape of her mother by her mother's slavemaster. Terrell was born to mulatto parents in a union of choice. Cooper sympathized with the sexual vulnerability of poor Black working women. She refers to her mother as the finest woman she ever knew, but writes that she owed her biological father "not a sou." She saw Black women domestics, like her mother, as victims of sexual violence. Terrell suggests disdainful judgment of working women's sexual vulnerability and survival ethic. Cooper judges the abuser, not the abused. Cooper, known for her work as president and registrar of Frelinghuysen University, which was for working students, also directed an annexed school named after her mother called the Hannah Stanley School for Opportunity, created for working women. Terrell and Cooper worked out of very different motivations. Cooper worked actively to give something back to women like her mother, who gave her moral support through her years of schooling. Terrell had no profound experiential connection to poor Black working women. It made a difference in their outlooks.

As we examine the life and writings of leaders like Cooper and Mary Church Terrell, it is important to examine distinctions between them as we engage in constructive and critical analysis of their leadership styles and social ethics. Some comparison of Wells-Barnett and Terrell has been made, but little of Cooper and Terrell. Womanist scholarship would benefit from considering various leadership styles and social ethics among Black nineteenth-century women leaders in the women's club movement.

There is much to be learned from such women. We can learn from Cooper's mistakes — the ways in which she fell short on the issue of classism — as well as from her positive contributions. Cooper worked her way through educational systems to become the most highly educated Black woman of her time. She was like many womanists today, who find themselves in elite institutions with relative socio-economic privileges in relation to the masses. As Delores Williams and Renita Weems have noted, womanist religious scholars, who are primarily middle-class by virtue of educational and professional status, must be accountable to our own capacity for oppression, both in terms of classism and also in terms of heterosexism, which was not addressed by nineteenth-century African American women.[48]

This leads to the writings of Toni Morrison, which reflect much of Black experience in America. Her literature considers the Black community's complicity in evil. She reminds us that the entire community participates in evil by scapegoating, acting out of envy, internalizing racist and sexist beliefs, participating in an erasure of African and African American myth and history, and feigning ignorance in the presence of evil. She considers the issue of paradox around problems of good and evil. In Morrison's novel

Beloved, for example, there are no saints. The race that enslaved Sethe saves her from the gallows. The Black community that shuns her returns to heal her. The task of the Black community, then, is to recognize its complicity in evil and its capacity for good.

While womanists, feminists, and liberation theologians have much to learn from Cooper's concept of and commitment to freedom and equality, it is important in our age to push her thought further on the matter of complicity in the problem of oppression. Cooper was an optimist. She deeply believed in the Social Gospel concept of society as organic, unfolding, progressing. Cooper's description of "progress in the democratic sense" as "an urge-cell, the universal and unmistakable hall-mark traceable to the Father of all," reflects her participation in a Social Gospel concept of society as an organism with God symbolized as the Father (!) of all.[49] Social progress for Cooper was both organic and divinely, universally ordained. Today Black women and men no longer see society as inevitably progressing toward freedom in the way that Cooper did. We are all too aware of humankind's complicity in our own destruction. We are beginning to question exclusively masculine symbolizations of God. It is necessary to build on Cooper's concept of a God of freedom and equality whose spirit is within humankind. At the same time it is necessary to extend Cooper's analysis of evil to include the complicity of African American women and men in our own oppression through practices such as classism, political apathy, and intra-community violence.

There is much we can learn from Cooper's concept of women's voices and of God's voice within humanity as well as from her social ethic of freedom and equality for all across racial, gender, national, and religious lines. We can also learn much from Cooper's mistakes — the ways in which she fell short in her analysis of classism.

Cooper's Legacy and Beyond: Foundations for a Womanist Theology

As Delores Williams has noted, womanist religious scholars, who are primarily middle-class by virtue of their educational and professional status, must be accountable to their own capacity for oppression. Clergy and religious scholars across the board, male or female, of color or White, must recognize a moral responsibility to remain connected with those who form the center of their bodily and spiritual life, the masses of anonymous women and men. Realistically, this does not mean that theologians and ethicists must choose between the academy and the Church. It is important to honor and respect theological education as a valid form of ministry in itself. Moreover, teaching and scholarship, like pastoring, are more than a full-time job if done seriously.

Black women in particular have been excluded from positions in scholarship and higher education for far too long to be berated for choosing such vocations. To challenge their choice for scholarship and teaching belittles the necessary contributions Black women in academic institutions must make if history, ethics, theology, and the present society are to be re-visioned. America and the globe in their diversity cannot know who they are or what they ought to become, without engaging in inclusive historical, theological, sociological, and ethical research by Black women and others who historically have been excluded. To put African American women in a position of questioning whether the academy is really the best place for them is an insidious but obvious revision of the old racially construed stereotypes of Black women's roles in society. It perpetuates an all too familiar oppression. Rather, all religious scholars can do some small thing to move society toward fuller freedom and equality by practicing what Katie Cannon calls "pebble ethics."[50]

The idea of pebble ethics is drawn from a poem by Nikki Giovanni, in which she writes that "one ounce of truth benefits like ripples on a pond" — the effect of a pebble tossed into the water.[51] The premise of pebble ethics is that the small everyday acts that individuals and individual groups make in support of social justice spread out like ripples on a pond, having a profound effect on the larger society. Moreover, each small act for social justice adds up, with lasting, positive repercussions. More people than we can imagine benefit from one truthful act or word.

To use another metaphor, the process of pebble ethics is something like "stone soup," a story I heard as a child. In this story, there was a poor old woman who had only a stone and a pot of hot water. Hungry but wise, she told her neighbors she was making a delicious "stone soup" and wanted each of them to contribute something. The stone was a very special ingredient. Like a magnet, it drew everyone to the old woman's home. After each of her neighbors had contributed a vegetable or other ingredient, they all had a delicious meal. The old woman did not go hungry and she increased love of neighbor in her community. If each member of a community or of a society contributes something, all benefit and none need go hungry.

To put it plainly, it is not a matter of one religious scholar or lay person spending countless hours volunteering in social justice ministries. Nor is it a matter of one Church focusing on social justice ministries to the exclusion of internal congregational concerns. To do so would be to buy into the "hero" model of the salvific individual whose actions set him or her apart from the many. It is too easy to look for saviors or attempt to become one. But people who become saviors tend to be short-lived; the world has had enough individuals die in the name of truth, righteousness, love, and justice. The search for saviors too often has resulted in despair and varying degrees of socio-political apathy when individuals like John F. Kennedy, Martin Luther King, Jr., and Robert F. Kennedy died for their beliefs in freedom and equality. Christians, in particular, must ask if it is indeed idolatrous to desire savior figures who will solve our problems for us. If Christians genuinely have faith in one savior, Jesus Christ, who died for humankind, the search for savior figures is idolatrous. During the Civil Rights movement of the 1960s, Ella Baker, who helped organize the Student Nonviolent Coordinating Committee, recommended a move away from a leadership centered in one charismatic leader to group-centered leadership, whereby an entire people takes responsibility for addressing social justice issues. It is time for Americans of every color and gender to live for justice by taking responsibility for a fuller realization of social justice as a people.

Such responsibility must be realized at institutional levels. For example, in the private and religious sectors, if each member of a faculty or congregation, or at least a majority, participated even occasionally in community improvement activities as individuals or small groups at regularly scheduled times throughout the year, that faculty or congregation could make a profound impact for social change. The family, which is undergoing rapid change, is another institution where such responsibility can and must be realized. Education about social responsibility must begin at home with one's self and one's children or significant others.

There is no one person or one small group of people who can single-handedly make the world a better place. The most minimal realization of our utopic visions requires small but massive efforts by the many. Garth Baker-Fletcher refers to this kind of activity as contributive ethics.[52] Whereas distributive ethics presupposes a small group of governing individuals who distribute socio-economic resources to the many, contributive ethics presupposes that each person in a society has a unique gift to offer others. It does not require the dismantling of distributive ethics, but works alongside it. It does not let government off the hook. It remains important to persuade elected government institutions to implement programs and legislation for providing greater socio-economic opportunities for all Americans, including those who have historically been discriminated against and disadvantaged.

Contributive ethics is not simply a matter of contributing monetary donations to charitable causes, which is important. Rather, contributive ethics goes beyond that to require a sharing of one's own talents. It is grounded in older meanings of the Christian concept of "charity," involving not paternalistic material donations, but a wholistic loving of the other (materially and spiritually) as part of the body of Christ.

A contributive ethic, whether we call it "pebble ethics" or "stone soup ethics," does not assume that God reaches from on high to eradicate evil. Rather, transformation of society requires the commitment of human hearts and hands. It is important to note that Cooper was not a thoroughgoing optimist. She did not believe that God alone would reform society. Human agency was essential. Humankind required God's movement and guidance to direct it toward the establishment of full freedom and equality. Because humankind is bumbling and ignorant, this would take millennia. She possessed a strong measure of realism in her analysis. God's movement for freedom takes place in the here and now in the midst of people who possess finite knowledge about what the movement for freedom entails. I suspect she would want to see contemporary theologians push her thought further to consider issues like child abuse, the pervasiveness of sexual violence, classism among Black women and men, ableism, the shifting character of sexism, and nihilistic behavior in the Black community and the larger American society.

Moving beyond Cooper does not simply mean addressing new issues. It involves addressing similar issues in new ways. Like Cooper, feminists and womanists today have criticized the silencing of women, particularly the silencing of Black women. Feminists and womanists are aware of the subjugation of women's voices in political, philosophical, and theological conversations. Carol Christ's *Diving Deep and Surfacing* poignantly recognizes the pain of this particular aspect of women's oppression. And if we look to historical sources, the autobiographies of Black women evangelists like Jarena Lee, Amanda Berry Smith, Rebecca Cox Jackson, Zilpha Elaw, and Julia Foote, as well as political leaders from Maria Stewart to Ida B. Wells-Barnett to Angela Davis to Shirley Chisolm echo the problem of men's efforts to silence the voices of Black women. In the 1990s we have seen efforts to silence outspoken Black women like Anita Hill and Desiree Washington. In spite of the efforts to suppress their voices, Black women still rise up in bold, often audacious, courageous speech. But Black women have not yet organized en masse to demand full socio-economic freedom and equality.

Cooper recognized very clearly that communities across race, culture, gender, and nationality shared responsibility for and accountability to one another. She demonstrated this sense of responsibility and accountability in her life. Throughout her life she actively recognized her connectedness to others — to the illiterate, the poor, the needy. What is significant about Cooper is not that she was middle-class and highly educated and moved among culturally elite circles, but rather the way she employed these advantages to forward social transformation.

Cooper's passion for freedom from domination and her outrage at injustice gives her work both a timeless and a contemporary value. Cooper referred to the voice of the Black woman of the South, her own voice, as but a cry. Quoting George Eliot, she suggested that women's voices have value even when able to give only a moan in solidarity with suffering. The cry of outrage, the moan of identity with suffering gives her voice a ring of verity. Cooper wrote with the confidence of a woman who was actively involved in efforts at reform. She lived what she spoke — a life of altruism dedicated to a reformation of society and the regeneration of the race. Her experience of and exposure to various injustices motivated her appeal for justice.

Perhaps it is only in the passion for justice, freedom, and equality and the outrage at the injustice of domination that the voices of middle-class Black women in America can resonate with the voices of women across classes and cultures. We need not expect the passion of each voice to have the same depth or tone. Cooper was careful to point out that only Black women can speak with the exact voice of the Black woman. White women, White men, Black men, cannot speak on Black women's behalf. Today it is necessary to take this observation further. One must question the notion that there is such a thing as the "exact voice" of the Black woman. There are many voices among Black women — as many voices as there are Black women. Theologians today must find ways of bringing these voices out of anonymity to hear the uniqueness and variedness of Black women's wisdom. One way of doing this is to turn to literature that mirrors the folk wisdom of Black women, as womanist theologian Delores Williams has done. Ethicist Katie Cannon similarly accesses Black women's folk wisdom through the works of Zora Neale Hurston and other African American women writers.[53] Oral-aural histories are another important resource. In taking such resources seriously, one need not exclude the voices of educationally privileged Black women like Mary Church Terrell, Ida B. Wells-Barnett, Frances Ellen Watkins Harper, or Anna Julia Cooper. Rather, it is necessary to include a variety of voices.

A contemporary womanist theology recognizes that each community as well as each individual has its own voice — its own song identifying the particularities of the problems of oppression from that community's own experience. And within each group, each community of Black women, each individual voice has a different tone, pitch, and depth dependent on its individual heritage and experience and the extent to which it engages in praxis for reform. There are different levels of experiences and awarenesses of the problem of oppression. Moreover, while my own focus and the focus of other womanists has been on African American women, there is much in the wisdom of the Diaspora of Black women globally that has yet to be learned. We must respect the value and integrity of the passion and outrage of the voices of each particular community of individuals.

The theme of coming to voice is foundational for womanist theology. It goes hand in hand with experience. Jacquelyn Grant suggests that the starting point for womanist theology ought to be contextualization, the social-historical experience of Black women. Language and experience are interrelated and cannot be separated. Language is vital for giving voice to experience, whether literally through vocal speech or figuratively through writing, sign language, or various art forms.

What kinds of experience have Black women in America articulated? Black women have experienced injustice and justice, bondage and freedom, suffering and healing, evil and goodness. This experience has been and continues to be articulated in writings by and about Black women. The negative aspect of Black women's experience is racism, sexism, and classism. Black women's experience in its positive aspect is their constructive, creative activity for overcoming oppression as well as their relationship to others engaged in such activity with whom they have shared a relationship of mutuality and solidarity.[54] Black women's celebrative experience includes survival skills, the ability to create something out of nothing and beauty out of ordinary things, and freedom of mind and spirit in the midst of bondage. In order for Black Christian women to voice the truth of their reality, they must reach into three different areas of experience: (1) their experience of oppression and despair and (2) their interpretation of scripture as giving a message of hope for social regeneration that leads to (3) the experiences of survival, liberation, and celebration. These three kinds of experience are foundations upon which one can build a womanist theology.

Black women cannot enact change without voicing the experiences of oppression that make social change necessary. Voice is powerful. Voice calls attention to pain and suffering. Voice criticizes injustice. Voice offers solutions to problems. Voice cries out in anger and outrage. Voice motivates others to follow. Voice shocks and touches people into action. Voice challenges subjugative social practices. Voice has the power to resist oppression. Historically, resistant voices have been the reasons for thousands of persecutions and executions. Calls for social transformation by the dominated have often evoked a will to silence them. If such voices were not powerful, there would be no desire to suppress them. The voices of the silenced have the power to challenge and the potential to change social patterns that are racist, sexist, heterosexist, or ethnocentric. Cooper recognized the power of voice.

NOTES

1. See Katie Cannon, *Black Womanist Ethics* (Atlanta: Scholars Press, 1988); Jacquelyn Grant, *White Women's Christ and Black Women's Jesus* (Atlanta: Scholars Press, 1989); Delores Williams, *Sisters in the Wilderness* (Maryknoll, N.Y.: Orbis Books, 1993); Emilie Townes, *Womanist Hope/ Womanist Justice* (Atlanta: Scholars Press, 1993); and Theressa Hoover, "Black Women and the Churches: Triple Jeopardy," in *Black Theology: A Documentary History: 1968–1979*, ed. James Cone and Gayraud Wilmore, (Maryknoll, N.Y.: Orbis Books: 1979), 377–88.

2. Jacquelyn Grant, "Womanist Theology," in Gayraud S. Wilmore, ed., *African-American Religious Studies* (Durham: Duke University Press, 1989), 212.

3. Jacquelyn Grant uses the terms "Black" and "White" in reference to African Americans and Euro-Americans, respectively. Grant reflects the language of Black liberation theology, best exemplified in the work of James Cone and influenced by the Black power movement in America. The value of these terms is their distinctive indication of the oppositional power relations between Caucasians and people of color, not only in America but worldwide.

4. Ibid., 212.

5. Ibid., 212–13.

6. Ibid., 213.

7. Ibid.

8. See Sarah Bradford, *Harriet Tubman: The Moses of Her People* (Gloucester, Mass: Peter Smith/Corinth Books, 1981).

9. See Cheryl Sanders, "Christian Ethics and Theology in Womanist Perspective," in *Journal of Feminist Studies in Religion* 5 (Fall 1989): 85–91. Sanders is, to my knowledge, the first to observe that Walker's earliest definition of womanism appears in her article on Humez's discussion of Rebecca Cox Jackson.

10. Jean Humez, *Gifts of Power: The Writings of Rebecca Cox Jackson, Black Visionary, Shaker Eldress* (Amherst: University of Massachusetts Press, 1981).

11. See Walker, "Gifts of Power," *In Search of Our Mothers' Gardens* (New York: Harcourt Brace Jovanovich, 1983), 71–82. See also Sanders, "Christian Ethics and Theology in Womanist Perspective," 85–91.

12. See Delores Williams, "Womanist Theology: Black Women's Voices," *Christianity and Crisis,* March 2, 1987, 67–68.

13. Cheryl Sanders, "Afrocentrism and Womanism in the Seminary," *Christianity and Crisis,* April 13, 1992, 124.

14. Ibid.

15. Jacquelyn Grant, *White Women's Christ and Black Women's Jesus,* 194.

16. Ibid., 199.

17. Ibid., 201.

18. Ibid.

19. Delores Williams, "Womanist Theology: Black Women's Voices," 67–68.

20. Ibid.

21. Ibid.

22. Ibid., 68.

23. Alice Walker, *In Search of Our Mothers' Gardens* (New York: Harcourt Brace Jovanovich, 1983), xi–xii.

24. Welch does not mention definitions of liberation and sin by womanist theologians such as Jacquelyn Grant.

25. Sharon Welch, *Communities of Resistance and Solidarity* (Maryknoll, N.Y.: Orbis Books, 1985), 48.

26. Anna Julia Cooper, "Equality of Races and the Democratic Movement," privately printed pamphlet, Washington, D.C., 1945, 10.

27. Freedom and democratic progress are *a priori* ideals for Cooper.

28. Mary Helen Washington, introduction to Anna Julia Cooper, *A Voice from the South,* ed. Mary Helen Washington, Schomburg Library of Nineteenth-Century Black Women Writers (1892; New York: Oxford University Press, 1988), xxxix.

29. Jacquelyn Grant, "Subjectification as a Requirement for Christological Construction," in Susan Brooks Thistlethwaite and Mary Potter Engle, eds., *Lift Every Voice: Constructing Christian Theologies from the Underside* (San Francisco: Harper & Row, 1990), 201–3.

30. Class lecture notes, Katie Cannon's course, "Black Women's Literature as a Resource for a Constructive Ethic," Harvard Divinity School, Spring 1984.

31. See Letty Russell, *Inheriting Our Mothers' Gardens* (Philadelphia: Westminster Press, 1988).

32. Ada Maria Isasi-Diaz, "Solidarity: Love of Neighbor in the 1980s," in Thistlethwaite and Engle, eds., *Lift Every Voice,* 31–40.

33. Grant, "Subjectification as a Requirement for Christological Construction," 211.

34. Ibid.

35. Ibid.

36. Grant, 214, from Olive Gilbert, *Sojourner Truth: Narrative and Book of Life* (1850, 1875; reprint Chicago: Johnson Publishing Company, 1970), 118–19.

37. Welch, *Communities of Resistance and Solidarity,* 81.

38. Ibid.

39. Ibid.

40. Ibid., ix.

41. Jacquelyn Grant, *White Women's Christ and Black Women's Jesus* (Atlanta: Scholars Press, 1989), 221.

42. Grant, "Womanist Theology: Black Women's Experience as a Source for Doing Theology, with Special Reference to Christology," 215.

43. See Washington, introduction to *A Voice from the South*, xlv–xlvii.

44. See also Delores Williams, *Sisters in the Wilderness*, 122–30. Williams, while appreciating the work Cooper did in the community and in her scholarship, criticizes her classism. Moreover, she writes that Cooper, Lucy Wilmot Smith, and Virginia Broughton employed language that "inadvertently supported elite, educated black men's 'Virgin Mary taste' and their preference for the Victorian 'true woman,' whose place was in the home and not in the arena of political activism." I agree with much of Williams's assessment of Cooper's inadvertent classism and appeal to elite Black men. Cooper employed much of the rhetoric of true womanhood to make certain progressive ideals palatable to a middle-class audience. She played with her audience by playing with the language of "true womanhood," weaving her appreciation of it in with her criticism of it. However, she writes in the genre of a "true woman," while criticizing its prejudices, particularly the notion that women belong in the home and not in the arena of political activism. She unabashedly described Black men as being "in the dark ages" on such issues. She was, after all, an activist herself. It is important to ask what factors in their social-historical context motivated such women to employ rhetoric that was inadequate and confining.

45. See Washington, introduction to *A Voice from the South*, xxx–xxxi.

46. See Mary Church Terrell, "The Duty of the National Association of Colored Women to the Race," in Beverly Washington Jones, *The Quest for Equality*, vol. 13 in *Black Women in United States History*, ed. Darlene Clark Hine (New York: Carlson Publishing, 1990), 144–45.

47. Mary Church Terrell, *Colored Woman in a White World* (Salem, N.H.: Ayer Co., 1992), 64.

48. Delores Williams, *Sisters in the Wilderness*, 186–87.

49. See Cooper, "Equality of Races and the Democratic Movement," 4–5.

50. Katie Cannon, "Betraying Our Daughters," Oreon E. Scott Lecture at Christian Theological Seminary, March 3, 1993, Indianapolis.

51. Nikki Giovanni, "[Untitled]," *My House* (New York: William Morrow & Co., 1972), 38.

52. Conversation with Garth Baker-Fletcher, January 8, 1993.

53. See Delores Williams, "The Black Woman Portrayed in Selected Black Literature and Some Questions for Black Theology," M.A. Thesis, Columbia University and Union Theological Seminary, 1975, and Katie Cannon, *Black Womanist Ethics* and "Moral Wisdom in the Black Women's Literary Tradition," in *Weaving the Visions: New Patterns in Feminist Spirituality*, ed. Judith Plaskow and Carol Christ (San Francisco: Harper & Row, 1989).

54. See Isasi-Diaz, "Solidarity: Love of Neighbor in the 1980s," for a *mujerista* ("womanist" in Spanish) discussion of mutuality and solidarity.

7

Black Women's Narrative as a Resource for a Constructive Theology and Ethics

HERE WE ARE in the dusk hours of the twentieth century, preparing for the twenty-first century, and women's ministry in the Church is still questioned by dominant culture, whether we are talking about women's lay ministry or ordained ministry. This is a problem that crosses denominations. It is a problem in Black churches and White churches alike. Many Black denominational churches remain particularly conservative in their perspective regarding the ordination of women, although its congregations tend to be predominantly female in the range of 75 percent and more.

Whether women are ordained or not, women, disproportionately to men, are placed in positions where there is little movement across established gender roles and limited power when they are able to move outside traditional ministerial roles for women. Another problem that many had hoped would be eradicated by the end of this century is the color line. W. E. B. Du Bois, in *The Souls of Black Folk*, identified the problem of the twenty-first century as the problem of the color line. Anna Julia Cooper, Du Bois's senior and contemporary, thought that the 1890s and beyond would be Woman's Era, that socio-economic inequalities along gender lines would be eradicated. Such is not the case. While some gains have been made, they all too often are token gains. It is necessary to move beyond tokenism, with its grudging respect of the other, to a truly inclusive model where the other is genuinely respected for her gifts.

Whether highly educated in formal institutions like Anna Julia Cooper or educated in the schoolroom of everyday life, Black women in America have generated spiritual, intellectual, and material life in the midst of social death. These activities are recorded in African American women's historical writings and narratives, in their contemporary literature, and in the oral-aural tradition practiced by well-known and anonymous Black women. Each of these resources represents a variety of African American women's voices.

I suggest, therefore, that womanist theologians lift theological themes out from such resources — historical and contemporary — to analyze, critique, and then build on those themes that meet contemporary needs and concerns.

Narrative as a Resource for Theology

Carol Christ writes that without women's stories there is no articulation of women's experience. Christ describes the woman without stories as "closed in silence." She cannot value her struggles, celebrate her strengths, or comprehend her pain. For Christ, if women's stories are not told, then the depths of women's souls will not be known. By stories, Christ has in mind "all articulations of experience that have a narrative element, including fiction, poetry, song, autobiography, and talking with friends."[1]

For Christ this storytelling is important for the spiritual quest of all women, whether White or of color. I agree that storytelling is essential to women's spiritual quest. It is elemental to the construction of womanist and feminist theologies. Black women come to voice when they tell their stories. By stories I have in mind, like Christ, all articulations of experience that have a narrative element. This would include not only those that Christ mentions, but scholarly essays such as Cooper's that reveal Black women's experience and appeal for practical reform of social situations of oppression. Further, the findings of sociological studies that recount Black women's thought and experience are part of the narrative tradition that womanist theologians can refer to for a constructive theology.

Not all of the literature womanist theologians turn to as resources for theological construction needs to be self-consciously or formally theologically focused in its intent. Historically, women have written their thought in narrative form rather than in formal theological treatises. Women until very recently have had minimal access to formal theological training and have been excluded from the canon of formal theological scholarship. Often it will be necessary to tease theological themes out of narrative materials written or dictated by women.[2] This is what I have done with the literature of Anna Julia Cooper.

Cooper saw herself first and foremost as a teacher. She spent most of her working life teaching classical and modern languages and literature. But Cooper saw herself as a special kind of teacher. She looked upon teaching as an act of altruism. It was a missionary role for her. Cooper was dedicated to what she saw as a calling to teach the needy. As a writer, Christian religious and moral principles pervaded much of the ideological impetus that motivated her. Theological ideas were a substantive aspect of her thought as a teacher, public speaker, scholar, intellectual, and writer.

Theologian Richard R. Niebuhr observes that theology is written in a variety of forms: formal theological treatises, sermons, liturgies, hymns, poetry, graphics, and narrative.[3] The *Confessions* of Augustine are a form of narrative, as is *The Life of Teresa of Avila, The Book of Margery Kempe,* John Bunyan's *Pilgrim's Progress,* Emerson's poetry and essays, Melville's *Moby Dick,* Flannery O'Connor's short stories, *The Journal of Mrs. Jarena Lee,* or the political essays of Maria Stewart. Cooper's *A Voice from the South* is theological in this sense. Some of Cooper's essays are more self-consciously theological in their focus than others. "Womanhood a Vital Element in the Regeneration and Progress of a Race," delivered before colored Episcopal clergy has a religious, theologically trained audience in mind. Cooper shaped her essay accordingly by emphasizing Christian principles.

Cooper never dropped the importance of Christian principles in her literature. In *A Voice from The South,* as well as in many of her pamphlets, letters, short stories, and poetry, the importance of the vitalizing force of religion, particularly Christianity, recurs in her thought with a regular pulse. It is the vitalizing principle of Cooper's life and thought. She frequently returned to Christian principles in her writings because in religious belief she found hope for the reform that she challenged America to engage in.

What one finds in her writings is emphasis on belief in the creation in the likeness of God of Black women, along with all of humanity. This is foundational for constructive womanist theology and ethics, because if women generally have been excluded from understandings of human being in classical and liberal Christianity, Black women have been excluded to the point where their very womanhood has been questioned.

Gifts of Power for Survival and Wholeness in Black Women's Narratives

Much has been said about Black women's situation of oppression and the denial of their humanity that emerged out of White supremacist and sexist ethics. But what of Black women's gifts of power for survival and wholeness in the midst of such oppression and dehumanization? And what can we learn about such powers from Black women's narratives? *Gifts of Power* is Jean Humez's title for her publication of the autobiographical writings of Rebecca Cox Jackson, who painfully taught herself to write and read so that she could write letters in her own words, without depending on others who might change her meaning.[4] Jackson referred to her ability to read and write as a gift from God. While she also wrote of gifts of the power to heal others, the gift of writing gave her power to name reality as she experienced it in her own words. There are a multiplicity of gifts of the power of survival and celebration in Black women's social-historical experience. Black women have survived in the midst of an oppressive social system historically, beating the odds and generating spiritual power in the midst of political-economic powerlessness.

Womanist theology emerges out of the experiential depths of creating life where it seems none could exist, the power to make beautiful what could be ugly, the power to share wisdom of survival and liberation with others,[5] the ability to pray and to heal. These are generative powers, inclusive of but moving beyond physical childbearing and nurture in the traditional sense. I will consider five powers of survival and liberation that reflect Black women's creation in the likeness of God: (1) the power of voice, (2) the power of making do, (3) the power of memory, (4) the power of holding things together, and (5) the power of generation.

I draw on several forms of Black women's narrative, beginning with Cooper's historical contributions but moving beyond them to consider my own mother's wisdom and contemporary Black women's literature to engage in a womanist generational reconstruction of Black womanhood.

The Power of Voice

From her brief personal, autobiographical fragments, to her articulation of the experiences and contributions of Black women in America, to her prescriptive analyses of how to solve the problems of racism and sexism in America, Cooper's narrative expositions reveal new interpretations of human nature and the Black woman in Christian culture. Most importantly, Cooper established that Black women are included in the range of human voices. During the nineteenth century, Whites questioned whether persons of African descent were human in a society in which Black men counted as three-fifths of a person. Today, White supremacist groups make similar assertions. We too often forget that racism in America has questioned whether Black Americans are distinguishable from apes. Cooper asserted that voice distinguishes human beings from apes. Moreover, she asserted that Black women, all women, in America have a voice. She thereby asserted the equal status of Black women as members of the human race.

Cooper drew Black women of the South out of anonymity and invisibility by speaking out, by writing, and by demanding an audience and a readership. That Black women possessed voice was rendered permanently concrete by Cooper through the medium of writing and publication. Her own words stand out on paper in black and white as a reminder of her voice. By "voice," Cooper did not mean simply the sound of human vocalization, but the language chosen by individuals to articulate their experience. She argued that the voices of Black women needed to be heard on the issues of domination, sexism, and racism because they were among the most dominated of the dominated in American culture. Neither White women nor Black men could be "expected fully and adequately to reproduce the exact Voice of the Black Woman." Only Black women could speak for Black women.[6]

Black women, she argued, were best "able to grasp the deep significance of the possibilities of the crisis" of domination of the weak by the politically, economically, and militaristically strong. Therefore, the world needed to listen to their voices. She spoke from the standpoint of Black Christian womanhood, aware of her particular dignity in the midst of race and gender oppression. She also recognized the interrelationship of the problems of Black Christian women and women of diverse cultures and religions. Cooper saw the women's movement as a particular embodiment of a universal good. In the process it was necessary to remember one's interconnectedness with the good of others across racial, class, and gender boundaries. She proclaimed freedom and equality of a particular group while at the same time proclaiming freedom and equality as universal human rights. Today, a diversity of women of color are making similar claims. Freedom, many would agree today, is a universal birthright of women and men, of Blacks and Whites, of people of every color, gender, and ethnicity.

Cooper argued against theories that democracy, progress, and equality were manifested only in Western European civilization. These principles were not the property of a superior race. Rather they were principles innate in humankind; they were "an inborn human endowment," a "shadow mark of the Creator's image," an "urge-cell."[7] This urge for freedom and equality, this Singing Something within humanity, can never truly be suppressed by a dominating race or nation. It eventually rises up, comes to voice, and actively moves in the world to demand social reform. To be created in God's likeness is to be created in freedom and equality. With a keen sense of the rights and dignity of the individual, Cooper argued for the consecration of "the image of God in human form" across color lines.[8] Humankind is created in the image of God and that God is the Creator of human being. To be created in God's image is to be created in freedom.

Voice continues to be important for the contemporary world.[9] Moving beyond Cooper, I would argue for a call-and-response concept of our relationship with God. We are called to respond to God's message of freedom and equality by raising our voices to call for social, political, and economic freedom. Cooper's work teaches us the power of voice. God's voice is a voice of freedom. God's voice, we might say, is a voice of liberation. We are not alone. We possess the power of God's liberating voice within us. The problem is, as Cooper pointed out, that Black women's voices have been like a muted note in the debate around issues of power and domination. It is vital that the Church, especially women in the Church who are awakened to the power of their own voices, help awaken women of every color to the power of the Singing Something of freedom and equality within them.

Why is voice so important? What does it mean to speak of "the power of voice"? Voice has to do with the articulation of experience and the subsequent conceptualization of self and the world, whether in writing or in public speaking. Symbolization or conception of self, community, God, and the world requires language.[10] I understand symbolizing activity here to be a *community* event that requires communication to be understood. This may be in words, images, graphics, or other forms human beings use to communicate, such as sign language and dance.

All of our ideas about human nature are founded in language. Our words about self, community, God, and the world predetermine the symbol systems or conceptualizations that we go on to construct. Cooper challenged a dominant system of thought based in pejorative language that misrepresented Black women as lazy, promiscuous, and immoral by replacing it with a system of thought based in positive language that represented Black women as hardworking, chaste, and moral. She corrected the misperceptions and misrepresentations of the dominant culture. The publication of Cooper's writings has preserved them and made them retrievable.

One of the most fascinating aspects of Cooper's discussion of voice is that she frequently used metaphors from music theory. She further described the voice of the Black Woman of the South as a testifying voice, a voice that bears witness in the judicial process regarding the rights of Black women and men in America. One is left with the image of a Black woman or Black women singing *soprano obligato* in testimony to the experiences of Black women of the South. Freedom and equality, a universal birthright, sing within the human soul, "a hallmark" that is directly traceable to the Creator. For Cooper humankind's creation in the image of God is more than merely imagistic. It is vocal. It is musical. It is auditory. She was not interested in a merely imagistic model of

God. She was interested in the sound, the words, the composition of God's voice. Cooper was concerned with harmony among human beings. How does one find harmony with one's neighbor? By becoming in harmony with God. It is in song, in voice, that humankind is created in the image of God, or better, in the sound of God.

Cooper did not emphasize human being as being in God's likeness in the sense of outer, physical appearance. She pointed to a likeness of voice, of tone, of words. She also used the metaphors of "divine Spark" and "shadow mark." Whereas feminist and womanist scholars today raise questions of God's embodiment in human being, whether God is black, of color, or female, Cooper moves beyond the outer appearance of the body to the voice of God and the voices of human beings.[11] Cooper's primary goal was to get at God's message and the vocalization of that message in Black women, so that it could and would be heard by her auditors and understood by her readers. She recognized the outward physical beauty of Black women, but as part of a critique of culture.

Cooper criticized America for abusing the physical beauty of Black women in the South. She also raised the importance of education for women, arguing that women, regardless of race, must be encouraged to develop their minds rather than devote all their time to being pretty. Today, precisely because of the abuse of women's bodies historically, womanist and feminist theologians are concerned with a positive valuation of women's bodies. Today Black women and men find it necessary to recognize and affirm the beauty of color. Cooper shared concern for the sacredness of women's bodies, but she found it necessary to draw attention away from mere physical appearance in order to overcome undue negative attention to skin color.

Cooper's metaphor of voice involves the body in a very expressive sense. The entire body is engaged in voice: the lungs, the diaphragm, the voice box — the very breath of human being, which is often symbolically equated with spirit.

Cooper's metaphor of a *Singing* Something points to the sacredness of human being as an energy and force that move the body to action regardless of conventional notions of beauty and appearance. Through voice one can assert the sacredness and beauty of the body. What makes one human is one's inner voice, the voice of equality and freedom that is directly traceable to God. The Voice of God, in this sense, sings through the human spirit and calls humankind to action, growth, development, reform. There is movement involved in the act of vocalization. One can build on Cooper's use of metaphor to suggest that when Black women speak in the voice of equality and freedom, when Black women speak from a *Singing* Something, Black women repeat the sounds and lyrics of God's voice. Black women in raising their voices participate in an antiphony.

Antiphony has always been very popular in the Anglican tradition Cooper was a part of. Moreover, in traditional Black churches the practice of call and response between preacher and congregation during prayers, sermons, and singing is integral to the service. Black women raising their voices to call for freedom and equality are engaged in call and response with God, repeating God's words and ideals in the Black church tradition.

Singing is an important aspect of voice because it is creative and expresses human thought and feeling in an aesthetic form. Music expresses speech in lyric form. I concur with Richard R. Niebuhr that song also is often a theological form. In the African American tradition, it is an important source of narrative, relating the experience of oppression and the desire for freedom. Susanne Langer, in her study in symbolism, *Philosophy in a New Key,* writes on the significance of music. Her emphasis, however, is on instrumental music, rather than on vocal music. She is interested in music as a tonal phenomenon. Langer finds vocal music unreliable, because "words and the pathos of the human voice are added to the musical stimulus."[12]

Langer moves beyond the understanding of music as expressive of human emotion and feeling, a view widely accepted by both musicians and philosophers, to discuss the history of music as a history of increasingly "integrated, disciplined, and articulated *forms,* much like the history of language, which waxes important only as it is weaned from its ancient source in expressive cries, and becomes denotative and connotative rather than emotional."[13] Music like language has an emotional content only symbolically, just as language has conceptual content only symbolically.[14] For Langer, "music articulates forms that language cannot set forth."[15] It is untranslatable and nondiscursive, and that is its strength. For Langer, music is "an unconsummated symbol," a "significant form without conventional significance."[16] It articulates, but it does not assert. It is expressive, but it is not expression. It cannot be reduced to emotion, feeling, expression.

I agree with Langer that music expresses human feeling only symbolically and that it cannot be reduced to emotion, feeling, or expression. But she misses the significance of vocal music.[17] It is precisely the assertiveness and pathos of the human words and voice that give vocal music a power to move people to action. Moreover, lyrics, like the musical score, can reflect or challenge conventional culture. In American history, this has been evident in the songs of the Civil Rights movement. Moreover, Cooper's work suggests that there is much meaning in the simplest moan or cry. Why wean music utterly away from moans of despair or cries of joy? The pathos and celebration such expressions add to song are persuasive and lend weight to the lyrics.

Cooper was familiar with all kinds of music; she enjoyed Bach, Beethoven, Mozart, Handel. But she pointed to the significance of vocal music. She placed an emphasis on singing. Perhaps she had in mind the Negro Spirituals of the South, as well as the oratorios of Handel, when she entitled her chapters on Black womanhood "Soprano Obligato." Womanist theologians must turn to African American song as one of the cultural forms in which Black Americans have expressed and recorded their feelings and thought about Black experiences in America. W. E. B. Du Bois referred to the Negro Spirituals as the "Sorrow Songs." Ironically, White people hearing these "Sorrow Songs" often misinterpreted the slaves as being happy because they were singing.

Clearly, the slaves were unhappy, as is evident in the words of the songs, slave narratives, and slaves' attempts to escape their condition. Moreover the songs were created in community both by an individual and a group, and thus were expressive not simply of subjective experience but of communal experience. Complex harmonies were added to the main melody as slaves joined in together to create a new song, singing in many voices as one voice. There was communal agreement about the significance of the songs' lyrics, rhythm, and tones.[18] Langer's suggestion that the emotional content of song is subjectively interpreted, then, proves wrong in the context of African American folk music.

That slaveowners and other White Americans associated the songs of slaves with happiness does not show the ambiguity of the symbolic function of music, as Langer's analysis of music suggests, but the insensitivity and cultural limitedness of the auditors. The slaves, of course, used this to their advantage. They used songs like "Steal Away to Jesus" as a coded language to refer to escape on the Underground Railroad, knowing that Whites, with their naive interpretations, would not break the code. Songs like "Go Down, Moses" voiced the slaves' sorrow and hope for deliverance from oppression. The songs voiced more than cries and moans, although cries and moans were often an integral part of the music. The songs voiced an articulation of the problem of oppression and the desire for freedom. Moreover, some songs were celebrative and expressed hope, jubilee, joy.

Cooper moved beyond cries, moans, and broken utterances to a full articulation of the experience of Black women and men in America and a demand for human rights. But her work suggests that even cries, moans, and broken utterances have important symbolic functions. She was open to a diversity of vocalizations regarding justice, freedom, oppression, celebration. She was right to compare her articulation to music and song. Her attention to the themes of the sorrow and tragedy of oppression and the call for freedom emerges out of and is echoed in the songs of African American culture.

The Power of Making Do

In addition to the power of voice there are other powers of survival and wholeness that have been named in Black women's narratives. One of these is the power of "making do," a power of survival and creativity in the midst of scarce, often hostile forces. As an example of this power, I begin with a metaphor.

In the Spring of 1992, Hurricane Bob raged along the North Shore in Massachusetts. The wildness of the ocean, in a tempestuous play with the wildness of the wind, met with the wildness of the land. To all appearances the lush, deep pink wild roses gave way to the fury of the ocean, and there were few wild rose bushes left standing. But rose bushes struggle to reemerge. There is something unruly and persistent about these wild roses. Their roots run deep and tap into a hidden source of life. For me, they are a symbol of the grace with which all creation is blessed. They are radical. They defy obsession with tameness and domestication. They are survivors, warrior plants.

Alice Walker writes of "revolutionary petunias," which are glorious in their wild growth.[19] Her mother's petunias and other flowers were so wildly and thickly flourishing under her creative hand that perfect strangers stopped by to admire and walk in her garden.[20] To rejoice in the earth and the nurture it gives to lushly growing annual flowers like petunias, is, as Walker asserts, deeply womanist. But the wild rose reminds me of the womanist herself, who is able not only to survive but ultimately thrives in the most rugged of environments. Walker's *The Color Purple* reminds readers through Shug that it upsets God if we don't admire the color purple, which grows wildly in the fields.[21] The planting and artistic nurture of petunias symbolizes well Black women's capacity for nurturing others. The wild rose, or the freely growing color purple in a field, in its beauty and irrepressibility, recalls the capacity for self-nurture in the midst of harsh circumstances. It recalls the capacity for survival and wholeness among women from Africa, forced into a new culture during the slave trade — a culture that too often has been hostile to the very being of Black folk.

When Europeans encountered Africans in the fifteenth century, they thought of them as wild, heathen savages in need of domestication. Over the next four centuries, they systematically raped and colonized Africa and America. While Europe all but exterminated the American Indians, they raped Africa of millions of its people. In the name of "ownership," White slavemasters raped Black women just as they had raped the land of Africa of its people, and just as they have continued to rape Africa of its natural resources of gold, diamonds, and produce. Slave mistresses often further abused Black women by punishing them for their own rapes. The prevailing moral ideology held that Black women were naturally immoral, wild, lascivious. Black women were conceived of as less than fully human because they were women; less than fully women because of their African ancestry.[22] They have struggled to fight against internalizing negative stereotypes of Black womanhood. They have survived with brilliance and beauty by affirming their freedom, equality, and humanity in subtle, subversive ways to create a survival ethic and wholistic concept of life passed on from mother to daughter.

Since womanist theology and ethics value the wisdom of one's ancestors, beginning with one's immediate context, I will discuss an example of survival ethics learned from the women in my family, an example that has been discussed in similar terms by womanist ethicist Katie Cannon. From my mother I learned the art of preparing a healthy meal with scarce resources. It wasn't that we were poor in any real sense. We were middle class, as were her parents. But because her parents had survived the Depression and segregation, she had learned the value of making things from scratch and producing abundance from scarcity. My paternal grandmother has named this survival skill "making do." She has passed on the ethic of making do to her children, grandchildren, and great-grandchildren. "Making do" is a creative activity. It is similar to what Cannon has called "making something out of nothing."[23] It is the art of making beauty out of scraps of material, of making mouth-watering meals in the midst of scarcity, of making a dollar stretch, of creating a healthy and nurturing environment in the midst of unjust socio-economic circumstances, of knowing how to work from scratch. When we were growing up, no matter how well we did in school, my grandmother did not consider us to be truly educated until it was clear that we had grasped the principles of "making do." In relatively successful financial times, she and my grandfather warned that we must always put aside some "rainy day" money, because you never know when hard times might come. My grandmother made housecleaning products, drapes, clothes, and cakes from scratch. Weaker in body now, she rarely does this today. But she can throw something together in a pinch if she needs to. She has passed on the tradition.

A presupposition of the "making do" ethic is that no matter how well educated or economically successful one may become, the reality of Depression, recession, and job loss mixed with racism and the vicissitudes that are part of human life require one to be prepared to make something out of nothing. In the midst of scarcity this ethic functions as a power of material survival and spiritual thriving. In the midst of relative abundance, it works as a power of material and spiritual thriving. "Making do" is a kind of power. It is a form of creative power, passed on from mother to daughter. It is also a kind of freedom in which Black women have engaged in the midst of limited opportunity and limited socio-economic and political freedom. The creative power of making do is essential for strengthening self, family, Church, and community. Not only has "making do" been a method of survival, but it has been a subtle form of defiance that flies in the face of false ideologies regarding Black women's humanity. It is evidence that human creativity cannot be thoroughly squelched or suppressed. Making do is related to what Delores Williams has referred to as the womanist concept of a God who makes a way out of no way.[24] To make do, creating sustenance and sometimes abundance out of scarce resources, is to walk in the empowerment of such a God. Black women's creative power of makin' do is a form of the *imago Dei*. Black women in their creativity reflect the likeness of God, Creativity-Itself.

In the midst of the most oppressive circumstances, Black women have claimed the power and freedom of creativity. As the twenty-first century begins to dawn, it is important to continue to employ such power to fully claim one's creation in the image of God. To do so is a kind of faith walk in which one practices faith in the creative power of God, self, and community. For the African American Church and community to survive and be truly whole, African American women must fully claim God's creation of Black womanhood in freedom and equality. Finally, this creative power, which is understood in a particular way in relation to African American culture, has global significance. All are created in God's likeness and are capable of more fully realizing God's creative power of making do, of making something out of nothing, of making a way out of no way. In global solidarity, humankind has the capacity to transform evil into good, to transform injustice into justice.

History, Myth, and the Power of Remembering

Katie Cannon has observed that the Black women's literary tradition is an important canon for womanist theologians because it preserves much of the moral wisdom of Black folk culture and a survival ethic that has been passed on through an oral/aural tradition.[25] Such wisdom is found in diverse literary forms: in novels, essays, and historical narratives. I find Cannon's analysis of Black women's literature important in considering womanist sources. Delores Williams, also, has pointed to Black women's literature as a preserver of cultural codes that are passed on from mother to daughter.[26]

Alice Walker and Toni Morrison explore Black women's remembering through research-based fiction to call attention to Black women's ancient culture and spiritual properties. They each consider both history and myth, the powerful stories that provide structure and meaning for communities, in their remembering. Alice Walker considers women's embodiment as an essential aspect of women's full humanity by critically engaging in memory of the dehumanizing effects of the rituals of clitoridectomy and infibulation. Clitoridectomy and infibulation have been performed on 85–100 million women around the world, particularly in Africa and the Middle East.[27] Clitoridectomy involves female circumcision of the clitoris. The purpose of infibulation, the sewing together of women's inner labia, is to increase male pleasure, while keeping women from being "loose." But "loose,"one of Walker's characters implies, means simply to set free to grow, thrive, flourish. It has nothing to do with morality, but with women's freedom to be loosed from bodily mutilation. Contrasting patriarchal practices with women's rituals, the novel also appeals to an older, ancient African women's culture where women valued all parts of their bodies, including their menstrual cycles, as sacred. In *Possessing the Secret of Joy* Walker challenges women to engage in a process of healing through memory, reaching not only into our own immediate pasts and those around us, but to a more ancient time when women's bodies were held sacred.

Both Morrison and Walker toy with terms like "loose" and "wild" as metaphors for freedom. In her novel *Jazz*, Morrison writes of a character called "Wild."[28] For Morrison, wildness is more ambiguous, paradoxical, than Walker's looseness. Wild is a mysterious woman who lives in the wilds of the forest in Virginia, home of Joe Trace, the male protagonist of *Jazz*.[29] Wild is Joe Trace's mother. Wild cannot be caught, is rarely seen, and is a source of local myth. She is elusive and mysterious and there is ambiguity as to whether she is good or evil. On the one hand she is a source of life; she is the mother of Joe Trace. On the other hand, she chooses not to live in "civilized" society or to "mother" Joe Trace.[30]

The character Beloved, in Morrison's novel *Beloved,* has a similarly elusive identity. There are several references to Beloved with regard to necks. Her own neck was cut by Sethe when she was a baby to save her from slavery. As a ghost, Beloved finds it difficult to keep her head on her neck. Beloved's anxiety about necks extends to Sethe. She is concerned that Sethe have no iron collar around her neck.[31] At the end of the novel Beloved manifests herself as tall, black, with hair like vines. She is last seen running off into the woods, with fish for hair. She is reminiscent of the "snake"-haired African goddess, Medusa, who was beheaded and coopted by the Greeks.[32]

Both Wild and Beloved are mythological figures. Like traditional African goddesses and gods they represent an ambiguity of creativity and destruction. For that matter, they have something in common with the God of Judaism and Christianity named variously El-Shaddai, Elohim, Yahweh, and God the Father, who is capable of both wrath and nurture. Who are these evasive, wild, mythological, forgotten women that Morrison writes about? In Africa, the Medusa, whom Beloved resembles, is related to the Egyptian Maat, the mother of all life. Who is this African goddess? What is her real name? She has been "disremembered" and "unaccounted for." As far as womanists are concerned, who were our mothers' mothers' mothers' mothers? Morrison's writings challenge her readers to ask such questions, to reexamine the past and engage in a process of rememory in part by remembering and reexamining African American myths. Morrison sees herself as dusting off myths to uncover their deeper meaning.[33] She strives to recover the way tales were told in the small town she grew up in, explaining that in leaving the towns where we were born myths get forgotten or are "misunderstood."[34]

Morrison conceived Sethe's and Beloved's story after reading about a historical Black woman named Margaret Garner, who tried to spare her children the brutalities of slavery by killing them. We need only open our daily newspapers to see similar accounts of Black women and men, boys and girls, engaging in desperate acts of violence against one another today. Just as the community in *Beloved* criticize Sethe for killing a baby daughter in the name of freedom and just as the narrative criticizes the community for not warning Sethe of the approach of slave catchers, so must we criticize nihilistic practices among Black women, men, and children today.

Morrison reworks ancient myths to challenge the way we think about our complicity with good and evil. The power of memory is important both for celebrating our creative, liberative gifts and for recollecting our own complicity with oppression. Remembering our mythic and historical ancestors is vital for building on our strengths and correcting our weaknesses. *Beloved* notes the importance of remembering to forgive and receive forgiveness for acting in complicity with oppression.[35] Moreover remembrance is vital for understanding exactly what we need to be delivered from. The power of remembering is another aspect of our creation in God's likeness. Just as God remembers so we must remember to participate in God's liberating activities of forgiveness and deliverance. We must engage in what Morrison's characters in *Beloved* refer to as rememory in community. As the character Sethe demonstrates, the wealth and pain of the past are too overpowering for an individual and can lead to madness. The powers of "making do" and of "voice" are necessary balancing powers that must go along with it. Moreover, through collective rememory we can regain powers like the power to hold things together — what Morrison's character Marie Therese in *Tar Baby* calls our "ancient properties" and what Morrison calls "tar."

Tar and the Power of Holding Things Together

In *Tar Baby,* Morrison dusts off the "tar baby" myth to re-vision the African origins of the Southern folk tale of Br'er Rabbit. According to Morrison, the "tar baby" of Southern folklore originates from a myth of a "tar lady" in Africa,[36] a powerful symbol of Black womanhood. Morrison suggests that myths that are African in origin have been reinvented from one period of history to the next by Blacks and Whites, so that we must uncover their earlier meaning to consider possible meanings for today.

Morrison explores what it means to be a tar baby according to the plantation, Westernized version of the story and what it may mean to be a tar baby from a more ancient African perspective. Morrison explains that the Western version has a tar baby used by a White man to catch a rabbit. Tar baby is a name similar to "nigger." White people call Black children "tar babies," especially Black girls. But at one time, Morrison argues, tar was considered sacred: "At one time, a tar pit was a holy place, at least an important place, because tar was used to build things. It came naturally out of the earth; it held together things like Moses's little boat and the pyramids."[37]

Tar, in this interpretation, has a sacred quality because it has played an important role in the building up and preservation of structures that uphold and contain that which is sacred. Morrison suggests another aspect regarding tar's sacred qualities. The myth of the "tar baby" reveals Black women's ancient properties of "holding things" together: "For me, the tar baby came to mean the Black woman who can hold things together. The story was a point of departure to history and prophecy."[38]

Tar's power to hold together and preserve that which is sacred — life, family, community — is embodied in Black women. It becomes a symbol of the strength and wisdom of Black women. Although the meaning of "tar baby" has been distorted by White culture, it can be redefined by Black women. Tar is good and natural and upholds sacred structures. It preserves cultures, communities, and life itself. The African tar lady in Morrison's reconstruction represents Black women who know their responsibility to the generations — elders, peers, and youth. She functions as a culture-bearer who preserves and passes on African American cultural values. The powers to nurture and hold things together are sacred properties.

Lest the tar lady begin to seem like a superwoman, concerned with others to the exclusion of her own liberation and wholeness, Morrison has clarified that no Black woman "should apologize for being educated." Likewise, Morrison implies that the character Jadine in *Tar Baby* should not apologize for her access to greater economic opportunity and freedom. There is a problem, however, in not paying attention to the "ancient properties."[39] For Morrison, Black women who neglect remembrance of their ancient properties are incapable of being an anchor to the past and holding together that which would otherwise fall apart.

Theressa Hoover writes of Black women as being "truly the glue that held the churches together."[40] In Morrison's work we find a metaphor for referring to a similar understanding of Black women's collective, coalescing strength that is essential for coalition building. The "tar lady" metaphor is an important one for considering Black women's power to generate cohesiveness and solidarity. One might employ Morrison's "tar baby" metaphor to represent Black women's ability to build coalitions in Church and community, which is part of liberating praxis. Such a metaphor represents Black women's ability to build coalitions with other oppressed groups, as well as members of oppressor groups who see themselves as standing in solidarity with the oppressed. The story of the tar lady who holds things together and the story of Beloved, who was violently dismembered and disremembered, calls to mind the necessity to resolve the tensions created by complicity with violence against self and community. The story of Beloved presents a challenge to value the power of memory. The story of the power of tar presents a challenge to stand in community to hold one another up in the process of making sense of sometimes dangerous and sometimes loving memories.[41]

Morrison's work, like Walker's and unlike Cooper's, is not Christocentric. She presents a combination of Christian and pre-Christian worldviews. Moving beyond Morrison, Christian womanists might argue that in the ancestral community of Moses, Zipporah, Jethro, Hagar, Nat Turner, Harriet Tubman, Anna Cooper, and Sojourner Truth, Christ perfectly embodies the power of the God of Moses, "I Am," Being-Itself to save lives and hold together that which would otherwise fall apart. Historically for Black women, Jesus embodies the God who "makes a way out of no way," who provides deliverance from oppression. Not only are Black women created in the image of God, in their gifts of creativity, liberating voice, and memory, but Black women are also created in the image of God in their ability to coalesce. Coalescence is vital for generating coalitions and solidarity, not only with other Black women, but with the entire Black community and with all those who choose to stand in solidarity with the oppressed. These are salvific activities that can generate not only survival, but wholeness.

The Power of Generation

For me a tar lady is a womanist who generates theological-ethical principles of survival and wholeness. Womanists are Black women who pass on the gift of holding things together from generation to generation. To be revolutionary in a womanist way is to pass on the gifts of makin' do, holding things together, and calling for social reform, which is to be generational in a liberative way. This goes beyond traditional notions of childbearing and child-rearing to a broader, inclusive, liberative praxis of regeneration and nurture that is not only familial but social, economic, and political. It includes aunts, uncles, friends, cousins, and biological and nonbiological parents.

Too many girls and boys, of every race in America, are dying spiritually and physically because of misconceptions about their powers of generation. We require a new understanding of generation. We must teach youth that sexuality is a God-given generative power. We are created in God's likeness in our ability to generate new life. But the power to generate new life is more than making babies; it is a physical, spiritual, and political power. It enables African Americans and all peoples to stand in solidarity with one another, to participate in God's creativity, and to call for progressive socio-economic reforms. The power of generation, passed on by historical and mythic ancestors, is vital to the renewed existence of faith communities.

Conclusion

We must learn from the wisdom of our historic and mythic ancestors. But we cannot actually live in the realms of the past or of myth. For Morrison, myth is "a departure to history and prophecy." That is, it reveals experiential truth from the past in symbolic form and thus provides insight into possibilities for future acts. Whether myth exaggerates or fills in missing gaps in historical events with fictitious details does not determine its truth-value. What determines the truth-value of a myth is whether or not it accurately depicts the true *feelings* about a historical community crisis of the people it represents. For example, Morrison's novel *Beloved* is based on extensive historical research about Margaret Garner, slavery, ex-slaves, and the horticulture of nineteenth-century Kentucky and Cincinnati. But the novel is more than a historical novel. It is a "ghost story" and a modern myth. The characters are larger than life. Morrison employs this genre to highlight the *feelings* of the *subjects* of the transatlantic slave trade crisis. The feelings evoked by this crisis have been passed on in subtle ways, often at subconscious levels, from generation to generation. The reemergence of such feeling and memory of pain outside of community is like a haunting — it can drive an individual mad. And yet the truth of the feelings is always present in the community in some form, whether recognized or not, and must be dealt with. Myth offers insight into a community's past and into possibilities for its healing and wholeness in the present and near future. History informs us about our past. Prophecy gives us new insight into our present and our future. What myth offers is a wholistic perspective on Black womanhood that unites past, present, and future ways of being in various social contexts. A wholistic womanist reconstruction of womanhood requires critical reflection on the past, the present, and God's call into the future.

These five gifts of power found among Black women are not limited to Black women, although they experience them and practice them in a unique response to particular social-historical and cultural experiences. Like the power of God's message of freedom and equality, the power of making do (creativity), the power of voice, the power of remembering, the power of holding things together, and the power of generation are available to all humankind. African American women historically have embodied these powers in unique ways in response to their context. Such embodiment reflects creation in God's likeness among Black women and anyone else who embodies them. Moreover, there are a multiplicity of gifts of power among humankind, which we have yet to fully name or realize. The naming and sharing of such gifts is an ongoing process that requires mutual listening and solidarity among diverse communities, working together for full freedom and equality. The gifts named here historically have generated survival and an abundant life for African American women and their communities. As co-generators and co-creators with God, elders, and ancestors, contemporary communities must learn to practice these gifts and pass them on, learning from each other as we work together for social justice. To do this is to move into a fuller sense of what it means to be created in freedom, with powers to create, to raise liberating voices, to coalesce, and to generate new life.

NOTES

1. Carol Christ, *Diving Deep and Surfacing* (Boston: Beacon Press, 1980), 1.

2. The slave narrative of Sojourner Truth, for example, was written by a biographer.

3. See Richard R. Niebuhr, "The Tent of Heaven: Theographia I," *Alumnae Bulletin, Bangor Theological Seminary* 52, no. 2 (Fall–Winter 1977–78).

4. Jean McMahon Humez, *Gifts of Power: The Writings of Rebecca Jackson, Black Visionary, Shaker Eldress* (Amherst: University of Massachusetts Press, 1981).

5. Delores Williams in *Sisters in the Wilderness* (Maryknoll, N.Y.: Orbis Books, 1993) argues that the God of ordinary Black women, like the God of Hagar, has been a God of survival, not a God of liberation. She acknowledges that womanists appeal both to this God of survival and the God of liberation. Jacquelyn Grant, for example, appeals to a God of liberation, which she sees in the narratives of Black women historically and in the present. I don't think we need to choose between these two Gods. For me God is both a God of survival and of liberation, of Hagar and of Zipporah, who circumcised Moses and led him to the God of the Mountain in Midian.

6. Anna Julia Cooper, "Our Raison d'Être," in *A Voice from the South,* ed. Mary Helen Washington, Schomburg Library of Nineteenth-Century Black Women Writers (1892; New York: Oxford University Press, 1988), iii.

7. Cooper, "Equality of Races and the Democratic Movement," privately printed pamphlet, Washington, D.C., 1945, 4–5.

8. Ibid., 118.

9. Systematic theologians such as David Tracy have also indicated the importance of being inclusive of a plurality of voices in theological conversation. Tracy highlights the problem of ambiguity and fragmentation of conversation in a pluralistic society. He seeks to listen to new interpretations of religion from the Third and Second Worlds. In his emphasis on preserving the "religious classics," however, he does not adequately question the power relations involved in who determines what constitutes the religious classics and who will determine the classics of the future. See David Tracy, *Plurality and Ambiguity:*

Hermeneutics, Religion, and Hope (New York: Harper & Row, 1987), 7–27, 82–114.

10. See Ernst Cassirer, *Language and Myth* (New York: Dover Publications, 1953), 28, who writes that all concepts of theoretical knowledge are founded in language: "Before the intellectual work of conceiving and understanding of phenomena can set in, the work of *naming* must have preceded it, and have reached a certain point of elaboration." In his *Essay on Theological Method* (Missoula, Mont.: Scholars Press, 1975; rev. ed., 1979), Gordon Kaufman argues that there is no experience without language; experience is conceived, interpreted, and articulated through language. See also Gordon Kaufman, *The Theological Imagination: Constructing the Concept of God* (Philadelphia: Westminster Press, 1981), 23–57. I differ with Kaufman and Cassirer as to whether experience precedes language. Experience and the development of language are too deeply intertwined to separate except in theories that are radically separated from human reality. Thanks to Kathy Black, my colleague at the School of Theology at Claremont, for alerting me to the importance of a broad concept of language that includes hearing-impaired persons.

11. As for whether God is black, white, red, or yellow, I find the biblical symbol of the rainbow or Alice Walker's understanding of universality as a flower garden to be more appropriate imagistic metaphors of God's affinity with both genders and with a multiplicity of races. One might also refer to a "human rainbow" as a metaphor or image that points to God's embodiment in human being. Attempts to construct images of a black God, white God, red God, or yellow God are inadequate in isolation. The beauty of God's embodiment in human being is seen in a multiplicity of images. It is important, however, to remember that all images and metaphors merely point to God and God's nature. Cooper describes God as infinite and suggests that God is infinitely loving, merciful, compassionate. It seems, then, that one would require an infinity of symbols and symbol systems to represent God. Human beings can begin to grasp this infinite multiplicity of symbolizations only within the process of human history and never within a lifetime or era.

12. Susanne Langer, *Philosophy in a New Key,* 3d ed. (Cambridge, Mass.: Harvard University Press, 1982), 212.

13. Ibid., 219.

14. Ibid., 218: "It is not usually derived *from* affects nor intended *for* them, it is *about* them."

15. Ibid.

16. Ibid., 241.

17. Although Susanne Langer makes some reference to song, particularly folk song, its value in popular culture, its ties to rhythm, dance, and other art forms, as well as its origins in religious ritual, she essentially dismisses the significance of vocal music.

18. See John Lovell, Jr., *Black Song: The Forge and the Flame* (New York: Paragon House Publishers, 1986), 201. Lovell writes that there has been argument about how much of the individual and how much of the communal was in the African American spiritual. He concludes that sometimes the songs were written with greater emphasis on the group, sometimes with greater em-

phasis on the individual. Both participated. But Lovell concludes that for the most part the artistic skills demonstrated suggest a predominance of an individual composer, most likely the Negro preacher. Lovell points to James Weldon Johnson, who showed strong parallels between sermons and spirituals: narrative technique, picturesqueness and concreteness, an emphasis on personal characteristics, as well as familiarity with the deity.

19. See Alice Walker, *Revolutionary Petunias* (New York: Harcourt, Brace, Jovanovich, 1983), 27–52, 70, and "In Search of Our Mothers' Gardens," in *In Search of Our Mothers' Gardens* (New York: Harcourt, Brace, Jovanovich, 1983), 238–41.

20. Walker, *In Search of Our Mothers' Gardens,* 241.

21. Alice Walker, *The Color Purple* (New York: Harcourt, Brace, Jovanovich, 1982).

22. See Barbara Andolsen, *"Daughters of Jefferson, Daughters of Bootblacks": Racism and American Feminism* (Macon, Ga.: Macon University Press, 1986), and Katie Cannon, *Black Womanist Ethics* (Atlanta: Scholars Press, 1988) for a discussion of physical and mental abuse by slave mistresses against Black women and White supremacist concepts of Black women among White women during the Reconstruction and Jim Crow eras.

23. See Katie Cannon, course lectures, "Black Women's Literature as a Resource for a Constructive Ethic," Harvard Divinity School, Spring 1984.

24. See Delores Williams, *Sisters in the Wilderness* (Maryknoll, N.Y.: Orbis Books, 1993).

25. See Katie Geneva Cannon, "Moral Wisdom in the Black Women's Literary Tradition," *Weaving the Vision,* ed. Judith Plaskow and Carol Christ (San Francisco: Harper & Row, 1989), 281–84.

26. See Delores Williams, "Womanist Theology," 67–68.

27. See Alice Walker, *Possessing The Secret of Joy* (New York: Harcourt, Brace, Jovanovich, 1992).

28. See Toni Morrison, *Jazz* (New York: Alfred Knopf, 1992).

29. Ibid., 160–67, 171, 175–79.

30. Ibid., 166ff.

31. Toni Morrison, *Beloved* (New York: Alfred Knopf, 1987). The narrative refers to "the tip of the thing she [Denver] saw when Beloved lay down or came undone in her sleep" (120), Denver's fear that Sethe would cut her neck too (206), Sethe's cutting of baby Beloved's neck, iron circles for the neck, and "the people of broken necks" (215, 211, 181). "It is difficult keeping her head on her neck, her legs attached to her hips when she is by herself. Among the things she could not remember was when she first knew that she could wake up any day and find herself in pieces" (132).

32. Ibid., 261, 264–65. Beloved becomes a mythic figure for the community. She is described as follows: "Later, a little boy put it out how he had been looking for bait back of 124, down by the stream, and saw, cutting through the woods, a naked woman with fish for hair" (267). Here Beloved, like Medusa, is associated with fish and children. By the end of the novel she "erupts into her separate parts" and is "disremembered," but there is a period during which "the rustle of a skirt hushes when they wake, and the knuckles brushing a

cheek in sleep seem to belong to the sleeper." From an Afrocentric ontological perspective, one might consider Beloved to have passed from the realm of the ancestors to the spirits whose names are no longer remembered.

33. Ibid.

34. See Thomas LeClair, "The Language Must Not Sweat," in *New Republic,* 184 (March 21, 1981): 26–27.

35. Morrison, *Beloved,* 258–59. In this section women who haven't approached Sethe's home for years come to pray for her and an atmosphere of forgiveness and deliverance emerges.

36. LeClair, "The Language Must Not Sweat," 26–28.

37. Ibid.

38. Ibid., 26–27.

39. Judith Wilson, "Conversation with Toni Morrison," *Essence* (July 1981): 85ff.

40. Theressa Hoover, "Black Women and the Churches: Triple Jeopardy," in *Black Theology: A Documentary History,* ed. James Cone and Gayraud Wilmore (Maryknoll, N.Y.: Orbis Books, 1979), 380–81.

41. I use "dangerous memory" here in the sense used by Sharon Welch in her feminist interpretation of Johann Metz's use of the term. See Welch, *Communities of Resistance and Solidarity* (Maryknoll, N.Y.: Orbis Books, 1985).

Index